Celebrating Christmas with…
Memories, Poetry, and Good Food

Celebrating Christmas with… Memories, Poetry, and Good Food

Editor

Donna Clark Goodrich

First Edition

Reflections on the Past is a division of **Hidden Brook Press.**
www.HiddenBrookPress.com
writers@HiddenBrookPress.com

Copyright © 2011 Hidden Brook Press
Copyright © 2011 Authors

All rights for stories, poems, recipes and characters revert to the author. All rights for book, layout and design remain with Hidden Brook Press. No part of this book may be reproduced except by a reviewer who may quote brief passages in a review. The use of any part of this publication reproduced, transmitted in any form or by any means, electronic, mechanical, photocopied, recorded or otherwise stored in a retrieval system without prior written consent of the publisher is an infringement of the copyright law.

Celebrating Christmas with…
Memories, Poetry, and Good Food

Editor – Donna Clark Goodrich
Cover Photographs – Sharen Pearson
Cover Design – Richard M. Grove
Layout and Design – Richard M. Grove

Typeset in Garamond
Printed and bound in U.S.A.

Library and Archives Canada Cataloguing in Publication

    Celebrating Christmas with-- memories, poetry, and good food / editor, Donna Clark Goodrich.

ISBN 978-1-897475-80-5

    1. Christmas--Anecdotes. 2. Christmas--Miscellanea. 3. Christmas cooking. I. Goodrich, Donna Clark

GT4985.C37 2011   394.2663   C2011-907563-6

Reflections on the Past, edits, ghost writes and publishes memoirs. Contact us if you have a family story you would like to bring to life.
Memoir Editor – Kimberley Grove – 1-613-475-2368 – kesgrove@yahoo.ca

Thank you to all of the contributors
for making this book possible.

One can find a longer bio
on each contributor on the website.
http://www.hiddenbrookpress.com/HBP.html

To Family and Friends
and the Traditions
that Bind us
to Christmas.

Celebrating Christmas with… Memories, Poetry, and Good Food

Table of Contents

Childhood and Teenage Memories

Not Mincemeat Pie Again – *Jennifer Kruse* – p. 2
Christmas Poem – *Maria Magdalena Agullo* – p. 4
Memories of a Swedish Christmas in America – *Karen Strand* – p. 5
In Memory of Candy Cane Cookies – *Liz Collard* – p. 8
Braised Stuffed Pork Chops To Die For – *Pat Rowland* – p. 10
A Special Surprise – *Juanita Nobles* – p. 11
The Christmas Spirit of Old – *Raymond Fenech* – p. 14
From a Child on New Year's Day – *Elaine Hardt* – p. 15
Up Front – *Terri Elders* – p. 16
A Remembrance of a Childhood Christmas – *Noreen Ophoff* – p. 19
Christmas Memories – *Freda Hatfield Tong* – p. 21
Italian Bowknots–A Post-Fast Treat – *Janis A. Van Keuren* – p. 22
Ignored Blessings – *Kathy Collard Miller* – p. 25
Christmas Magic – *Brendalyn Crudup Martin* – p. 28
A Cinnamon Toast Gift – *Annette Kathleen Hutchins* – p. 30

Family Memories

Easy Christmas Turtle Candy – *Debbie Cunningham Carpenter – p. 32*
Christmas Traditions and Treasures – *Joyce McCullough – p. 33*
A Blue Christmas Turned Bright – *Millie Barger – p. 34*
Our Family Christmas Custard Eggnog – *Joanne Hendrix – p. 35*
The Gift of Life – *Linda Boutin – p. 37*
Christmas Muffins – *Deb Kemper – p. 40*
Christmas Company – *Virginia Colclasure – p. 41*
The Best Pecan Pie in the World – *Cona Gregory – p. 42*
Teddy Bear in the Attic – *Suzanne Gene Courtney – p. 44*
Orange Blush – *Pat Rowland – p. 45*
Angels in Disguise – *Mia Lynn DeBruyne – p. 46*
Oatmeal Date Cookies – *Kathy Bruins – p. 47*
Plum Pudding – *Janet Ann Collins – p. 48*
Christmas—Ready or Not – *Betty Baker – p. 51*
The Fruitcake Mission: Three Decades of Giving – *Lisa Harris – p. 53*
A Southern Garden of Christmas Gifts – *Sandra Fischer – p. 57*
A Husband's Devotion – *Rebecca Carpenter – p. 58*
Christmas Wreath – *Joyce McCullough – p. 59*
Pumpkin Bread – *Joyce McCullough – p. 60*
Christmas Haiku – *John J. Han – p. 61*
Christmas Party Coleslaw – *Patti Schieringa – p. 62*
The Unexpected Christmas Gift – *Christine Henderson – p. 63*
Apple Crisp – *Jewell Johnson – p. 65*
Quilting Memories – *Gay Ingram – p. 66*
Bread Sauce – *Cora Holley – p. 67*
A Christmas Cinquain: As Years Go By – *Cassandra Wessel – p. 68*
The Stockings Were Hung – *Carin LeRoy – p. 70*
The Perfect Gift – *Joyce McCullough – p. 71*
Cheddar Cheese Logs – *Betty Arthurs – p. 73*
Behold the Sights of Christmas – *Debbie Carpenter – p. 74*
Yule Kage – *Bruce McLeland – p. 75*
Our First Christmas – *Danielle Mendenhall – p. 77*
Red Velvet Cake – *Diane Morgan – p. 78*
Christmas Forever – *Jewell Johnson – p. 79*
Baked Eggs – *Ellen Cardwell – p. 80*
Returned to Sender – *Sherri Murphree – p. 81*

Cathedral Cookies – *Carol Dee Meeks* – *p. 82*
Our Family Christmas Eve Soup – *Carol Dee Meeks* – *p. 83*
Crystal's Christmas Dove – *Ginger B. O'Neill* – *p. 84*
Marshmallow Nut Clusters - *Leola R. Ogle* – *p. 85*
Gingerbread Men – *Cherry Pedrick* – *p. 86*
Keep It Simple – *Jewell Johnson* – *p. 87*
The Making of the Cranberry Sauce – *Laurie Barker Copeland* – *p. 88*
Through the Years – *Connie Peters* – *p. 89*
A Memory Locked in Our Hearts – *Tammy Pfaff* – *p. 90*
Fennel Pistachio Cookies – *Peggy Blann Phifer* – *p. 91*
The Giving Spirit – *Annette Rey* – *p. 92*
Red Salad – *Anne Grace* – *p. 95*
The Old-Fashioned Way – Star and Moon Cookies – *Jane Riley* – *p. 96*
Angels, Roaches, and a Christmas Child – *Lorilyn Roberts* – *p. 98*
Christmas Chinese Rice – *Natalie Kim Rodriguez* – *p. 101*
Picture Perfect – *Janet Roller* – *p. 102*
Aunt Teddy's Snicker Doodles – *Joanne Sandlin* – *p. 104*
Surprise Christmas – *Verna Simm* – *p. 106*
Loss Brings Poignant Holiday Memories – *Deb Wuethrich* – *p. 109*
Christmas Cake – *Jane Riley* – *p. 111*

Memories of Mother, Mothers-in-Law, and Aunts

Love What Is Before It Isn't – *Carol Mottinger Ramirez* – *p. 114*
Great Aunt Hallie's Luscious Cake – *Barbara Boothe Loyd* – *p. 116*
Mom's Extreme Holiday Baking Project – *Emily M. Akin* – *p. 117*
What Mothers Do – *Bill Butler* – *p. 119*
My Mother's Gingerbread Recipe – *Paige Carpenter* – *p. 121*
Mama's Magnificent Meatless Mincemeat – *Rebecca Bruner* – *p. 123*
Lil's Sugar and Spice Cookies – *Lynn Hartke* – *p. 125*
The Unexpected Gift Exchange – *Carol Moncado* – *p. 127*
Ma's German Christmas Bread – *Elaine Hardt* – *p. 129*
Cranberry-Orange Relish – *Rhonda Brown* – *p. 130*
Mother's Large Custard – *Frances E. Luymes* – *p. 131*
Mother's Magic – *Barbara Russell Chesser* – *p. 132*
Lost Tradition – *Linda Rose Etter* – *p. 134*

Christmas Brunch – *Ashleen O'Gaea* – *p. 136*
Magical Windows of Christmas – *Nancy Julien Kopp* – *p. 139*
Mother's Cinnamon Rolls – *Kris Lindsey* – *p. 141*
Christmas Eve Buffet – *Diane Morgan* – *p. 144*
Spritz Cookies – *Rhonda Brown* – *p. 145*
The Perfect Gift – *Deborah G. Onderdonk* – *p. 146*
Christmas Brunch – *Debbie Schmid* – *p. 148*
A Sweet, Rich Tradition—Braided Cardamom Bread – *Liane Williams* – *p. 149*

Father Memories

Christmas Lights – *Kelly Combs* – *p. 152*
Daddy's Christmas Box – *Connie Coppings* – *p. 153*
Please Don't Sing – *Don Cunningham* – *p. 155*

Grandparent/Grandchildren Memories

Oh Tannenbaum – *Diane Ellenwood* – *p. 158*
The Best Christmas Present Ever – *April Smith Carpenter* – *p. 160*
Sugar Cream Pie – *Diane Morgan* – *p. 162*
The Perfect Duet – *Rebecca Carpenter* – *p. 163*
Grandchildren's Christmas Delight – *Willow Dressel* – *p. 164*
Memories in the Making – *Phyllis Qualls Freeman* – *p. 166*
Struggling with the Season – *Linda Gillis* – *p. 169*
Grandma's Peanut Butter Divinity—a Christmas Tradition – *Joyce Komar* – *p. 171*
The Christmas Sideboard – *Jerri Clark Legler* – *p. 174*
Head Cook at Junior High– *Diane Morgan* – *p. 176*
Festive Christmas Jell-O – *Diane Morgan* – *p. 177*
A Thrill and Miracle – *Loreen Kollmorgen* – *p. 178*
Pretty Birdie – *Loreen Kollmorgen* – *p. 179*
My Grandmother's Noodles – *Andrea Arthur Owan* – *p. 180*
Red Velvet Christmas Delight – *Donna Collins Tinsley* – *p. 183*
Grandma Fran's Christmas Rolls – *Cassandra Wessel* – *p. 185*
Peppernut Memories – *Christy Williams* – *p. 187*

Oh, Christmas Tree

The Beginning of Traditions – *Liane Williams* – *p. 190*
Every Good and Perfect Gift – *Nanette Thorsen-Snipes* – *p. 191*
The Christmas Angel – *Connie Poole Wesala* – *p. 193*
The Stolen Tree – *Cassandra Wessel* – *p. 195*
The Abandoned Christmas Tree – *Cherry Pedrick* – *p. 196*
A Fresh Pine Memory – *Betty Ost-Everley* – *p. 198*
Oh, Christmas Tree – *Cona Gregory* – *p. 199*
The Christmas Tree Parade – *Annette Geroy* – *p. 200*
Two Christmas Trees – *Margaret Dornan Gamber* – *p. 203*
The Day the Kids Bought the Tree – *Phyllis Ciarametaro* – *p. 205*
Oh Christmas Tree! – *Faye Braley* – *p. 208*
The Not-So-Perfect Tree – *Betty Arthurs* – *p. 209*
Paper Christmas on the Tree – *Maria Magdalena Agullo* – *p. 211*

Christmas in Other Places

Christmas in Portland – *Josephine Walker* – *p. 214*
O Little Town of Bethlehem – *Lucy Neeley Adams* – *p. 216*
Christmas in a Suitcase – *Debbie Burgett* – *p. 218*
Christmas Down on the Farm – *Carol Dee Meeks* – *p. 220*
Christmas in Wartime Scotland, WWII – *Margaret Dornan Gamber* – *p. 221*
Centuries Old Scottish Christmas Delight – *Margaret Albertson* – *p. 223*
A Christmas to Remember – *Anita Mellott* – *p. 225*
A Colorado Christmas – *Peggy Halter Morris* – *p. 228*
"Yah, Sure, Swedish Pancakes" – *Sharen Pearson* – *p. 232*
The Posada—A Southwestern Tradition – *Carol Mottinger Ramirez* – *p. 234*
Shiny, Happy Cards – *Coleene VanTilburg* – *p. 235*
An Arkansas Christmas – *Anna Roberts Wells* – *p. 237*
Poppy Seed Cake – *Suzanne Gene Courtney* – *p. 240*
Two Memorable Recipes from Historic Malta – *Raymond Fenech* – *p. 241*
Strufolli (Italian Honey Balls) – *B.H. Haropolous* – *p. 245*
Three Wise Decisions – *Reba Cross Seals* – *p. 246*

A Sweet Treat for My Sweetheart
  —Diabetic Date Nut Cake – *Alice King Greenwood* – *p. 250*

Unexpected Surprises

Megan and Zoe – *Rebecca D. Bruner* – *p. 252*
Behind the Mask – *John Brewer* – *p. 256*
The Christmas Visitors – *Michael M. Alvarez* – *p. 258*
I'll Be Home for Christmas – *Sandra Fischer* – *p. 261*
Mistletoe and the Bell – *Nikole Hahn* – *p. 264*
Christmas Riches – *Londa Hayden* – *p. 267*
The Gift She'd Always Wanted – *Leola Ogle* – *p. 269*
No More Stones, Please – *Jo Russell* – *p. 273*
Season of Guinea Pigs – *Jean Ann Williams* – *p. 274*
The Blue Woolen Blanket – *Lenna Wyatt* – *p. 277*

Christmas Miracles

Angel on Ice – *Barbara Russell Chesser* – *p. 282*
Like Precious Silver – *Patricia Childress* – *p. 285*
A Christmas Prayer – *Carolyn Griffin* – *p. 287*
Stolen Bikes and Grace – *Lynn Hartke* – *p. 289*
A House for Christmas – *Donna Clark Goodrich* – *p. 290*

Editor Bio – *p. 293*
Author Bios – *p. 294 – 301*

Childhood and Teenage Memories

*It is good to be children sometimes, and
never better than at Christmas, when
its mighty Founder was a child Himself.*
—*Charles Dickens*

Not Mincemeat Pie Again

Jennifer Kruse

It was frigid that day, I remember sitting close to the fire. The fire was beautiful but also necessary as it was the only heat in our house. I had pulled a chair near the hearth and was trying to read my book. Reading was my favorite thing and I looked forward to Christmas vacation which gave me the excuse to be inside and read. I turned twelve this year and was reading as many books as I could get my hands on. 1927 was a tough year for most Americans but I was certain a new book would be waiting for me on Christmas morning.

My mother and sister were in the kitchen cooking, preparing for the Christmas dinner that was now just two days away. My mother hummed Christmas songs softly as she padded around the kitchen, whispering instructions to my sister.

Our home was always a quiet home as my father was a minister and studied behind closed door in his den, which my sister and I were not allowed to enter. When he was working, Mother tried to maintain an atmosphere in which he could prepare his sermons. Easy for me, pick up a book and lose myself in another fantastic story of adventure and history. My sister, on the other hand, could hardly stay still long enough to enjoy a good book.

My mother made special efforts to keep my sister busy by asking for help in the kitchen. I could hear them discussing the ingredients needed for the mincemeat pie. I slowly closed my book and sat it on my lap, rolled my eyes, and breathed a deep sigh. Mincemeat pie? Yuck, I can't stand mincemeat pie. Why can't the tradition be something chocolate, my second love? I sat my book down on the coffee table, pulled my sweater up around my neck, and strolled into the kitchen.

Already knowing the answer I asked Mother, "What are you making?" She replied, "Mincemeat pie, of course." I couldn't help it anymore; I was nearly a teenager and felt my opinion needed to be heard. I knew my parents didn't have a lot of money and they raised us to be grateful for every bit of food we were served. However, I believed it was time for her to know that being served mincemeat pie was no treat or Christmas celebration for me. I hated mincemeat pie. My mother stared at me with her strong blue eyes, let me have my rant, and then continued making mincemeat pie without saying a word. I recognized the conversation was over and returned to my book.

The next day my sister and I were to help my father set up for Christmas Eve service at his church. We spent the morning sweeping, oiling wood, and making sure everything was in order. When we came home, an aroma filled our house that delighted my whole heart and soul. It was unlike anything I had ever smelled, but I will tell you it is the smell of Christmas. My mother called me into the kitchen where she showed me a little bowl of something wonderful sitting on the counter with a spoon next to it. "Lana, I hope you find this Chocolate Bread Pudding a treat for you. Try it and tell me, can you celebrate Christmas now?" The corner of her mouth turned up in a smile.

Feeling a little ashamed of what I had said the day before, I reluctantly picked up the spoon and took a taste. Amazing…Chocolate Bread Pudding. I had never tasted anything so warm, so wonderful, so full of chocolate, so…well, so Christmas. All of a sudden I did not care if there was a book under the tree tomorrow. For the first time ever, I was excited for our Christmas dinner.

My mother made Chocolate Bread Pudding every Christmas for us from then on, and I continued the tradition when I married and had my four boys. Many years I had the recipe memorized because I would make several batches a year (you can't imagine how much of that delicious dessert four growing boys can eat). My sons took the recipe to their families and now my grandchildren are making it for my great-grandchildren. This isn't just a recipe for us; it is a family tradition. A tradition—that when you smell it baking in the kitchen—takes you back to many wonderful memories of Christmases past. A tradition that at first bite causes you to close your eyes, smile, and be grateful that it isn't mincemeat pie in your mouth.

Chocolate Bread Pudding

Grease 2½ qt. baking dish
Mix in baking dish:

4 cups milk
1 tsp. salt
4 cups soft bread, cubed
1 cup chopped nuts
2 tsp. vanilla

Beat well 2 eggs

Mix 2 cups sugar with 2/3 cup cocoa, add to eggs, and stir until moistened completely.

Add this mixture to baking dish and stir to mix well.

Bake 1 hour at 350 degrees, and serve with whipped cream.

Christmas Poem

Maria Magdalena Agullo

heaven's lace upon the land
an angel's serenade
a winking star to crown the sky
a Baby heaven-made
This is Christmas time!

frosty winds that tag your face
villages of snowmen rise
balls of ice to throw at friends
red cheeks and twinkling eyes
This is Christmas time!

trees with gowns of glowing lights
yards with blinking shows
packages of mystery
songs the east wind blows
This is Christmas time!

Memories of a Swedish Christmas in America

Karen Strand

As a child, Christmas Eve was the highlight of my year. If we were lucky the cold, dark night would be brightened by mounds of snow. Bundled up in layers of warm clothing topped by a scratchy wool coat, our family (Dad, Mom, and older sister Janice) walked one mile to Grandpa Carlbom's house in my hometown of Tacoma, Washington. Once there, the small house quickly filled with relatives. And the more relatives that arrived, the more animated became the Amazon green parrot, Philip, who lived in a corner of Grandpa's kitchen. (Grandpa had been given the parrot by a Swedish seaman down on the docks. Having emigrated from Stockholm, it was one place where Grandpa could go to speak his native language.)

While my cousins joined me in Grandpa's living room to scope out the gifts under the tree (it rattles like Tinkertoys!) and scatter silvery tinsel all over the rug, my aunts bustled about a hot kitchen preparing the smorgasbord. Once, when Aunt Helen told an older aunt to "Rest a bit, you're doing too much," Philip promptly piped in with the very same words, causing laughter all around.

In the meantime, Uncle Nels and Uncle Frederik tended to the kettle of glogg, which simmered on a back burner. It was made with red wine, raisins, and spices such as cardamom, cinnamon, and cloves.

Then we gathered around the dining room table, and what a feast! The table was covered with a white linen cloth and held all the tasty morsels of our Swedish heritage—a platter of lutefisk, Swedish meatballs, sausages, bowls of pickled herring, boiled potatoes, hard-boiled eggs, plates of cheeses, hardtack, and an assortment of breads. There would be plates of Spritz, among other Christmas cookies. And Mom always brought pies, usually lemon meringue.

One time, after supper, Uncle Nels told us he had bought a new record called "I Yust Go Nuts at Christmas" sung by Yogi Yorgesson. He invited us down the street to his house to listen to it. Then he put on a polka, and the grownups danced in his living room. But that was only one time. Usually, after eating we gathered in Grandpa's living room for the presents. But where did the presents go? For my grandpa had somehow slipped in, scooped up the gifts, and put them in a large pack on his back. Then, as anticipated, a knock came at the front door and there stood Santa, fake beard and all, and on his back—all the presents. The gift I remember most was a charm bracelet made of miniature replicas of grocery items such as a can of Chase & Sanborn coffee, a checkerboard box of Ralston Purina, and a tiny can of Dutch Girl cleanser.

When the festivities were over, we retraced the mile home—Mom, carrying brown paper bags stuffed with presents, and Dad, hoisting a sleeping girl on his shoulders. Once there, Janice and I hung our stockings on the fireplace before climbing upstairs to our beds. Then I couldn't sleep, knowing that the next day held even more good times. Those limp stockings would be bulging with pencils and hair ribbons and candy canes. In a corner of the large dining room would be our tree, decorated with homemade popcorn balls wrapped in waxed paper and tied to the branches with red or green ribbon. Under the tree—more presents.

On Christmas morning we got to eat in the dining room instead of the kitchen. There was no wondering what breakfast would be: Julekaka (Christmas bread) with hot cocoa for my sister and me. In the afternoon we celebrated Christmas at my grandma Johnson's house, but it was quieter, and paled in comparison to the noisy crowd the day before with Philip the parrot chiming in, and having Santa actually deliver presents to the front door!

Good memories. Warm memories. Family memories, of a good ol' Swedish Christmas.

Julekaka (Christmas bread)

Turn on oven for 10 minutes at 150 degrees, then shut it off but keep door closed. This makes a nice, warm haven in which the dough can rise.

In large mixing bowl, put:

5 cups white flour
1 Tbsp. cardamom
2 cups candied fruit and citrus (chopped citron)
1 – 1½ cups raisins.

Mix well. Set aside. Combine the following:

2 cups milk, scalded (can be done on stove or in microwave)
1 cup sugar, dissolved in scalded milk
1 cup butter melted in the scalded milk

Let mixture cool to lukewarm. Pour some of it over:

1 Tbsp. active dry yeast

Mix. When smooth, add dissolved yeast mixture into main milk/sugar/butter mixture. Then add all of flour mixture, and combine to make soft dough. Knead together to make soft dough that doesn't stick to the sides of the bowl. Or, you can turn it out onto lightly floured surface for kneading.

Place in buttered bowl and turn over once so oiled side is up. Place cotton dish towel over top, and place bowl in warm, preheated oven. Leave for 30 to 45 minutes. Punch down and knead again. This time, separate the dough into 2 rounds and place them in round Pyrex pans. Cover with dish towel again and let rise once more for 30 to 45 minutes.

Once risen, bake in a 400 degree oven for 30 to 40 minutes.

In Memory of Candy Cane Cookies

Liz Collard

As soon as I came in the back door and saw the bowls of red and white dough on the kitchen table, I knew it was officially Christmas. My older sisters and I rushed to shed our snow-dusted outer garments and wash our frostbitten hands. It was cookie baking time! For the next several days we would help prepare the dozen or so recipes that had become family favorites.

After each batch was completed, they were packed between layers of waxed paper in five gallon ice cream buckets and stored on a shelf in the garage which served as additional freezer space in Minnesota during the month of December. On Christmas Eve, the centerpiece of the dining room sideboard was a large silver tray, displaying a tantalizing assortment of our efforts.

We started with the Candy Canes every year. Mom mixed the ingredients while we were at school. Our part was to roll them out and shape them. After they were placed in the oven, we waited anxiously for the "ding" of the timer, then looked on as Mom donned her oven mitts and withdrew the hot pans. We argued over whose turn it was to sprinkle them with the crushed candy cane and sugar mixture. When they had cooled just enough to pick one up, that first bite of a warm buttery-minty cookie was pure heaven.

My mother passed away shortly after the birth of my first child, but I have continued the tradition she began. It was always one of the highlights of the season for my children, as it had been for me. Even after they became teenagers and were too busy to help make the cookies, I soldiered on alone. They might have lost interest in the baking, but they still wanted to participate in the taste-testing.

Each member of my extended family has their own personal favorite from the assortment of bars, candies, and cookies we continue to make year after year. But for me, nothing evokes the happy memories and warm feelings of Christmas like a Candy Cane cookie.

Candy Cane Cookies

½ cup shortening
½ cup butter or margarine
1 cup powdered sugar
1 egg
1½ tsp. almond extract
1 tsp. vanilla extract
2½ cups all purpose flour
1 tsp. salt
½ tsp. red food coloring
½ cup crushed candy canes or peppermint candies, mixed with
½ cup granulated sugar

Mix the first 8 ingredients in order given. Divide dough into 2 equal parts and place in separate bowls. Color one-half with the red food coloring. For each cookie, use a 1-inch ball of red dough and a 1-inch ball of white dough. Roll the balls into strips about 4 inches long. Carefully twist the 2 strips together and form into a candy cane shape. Bake at 350 degrees for about 9 minutes, or until the cookies are firm but not browned. Immediately remove from pans and sprinkle with crushed candy cane/sugar mixture while cookies are still hot.

Tip:

It's best to keep the size of the cookies small so they won't break as easily after they're baked.

Braised Stuffed Pork Chops To Die For

Pat Rowland

This is a recipe my daughter always requests for Christmas. It's a nice switch from the usual turkey and dressing or ham. I learned to make these pork chops in high school, senior year (class of 1961) in Home Economics. The recipe was supplied by our teacher and came, I believe, from a Meta Givens cookbook.

At the end of our year, part of our grade was to plan and prepare a meal for the Agriculture boys. (At that time only girls took Home Economics and boys took Agriculture.) Following the meal, we were required to write a summary of the experience, another part of our final grade. We gave an overview of the meal and then broke it into what went as we had planned, what snags we ran into, and what adjustments we had to make in the process. It was truly reminiscent of the day when young girls dreamed of being Betty Crocker housewives.

The stuffed chops were such a hit then and continue to be for fifty years! I bake yams along with it, adding to the efficiency of the meal and good use of the oven heat.

Braised Stuffed Pork Chops

5 double-rib pork chops
1½ cup soft, coarse bread crumbs (use half loaf bread and half cornbread)
¼ tsp. poultry seasoning
½ tsp. salt
½ cup finely diced celery
4 Tbsp. melted butter
flour
milk
salt and pepper

Note: 1 cup chopped apples is also a good addition to stuffing, but I've never used it—too perfect the way it is!

Serves 5

Have butcher make pocket for dressing on inside of each chop, with opening between 2 bones. Wipe chops with damp cloth. Lightly mix together crumbs, seasonings, celery, and melted butter, and stuff chops. Sprinkle with salt and pepper to taste, roll in flour. Brown chops quickly in a small amount of oil. Place in a baking dish and pour in about ½ inch of milk. Do not cover pork chops with milk. Cover and bake in moderately slow oven (325 degrees) for 1½ to 2 hours or until chops are perfectly tender. Remove cover for last 30 minutes of cooking.

A Special Surprise

Juanita Nobles

This Christmas story happened in my husband's family and I have heard it many times. Of course, it is embellished.

It was December 23, and three tow-headed little boys looked out the window, waiting for their dad, Bill, to come in to eat supper. Their mom, Thula, had prepared beans and cornbread, but nobody could eat until Dad walked through the door. Their stomach growled as they watched Mom dish up the beans and pour the fresh milk. She had milked the cow that morning, then chilled the milk so they would have a nice, cold treat at suppertime.

Most of the time, beans and cornbread were the fare at their house. They killed a beef once in a while but the meat had to be used sparingly. More often, they butchered a hog. Then they had bacon, sausage, and ham curing in the shed. Mom sometimes put some of the pork into the beans. The boys all hoped to get pieces of meat with their beans when that happened. But they ate what was on their plate, and if they got lucky and had some meat, they were glad.

Their dad was foreman on a ranch just west of Fort Worth, and he was fortunate to have landed that job. Before they moved to that area, they were sharecroppers working farmland on the banks of the Brazos River, way down in south Texas. Times were better now, but still it was nothing special.

Christmas was just two days away, but the three boys knew not to expect much. They knew they would get an orange, maybe a banana, a pair of socks, and a small toy—probably something their dad carved out of wood for them to play with. But they didn't expect anything else, because that was the way it had always been. These were hard times in the 1930s in Texas during the Great Depression, and they were all used to it.

Ed was the first to see his dad. "Look, Thuriel, there he is!" he shouted. Ed was eight and the oldest of the boys. Thuriel was six and George was four.

All three boys clambered to get to the front door first, to grab Daddy around the legs and give him a hug. Ed, being the oldest, always got there first, but Bill had a special hug for the other two as well. He was a loving dad who didn't leave any of the boys out. Ed hugged him around the waist while the other boys each grabbed a leg to give him a proper welcome home. It was the highlight of Bill's day to look at his three boys and then to sit down and hold them on his lap for a few minutes before sitting down at the table. He was proud of his family.

That night, Mom had baked a cake for dessert. She dished up three slices and set them before the boys after their meal was finished. Thuriel looked at Ed's piece and said, "He got more than me." Ed grabbed his fork and began eating. Nobody was going to take his piece away, if he was quick at getting a bite of it.

"Just eat your cake, boys, and be glad you got it," said Thula, giving Bill his and putting hers on her plate. As she watched the boys she thought of a plan. Next time she baked a cake, she would let one boy cut it, and the other two would get first choice of the pieces they wanted. That will help them learn to be careful and it just might solve the problem of the rivalry, Thula thought.

They had filled up on the beans and cornbread, and before long it was bedtime for the boys. Then Bill and Thula sat quietly, cherishing their precious time together and making plans for Christmas. Bill showed Thula the little cars he had carved for the boys to play with, and she told him she had three oranges, one for each boy's stocking. Money was scarce, and there was nothing to be done about it. They would not go into debt; they would do what they could, and it would be as it always had been.

Bill and Thula did not get to go to church very often as it was a five-mile walk, but everybody at church knew they were regulars when they could get there. Sometimes a neighbor with a car would pick them up and take them. Not wanting to neglect their boys' Christian education, they read their Bible at home and told the boys stories about Bible heroes most every night.

The next day, December 24, Bill took the boys out and cut a tree from the woods around their house. They proudly trekked back, pulling the tree, and excitedly waited until their dad nailed it to a couple of pieces of wood so it would stand up, then their mom pulled out the box of decorations. The children were happily chattering and decorating the tree when they heard the sound of a car close to their front door.

Who could that be? Thula wondered. When she opened the door, three ladies from the church carried in a big box.

"We brought you this food," one of the ladies said. She set the box on the table and began taking out a turkey, home canned vegetables, and produce.

Bill and Thula were speechless as they considered the gift they were receiving. The boys knelt in chairs by the table as they pulled things out of the box, amazed at the bounty.

"Oh, we have more," another lady said. She opened the door and brought in toys—a truck, a play lawnmower, and a little car big enough for a boy to sit in! The boys looked at the toys, and each of them figured out which one was his. The car was too little for Ed and too big for George, but Thuriel fit into the seat perfectly. It was made for him. He pushed the pedals and the car began to move around the room. He was in little boy heaven. He had never had a gift like this one! Ed grabbed the truck and George began pushing the toy lawnmower.

On Christmas morning, the boys could hardly wait to play with their toys, then they took their stockings from the mantle and exclaimed over the oranges. Ed stuck his thumb into the thick skin and began sucking out the sweet juice. An orange was a rare and wonderful treat for them.

Thula roasted the turkey and made cornbread dressing, opened a jar of the home canned green beans, peeled potatoes for mashing, and made a feast for her family. They counted themselves among the privileged on that Christmas in 1934, thankful for people who cared enough to think of them and bring them gifts.

Cornbread Dressing

6 cups cornbread
4 cups biscuit or soft bread crumbs

Soak in 4 cups milk, stock, or water. Sauté in hot fat until golden brown: large onion, celery (part leaves). Add onions and celery to crumbs.

Add:
4 well-beaten eggs
2 teaspoons salt
½ teaspoon pepper
1 teaspoon sage or poultry seasoning.

Add 4 more cups milk, stock, or water. Taste and add more sage, if needed.

Stuff bird. Cook in medium oven about 25 minutes per pound.

The Christmas Spirit of Old

Raymond Fenech

Christmas is always a feast for senses;
it wakes human instinct, bringing to life all extrasensory perception.
When memoirs rally our hearts
and time becomes an insignificant fraction.

I pledged all my childhood to this feast of colour and lights,
smells of oven-baked macaroni, chestnuts cooked in caldrons,
that smoked Christmas ghosts from the warm fierce flames;
sizzling fried date slices that filled the air with aromatic flavours
of brandy and anise—so many Christmas sweet delights.

There were pine tree branches lit with minute lights like fireflies,
fairies flitting about their flaming wings shedding their glittering sparks,
fresh from their flamboyant magic wands.

The Holy Night was personified in the poor dimly lit crib
made of thick brown paper, or rustic stone and sand,
populated with clay figurines of heroes that live our daily lives,
struggling against mercenary politicians who abuse the weak
        and glorify evil.

This was a time for family to rejoice, singing Christmas carols together,
and many accompanied the procession of the newly-born Saviour
when lighted lanterns flooded darkness and wealth was measured
        by the spirit.

Even love in those days was platonic, romantic, harmonic.
It signified the true family values taking long to come but when it came
it was there to stay until the couple grew grey and even dementia
        was powerless
and could not take their immortal love away.

From a Child on New Year's Day

Elaine Hardt

We packed Christmas away,
we put it in a box
The lights that twinkled
the tinsel so shiny
little balls of different kinds
that hung on the evergreen tree
We packed Baby Jesus away
we put him in a box
with Mary and Joseph
his star so shiny
the shepherds and the three wise kings
that came to worship at the manger
We packed Christmas away
we put it in a box
the laughter, surprises
the good times together with
relatives from far away
Why can't that happiness last more than a day?

Up Front

Terri Elders

Even though Mama always warned me to be careful what I wished for, I had no doubt I wanted a padded bra for Christmas. I wished for one when I blew out the candles on my twelfth birthday, and when I split the Thanksgiving wishbone with my sister. Once I even sneaked outside late at night to search for a falling star to wish on.

I had skipped a grade, so felt dwarfed by the other girls in seventh grade who wore bras, whether they needed them or not. I'd seen a few stuffing Kleenex in their bras in the girls' restroom, but in the gym showers I recognized that most of the girls already had no need for such artifice. I did.

I'd heard of training bras, but thought that sounded like something for wannabe ten-year-olds, just one step up from an undershirt. I longed for the real article, a lacy 32AA with some slight padding to give me the illusion of curves. My older sister, Patti, had bras, and I wanted one too.

Actually, *wanted* might be too mild a word to describe how incredibly desperate I was to be able to look down and see something other than my slightly knobby knees. I pined, I yearned, and I hankered and hungered. Sometimes at night I'd pat a hand across my concave chest as I called for divine intervention. "Not too big," I'd whisper, "but just a little something to distinguish me from my little brother."

At first my parents scoffed at my request. "Christmas is a time for games, for things you really need. Coats, for example, not for underwear," Mama said.

"A bra? That's silly," Daddy said.

Patti agreed that she, for one, needed a new coat, a pea jacket just like the other girls were sporting that winter.

But I whined and wheedled, moaned and groaned, until finally Mama sighed, shook her head and said, "We'll think about it." Daddy grumbled, but I knew I had won. When Mama thought about something, it got well-thought, and I knew she wanted me to be happy. And to look nice. She'd always reminded me to wear clean shorts when I went to play tennis, and to wash my hair when I came home from the playground pool.

On Christmas morning Patti opened her present first, the biggest box under the tree. She pulled out a navy blue pea jacket, and squealed with delight. She threw it on and vamped around the living room as if she were parading down a catwalk. I had to admit she looked chic indeed in the stylish broad-lapelled coat with its slash pockets and big wooden buttons.

My old red wool jacket would get me through another winter, I told myself, even though I had noticed it was getting snug across the shoulders. I reached for my package, much smaller, but equally gaily wrapped. I opened the box, and spied, nestled among the tissue, not one, but two delicate brassieres.

My father and brother looked the other way when I pulled them from the box, but Mama and Patti smiled. I scampered into the bedroom to try one on and nearly cried for joy when I saw myself in the mirror. I had a bosom, at long, long last. For the next few hours I preened, pretending not to notice my brother's knowing smirks.

Later that day we prepared to drive to Grandma's for Christmas dinner. Since the temperature in late December had dipped into the low 40s, cold for Southern California, I threw on my old red jacket. But when I started to button it up I realized I had a problem. No matter how hard I tugged, the buttons wouldn't slip into the buttonholes. It fell about half an inch too short.

The culprit was my Christmas bra. The padding added just enough girth to my front to render the coat unbuttonable. And red wool did not fall into the category of a stretch fabric.

I had a choice. Either remove the bra or go to Grandma's coatless. I chose the latter, yanking the Army blanket from my bed and wrapping it around my shoulders. Nobody said anything when we piled into the backseat, but I couldn't help but notice how pretty and warm Patti looked in her new coat.

"She's really growing up," Grandma said, marveling at my enhanced figure, even though she'd seen me the week before and must have known I couldn't have developed that much that fast. Grandpa just did a silent double take.

When school started after winter break, I knew I'd have to put the bras aside until the weather got warmer. I couldn't substitute my Army blanket on the long hike to the bus, so would have to button my jacket against the chill. I thought about tucking a bra into my zipper notebook and sneaking into the restroom before classes, but remembered how embarrassed those girls had looked when I saw them with the Kleenex, so decided against making myself a laughingstock. The bras would wait for their school debut.

By spring I had grown two inches and gained ten pounds. On the first day balmy enough to head for the bus without my old jacket, I eagerly pulled one of the bras from the drawer where they had languished all winter. "So pretty," I thought, as I stuck my arms through the straps and reached behind to fasten the hooks.

I couldn't get it hooked. I took it off and stared at it in disbelief. The 32AA was now too small. Then my eye fell on something else, something softly rounded.

"Be careful what you wish for," Mama had said. Thank heavens my birthday was coming up soon. I knew exactly what to wish for. A new jacket in a larger size. Because it was suddenly clear that Mama and I would have to go to the store for underwear before then. Probably right away!

A Remembrance of a Childhood Christmas

Noreen Ophoff

On Christmas Eve 1958 I was eight years old. Long after going to bed, I quietly tiptoed down the stairs, stepping far to the left side to avoid the creaky noise of some of the steps. Mom had already gone to bed and my older brother, Don, and older sister, Cathy, were fast asleep too. I sat on the second step from the bottom and leaned forward to look at the Christmas tree in the living room to my left.

Santa hadn't been there. No presents were under the tree we all decorated the week before. Mom told us Christmas would be different this year because Daddy had died in April. I knew Santa brought the presents and I didn't tell anyone I was worried, because Mom didn't say what would be different.

As I sat waiting, I heard the back door open and footsteps come through the dining room. Then, through the crack of the open door at the bottom of the staircase, I saw Santa. He set down his big red sack and hung red and white peppermint candy canes all over the tree. Then he filled the stockings for my brother, my sister, and me. Nothing in our stockings was ever wrapped and he had his back to me so I couldn't see what he was putting in, but I was hoping for the usual comic book, coloring book and crayons, and small toys.

Santa then leaned over and placed a large stuffed black-and-white panda bear behind the tree. Big presents were never wrapped either. Finishing up, Santa put other wrapped boxes all around under the tree, piling them on top of each other.

I smiled and wasn't worried anymore. The Christmas present pile looked like it always had when Daddy was with us. I silently went back to bed and slept until Cathy woke me up, and we three kids ran down the stairs—excited to see our stockings full of the usual things: Bugs Bunny comic books, baseball cards for Don, and paperback books for Cathy. I got a set of tiny dolls, just the right size to ride horses I loved to play with. Don and I got books too, and other things appropriate to our ages of Don, fourteen, Cathy, twelve, and I was eight. Some of our presents were clothes and we were even excited to get sweaters and socks.

I had my sneak peek of watching Santa bring us our Christmas. Even though Daddy was in heaven, and I had asked Mom how we were going to get along without him, our Christmas was the same as always with lots of presents to open.

Mom even had her usual box of Whitman Chocolates. I had an unshakable sense that as a family we were going to be okay.

***

The years have flown since 1958, and my sister insists that I dreamt the whole thing. She laughs when I tell this story to my grandchildren and hers, and she says, "She was sleeping at the bottom of the stairs and it was a dream."

But I know the truth. I wasn't sleeping and it wasn't a dream.

Christmas Memories

Freda Hatfield Tong

It happens like clockwork every December
My mood becomes pensive. I find I remember

Childhood Christmases, so long ago
Secrets and fragrances, new fallen snow,

A scraggly fir brought in from the cold,
With presents beneath and a new doll to hold.

Well, maybe not perfectly new, I am guessing,
But new-to-me, sweet-faced, and always a blessing.

This is your brother's; this for you, honey!
We did our best, though there wasn't much money.

We'd pile into the old car on a bright snowy day,
To pick up our grandparents, sing all the way.

Grandpa always brought candy. Grandma made pies.
Anticipation glowed in our eyes.

Back to our old clapboard house before noon,
We'd find Mama stirring with the old wooden spoon.

The woodstove was stoked, the aromas were real,
For chicken and dumplings were part of the meal.

Yes, the wind whistled through cracks in the door.
And our feet were cold on the rough wooden floor,

But we were together, a smile on each face,
As we sat at the table, each child in his place.

True, our gift giving was meager and mild,
But Christmas brings joy to the heart of a child.

Celebrations so simple in every way
Began the sweet memories I treasure today.

Italian Bowknots– A Post-Fast Treat

Janis A. Van Keuren

The sweet smells of Christmas draw me back to my carefree childhood days perched on a kitchen chair beside my mother, watching her cut and twist paper-thin slices of cookie dough into bowknots, wreaths, figure eights, long slivers, and other shapes. I always begged her to let me twist and pinch the dough, making a letter "J" for my name. I knew it would be mine once she fried the sweet dough in bubbling olive oil, drained it, and shook the heavenly snow of powdered sugar all over it.

I grew up hearing this crisp, light cookie dough called by its Italian name, "Crestoli," pronounced in my childlike ears, "Crustel." It is better known as "Italian Bowknots" or "Italian Bow Ties."

My mom was the best cook in our family. My Aunt Ange was a close second and Christmas was always at her home. When Mom walked into the family Christmas dinner carrying her bowl filled with lightly dusted "Crestoli," all the cousins jumped up to give her a hand. "Oh, let me help you, Aunt Louise," they all chorused. Mom was usually bearing Italian entrée dishes as well—"veal scaloppini" or "veal and eggplant parmesan."

Christmas Day was the big feast with antipasto, lasagna, veal, and eggplant Parmesan, tossed green salad, ham, corn on the cob, three-bean salad, green olives, and those lovely pitted black olives. My cousin Eddie and I used to put the olives on our fingers (before the meal) and walk around the house eating them off our dainties, one by one. Mom was not very happy with that unladylike behavior in me. I usually got the "eye" or a quick grab on the wrist with a harsh whisper to my ear to stop doing that.

After fasting from meat on Christmas Eve and not eating until after church on Christmas morning (per the Catholic tradition in those days), we all eagerly awaited the blessing and passing of the food. As the youngest child at that time, I was relegated to the kids' table with my younger cousins. That usually meant the card table at the end of the dining room table which stretched into the living room on holidays. We could hardly wait for the next generation to grow up so that we could join the adults at the main table.

The men usually gathered in the kitchen to talk and play cards after dinner while the women and children washed the dishes (another tradition we looked forward to passing on). When dishes were put away, the aroma of desserts and coffee wafted into the dining room. At last, I could have some Crestoli—my favorite holiday treat. Fortunately, Mom made enough for us to have at home in the mornings with coffee during my Christmas school break.

My family did not cook by recipes but only by memory, letting the feel of the texture and the taste of what they were making guide them. However, I needed something in concrete. Mom obtained something written from an Italian friend of hers and we adjusted it to make it just like Mom's and her mom before her.

Whenever I make these light, crispy cookies, I use my grandmother's pastry cutter to trim the paper-thin dough into slices that can be pinched and curled into different shapes. With each stroke, I remember those years when we were one great big family, living just a few blocks from each other, and celebrating every holiday with great joy!

Italian Bowknots

3 eggs
1½ Tbsp. granulated sugar
1/8 tsp. salt
¾ tsp. anisette flavoring
1½ Tbsp. anisette liqueur
½ Tsp. almond flavoring
1½ cups flour
1 Tbsp. butter

2 cups of oil for frying, usually a combination of extra light or virgin olive oil mostly and a light vegetable oil

Beat eggs lightly; add granulated sugar, salt, flavorings, and anisette liqueur; blend thoroughly. Place flour on board; cut in butter; add egg mixture. If this is too sloppy, you can mix it lightly with a wooden spoon in a bowl.

Knead dough until smooth ball is obtained. If dough is too soft, gradually add a little flour to make a firm but not hard dough. Set aside for 30 minutes. Cut dough into 4 sections. Roll out one at a time on well-floured board until it is wafer thin. Cut with a pastry cutter into strips about 6 inches long by ¾ inch wide. Pinch once in the middle or make a bowknot (like a bow tie) after pinching.

Once dough is cut, lay it out on thin, cotton dish towels to dry. DO NOT USE TERRY CLOTH TOWELS as dough will stick to them. Leave it there for about 1 hour allowing the dough to dry so that it can fry up crisp.

Fry boughs about 3 minutes or until light brown in deep hot oil. You may want to flip the pastry while frying. Drain on absorbent paper; cool; sprinkle with powdered sugar.

Buon Appetito.

Makes about 4 dozen bowknots. Double recipe for more.

Ignored Blessings

Kathy Collard Miller

Karen and Chuck stood in the wood-floored hall near their bedrooms, getting as close as they could to the closed door that led into the living room where they could imagine the sparkling Christmas tree awaiting them. Nine-year-old Karen whispered, "Why are they taking so long?"

"Yeah," Chuck murmured back. "I don't know how long I can wait. I'm gonna burst."

They knew the routine—they had to eat their breakfast first. Mother's rule: no breakfast—no gifts! "Why doesn't Daddy come get us? I can't wait to get my new bicycle," Karen mumbled, even as she feared her parents didn't have enough money for it.

Suddenly, Daddy was there. "OK, who wants to go first?"

His question was a tease because everyone knew the youngest always went first. He scooped Chuck up into his arms, gently laid the blanket over his head, and whisked him through the door. Karen tried to peek into the living room, but her father closed the door too quickly. *Oh, why does Mommy have us eat breakfast first? If only the kitchen weren't on the other side of the living room. If only I didn't have to have the blanket over my head so I could see my presents. There are always unwrapped presents. Will the bike be unwrapped right by the tree? I just know it's going to be the first thing I see.*

Within moments, Karen had her turn with the blanket over her head. She knew better than to try to raise it. She would just have to eat her oatmeal quickly and then find her new shiny bike. In a flash, she envisioned and could feel the air against her skin, pushing back her flowing hair as she rode fast down the nearby hill at the park.

After they gobbled down their oatmeal, they both sprinted around the wall that separated the kitchen from the living room and gasped with delight. The tree blazed with colored lights. Karen's eyes scanned over the gifts, some wrapped, some not. But there wasn't any bike standing by the tree. *Where is it?* she wondered as her heart felt heavy. *Maybe they'll bring it out later. Oh, I hope so,* Karen pleaded silently as she raced to the edge of the tree where her presents were stacked. Trying to push her disappointment aside, she grabbed the unwrapped doll that sat on top of her pile. It was the doll she wanted—but it wasn't the bike!

"Karen," she heard her mother call, "please go to the hall closet and get me one of the folding chairs."

"But Mommy, I'm not done with my presents…" Her mother's warning look stopped her whine. She got up slowly. "Oh, OK." She wanted to scream, "Where's my bike?" as tears pooled in her eyes. *I guess there just wasn't enough money, but oh, I wanted that bike so much. I shouldn't have gotten my hopes up.*

She walked across the small living room to the hall closet and jerked open the door. Tugging at the chair inside, she pulled it out and carried it to where her mother sat. "Thanks, honey." Her mother grinned.

Moments later, Karen's shoulders slumped as she reached for her last present. It certainly wasn't anywhere big enough to be a bike. As she ripped the paper, she could hear the tittering of her parents. *Why are they laughing? It's not funny!* Her bike wasn't going to suddenly materialize from the small last present waiting for her.

Karen slowly peeled the paper from the present, hoping against hope that a bike would suddenly take shape. But it didn't. She held instead a stuffed white polar bear.

But it wasn't her bike.

"Karen, if you're done opening your presents, what do you say?" her mother asked.

"Thanks for my presents. They're nice." *But they aren't my bike,* she wanted to say, but knew better.

Then her mother spoke up again, "Karen…" but started laughing before she could say anything more. Before she could control herself, her father had burst into laughter too.

Her mother's giggling subsided and then she said, "Karen, would you please go to the front door closet again and stand there?"

She obediently trudged toward the closet and front door, and then jolted to a stop. There, right in front of her, leaning against the opposite wall, was her shiny, red bike decorated with a big red bow! As she stood transfixed with her mouth agape, everyone roared with laughter.

"Honey, why didn't you see it before?" her mother called out. "It's been there the whole time. That's why I interrupted you with that silly task."

Karen couldn't speak at first. *Her bike! It's real!* "It's been here the whole time?" She grinned as she ran over to the bike and touched it tenderly. Red! Just like she'd wanted.

As she jumped onto its red plastic seat that sported bright yellow sunflowers, she brushed away tears. "I guess I was so disappointed when I didn't see it near the tree that I just didn't notice it over here." She paused. "But it's here! My bike! I love it!" She ran to each one and hugged them.

I know that story is true because I'm Karen's older sister and I saw the whole thing. When I get disappointed by life and even other people, I remember that story and how blessings are often all around us, and yet we just don't see them. It only takes looking outside the box to consider other ways of thinking, like seeing a bike waiting just a few feet away.

Christmas Magic

Brendalyn Crudup Martin

The snowflakes drifted across the yard, creating a pattern of white dots in the air. I watched for a while before easing back to the warmth of the furnace. Christmas Eve…I thought about the times my brother and I waited for Daddy to come home with the gifts for the tree.

He always tried to hide some in the car to surprise us, pretending that Santa must have dropped them down the chimney. When I was small, I wondered how Santa came out of the fireplace, but everyone said it was magic. We had an artificial chimney so over the years that became a family joke. One year to confuse us, Daddy said, "Santa knocked on the door and I let him in." We had a lot of laughs over that.

I walked into the kitchen as the aroma of turkey and dressing, ham, potatoes, and greens teased my nostrils. Mom was putting the last touches on her famous chocolate sheath cake. She has made it every year for as long as I can remember, and has protected the recipe as a treasured heirloom to be passed on to me one day. The ingredients for the icing are cooked in a pan on top of the stove, then mixed with the powdered sugar and pecans, and poured over a warm cake. After a few hours, the icing tastes like delicious pecan fudge. When I was growing up, Mom always let me have the bowl when she was finished, making sure she left a little icing for me to spoon out with my fingers.

She laughed as I waited for her to finish. "Haven't you outgrown this yet?" she said with a smile. I shook my head as I reached for the bowl. I enjoyed the smooth feel of the mixing bowl as I ran my fingers around each side and back and forth across the bottom to capture every bit of icing. I couldn't remember how old I was the first time I did this, but over time it became a family tradition whenever she baked.

I turned at the sound of the front door. Ron and Daddy walked in laughing, trying to decide whether Arkansas or Texas would have the coldest Christmas. They seemed to be hitting it off pretty well. I was always Daddy's little girl, and even though I was married for nine years and a widow for one, he still covered me with fatherly wings. I wasn't sure how he would react to a prospective son-in-law right now; especially since I wasn't sure of my own feelings just yet. Maybe that's why I found so much comfort in surrounding myself with familiar things.

More than five years had passed since I spent Christmas in Arkansas. I missed the serenity of the Southern lifestyle, so much calmer than the frenzy of a big city. Phoenix had really grown since I moved there years ago. I had recently graduated and I think I was a little full of myself at the time, but aren't we all at that age?

I grew up in a protective environment, sheltered from the harsher realities of life. God blessed me with two very special people who did not wait until Christmas to show us we were loved. Mom and Dad made it a day-to-day process. They encouraged my brother and me to form our own opinions and they let us know our thoughts were important enough for them to always take time to listen to us. We didn't always get everything we wanted, but they made sure we had everything we needed.

We may have taken a few things for granted when we were growing up, but we never doubted their love and I'm sure they never doubted ours. I fell back into the couch and let the warmth of their love surround me now as I thought back over my life and all the happy memories.

I remembered my brother and cousin making their own version of a go-cart and sailing down the hill to end up in a heap of wheels, legs, and arms when they reached the bottom. I remembered the football games, the after-game parties, and marching in the band. I remembered field trips and hikes up the mountains to the Gorge, picnics on the lake, boat rides, and so much more.

I remembered the times my brother and I tried to stay up late to catch Santa, only to fall asleep on the couch with Daddy waking us to a tree filled with gifts and an empty plate of cookies to show that Santa had been and gone. No matter how hard we tried, we could never catch him.

I still had the Just Like Me doll that Santa left when I was six years old. I used to dress her in my clothes and tried to take her everywhere. One day Daddy came home and she was sitting on the couch. He thought it was me and asked if I had fun at school. I laughed as I remembered the expression on his face when he realized that he was talking to a doll.

I turned at the sound of a door opening and watched my brother and his family enter the house. Once more it was filled with the sounds of children's laughter as they circled the tree pointing at gifts, trying to guess what secret delight was in store for them. So many memories flooded my mind and once again, I was a child, caught up in the magic of Christmas, searching among the gifts under the tree, laughing with delight at each new prize, while outside, snowflakes drifted softly through the air, creating a very special Christmas magic.

A Cinnamon Toast Gift

Annette Kathleen Hutchins

Katie tiptoed down the dark hallway and peered into the living room. She gazed at the brightly wrapped presents under the Christmas tree and counted the tags that started with the letter "K". One...two...three...four. She had promised not to open a single gift until morning. The full moon still shone through the curtains. It was too early to wake everyone. She would have to wait.

Katie's growling stomach told her that she was hungry. Into the kitchen she went to search for a midnight snack. Cinnamon toast. She knew how to make cinnamon toast all by herself. She took out a loaf of bread and pulled out two slices, slipped them into the toaster, and pushed down the lever. While they were toasting, Katie opened the refrigerator, took out the tub of butter, pulled out the bowl of sugar, and brought out the tin of cinnamon from the spice rack. A butter knife, a teaspoon and a napkin—she was ready.

POP! Up shot the hot toast. Katie waited for it to cool a bit, then she lifted the slices out of the toaster and placed them on the spread-out napkin. She buttered each piece, sprinkled the sugar and cinnamon on top, and blended everything carefully with the knife. There! They were ready to eat.

Katie munched on the first piece hungrily. Yummy! As she picked up the second piece she considered someone else—she would like to give this piece to Jesus. Putting it back down on the napkin, she said, "This is for you, Jesus." She smiled and left the kitchen so Jesus could eat it when He was ready.

Katie nestled on the coach and gazed at the room full of Christmas until her eyes drooped shut. Later she awakened with a start and ran back to the kitchen to find out if Jesus had eaten her cinnamon toast gift. But there it sat untouched on the napkin.

Katie's heart hurt from disappointment. She had longed to see a miracle and the toast to be eaten and gone. Then a thought came to Katie. It seemed that Jesus wanted to tell her something: "Thank you, Katie. Thank you for My cinnamon toast gift. I love your gift and I love you, Katie. But I would like you to have it."

A smile spread across Katie's face, "Oh, thank You, Jesus," she whispered. She picked up the cinnamon toast gift and ate every last delicious bite.

Family Memories

*To us, family means putting your arms
around each other and being there.
—Barbara Bush*

Easy Christmas Turtle Candy

Debbie Cunningham Carpenter

This recipe shared one year at the Cunningham Ladies Christmas Tea soon became my favorite homemade Christmas candy. It is easy enough for children to help.

1 pkg. small pretzels
1 13-oz. pkg. Rolo candies (app. 60 pieces.)
1 package pecan halves

Preheat oven to 250 degrees. Unwrap candies. Cover cookie sheet with foil and place pretzels on foil in single layer. Place a Rolo candy on each pretzel. Cook for 4 minutes or until candy is soft but not melted.

While candy is warming, toast pecans in the microwave for 30 seconds. Then scramble pecans with your hands and toast for another 30 seconds.

Remove candy from oven and place one pecan in the center of each softened candy, pressing lightly. Let candy cool at least 20 minutes, then put it in the refrigerator for at least 20 minutes to help it solidify.

Christmas Traditions and Treasures

Joyce McCullough

I am from Little Golden Books and stockings filled with fruit.
I am from My Chatty Cathy, two Barbies,
and my sister's bride doll lay hidden in the attic.
I am from opening one gift on Christmas Eve
and reading the second chapter of Luke.
I love candlelight services and sounds of "Silent Night."
I am from dinner at AJ's and a table decorated with crackers
waiting to be popped.
We always play the latest board game.
I am from Christmas morning brunches with Mother's sticky buns
To Sunday lunches with cousins and casseroles.
I am from live cedar trees adorned with angel hair
To an artificial silver tree with a color wheel.
I am from a tall and slender Norfolk pine.
I play the piano, and we fill the great room with harmony.
I am from pumpkin bread and Christmas wreaths
To party mix and chocolate chip cookies.
I am from secret pals, fruit baskets, and live nativity scenes.
I pretend to be Mary or a shepherd.
I am from World Vision chickens, soccer balls,
and teaching supplies.
I adopt a Prison Fellowship angel.
I am from new generations that carry on the family name.
Instead of listening to the stories, I now tell them.
I am from a family with Christmas traditions and treasures.

A Blue Christmas Turned Bright

Millie Barger

It was Christmas Eve and I was feeling a bit blue. I missed my daughter Shirley and wished she and her husband Mike could be with us. But they lived in Canada, and traveling during the holidays was just too much of a hassle for them.

That afternoon, the doorbell rang. I answered it but nobody was there—not a delivery truck or car in sight, just a huge refrigerator carton. Puzzled, I called for my husband. He came outside and we examined the box. It was addressed to us but had no return label. We started to push it into the house when I heard a thud.

I jumped back. "Something moved in there!" I exclaimed. Suddenly, the top of the box flew open and out popped a laughing Shirley and Mike.

"Merry Christmas!" they shouted. And, believe me, it certainly was!

Our Family's Christmas Custard Eggnog

Joanne Hendrix

Our Family's Christmas Custard Eggnog is a recipe that has been enjoyed by our family for over 50 years. I remember my older sister first made it when she was about eleven for a 4-H demonstration, then I followed up and made it for a 4-H demo several years later. When I first tasted this eggnog, I couldn't believe anything could taste so wonderful. I was amazed that if you add a little sugar to "yucky" egg whites and whip them up, you'd get these heavenly billows of delight. And the custard was so smooth, rich, and warm, I'd dream about it until the occasional holiday when one of us would make it again.

The original recipe was found in a 4-H book, but it was lost years ago. My sister and I have both made it off and on throughout the years, trying to remember the exact recipe, but we could never get it quite right. I wanted to be able to pass it down to our daughters, so I researched many eggnog recipes until I finally developed this one that is very similar to the original one we loved. We now make it every Christmas Day evening in my family, as a little something to look forward to as we close the Christmas celebrations. I also buy my five daughters and one daughter-in-law soft pajamas and Christmas socks every Christmas. Those that can, gather Christmas night in our new pj's and socks, watch "White Christmas," and sip this marvelous hot eggnog.

Christmas Custard Eggnog

Eggnog

6 egg yolks
½ cup sugar
3/8 tsp. salt
½ tsp. nutmeg
4 cups whole milk
2 cups heavy cream
1½ tsp. vanilla
Sprinkle of nutmeg

Meringue

6 egg whites (best if they are at room temperature)
3-6 Tbsp. sugar (depending upon taste)
½ - 1 tsp. cream of tartar

Eggnog Procedure

Beat egg yolks on high speed of electric mixer until thick and lemon colored. Gradually add sugar, salt, and nutmeg, as you are beating, for a total of at least 6 minutes beating time. Set aside. Pour milk and heavy cream into medium saucepan, stir and bring almost to a boil. Pour the hot milk mixture into egg mixture a little at a time so eggs don't scramble. Then, pour the whole mixture back into saucepan and cook and stir over medium to low heat just until the mixture is thick enough to cover a metal spoon, or it reaches 160 degrees F. Do not overcook…the eggs will scramble. But, because of the unique procedure of heating the milk first, without the eggs, this probably won't happen.

It can be served hot or cold. It's delicious enough to be dessert! You can sprinkle a little more nutmeg to top to taste.

HOT: Serve hot with meringue (below) softly folded in well, or with meringue on top. We like it best hot. But, if there is any left over, we put it in the fridge and enjoy it cold the next morning.

COLD option: Put in refrigerator to cool. Gently fold meringue into chilled eggnog, or just serve with it on top.

Meringue Procedure

Sprinkle cream of tartar over egg whites. With chilled beaters, in a chilled, medium mixing bowl, beat egg whites till soft peaks form. Gradually add sugar and beat until stiff peaks form (about 7 minutes).

Yield: Approx 12, 4-6 oz servings.

The Gift of Life

Linda Boutin

I love Christmas Day, but this year I felt ridiculous, like everyone who saw me understood what a freak I had become. An eight-inch long, white, rubber tube hung out my nose, carefully taped to my left nostril. Called a Cantor Tube, it dangled awkwardly, yanking at my face and my self-esteem. The troop of young doctors thoroughly explained to me that it was meant to drain my intestines of excess fluid and gas. Understanding it did nothing to make its intrusion any more acceptable to me. Still I wanted to go to our family Christmas party.

I squirmed beside my husband, Gary, in the front seat of our little car, the first time I had been out of UCLA hospital in nearly a month. "I'm starving," he declared. How many times had I heard that comment in our two years of marriage?

"You probably better stop at a restaurant and get some lunch," I answered. "It's two and you had breakfast hours ago."

We got off the freeway in the San Fernando Valley and searched for an open restaurant, but to no avail. In 1979 no self-respecting restaurant stayed open on Christmas Day. Everyone would be eating at home with their families. After the fruitless search we drove back onto the freeway and continued on to my brother and sister-in-law's home where the Christmas party was already underway.

As we pulled up the long, winding driveway, Blanco, their huge white German shepherd, barked a greeting. He dropped his rimless tire at Gary's feet and my husband obligingly rolled it down the driveway for the dog to retrieve. The familiarity of the house and surroundings felt strangely out of place after being secluded behind hospital walls so long.

We walked in the door and received instant greetings from our family, all the adults that is. Everyone considerately ignored the strange protuberance I sported from my nose.

I knew it looked weird. (There was a reason the mirrors were kept small and out of the way in the hospital.) I chatted with my brothers and sisters who surrounded me with questions that overwhelmed me. As I wilted in front of them, one of my sisters ushered me over to the couch and I relaxed back into the cushions. The group moved over to the appetizer table and I sighed in relief. This was more activity than I had participated in in months and although I was only 24, I had no stamina after months in bed. Gary sat beside me and whispered an anxious, "Are you okay?"

"Yes, just tired. You go ahead and enjoy the appetizers." I dare not go near the food. The doctors and nurses both extracted many promises from me to not eat or drink anything and be back at the hospital within six hours. With my intestines paralyzed, I knew that anything I put into my stomach would just cause problems. The house smelled wonderfully, though, of Christmas treats. I could identify everything from prime rib and twice-baked potatoes to pies and cakes.

I turned away from the kitchen and focused my attention on enjoying the Christmas tree, the large Nativity scene, and the gifts scattered around the room. A Yule log burning in the fireplace made tongues of light flicker on the walls. This was the first Christmas since I was five that I hadn't purchased a single gift, but the Lord had given the doctors the most important gift—the information they needed to save my life. I pondered the significance of Jesus' birth until something else distracted my attention. Two pairs of eyes peeked around the edge of the couch, openly staring at this unfamiliar lady sitting so close.

When it came to interacting with my nephews and nieces I knew this territory. I had started babysitting for Launi when I was eleven and most of the children knew me well. But not Eric and Chris. At ages two and four, they didn't even attempt to disguise the curiosity about their aunt sitting alone in the living room.

As they stood transfixed, I leaned over to them. "You know what this is, don't you?" I quizzed them. Two solemn faces shook their heads no. "Well, come over here and I'll show you," I said patting the couch beside me.

They approached cautiously, keeping enough distance to run back to their parents while still getting close enough to take a better look. A moment of heavenly inspiration helped me break the ice. "It's my elephant trunk," I stated, picking up the end of the tube to show them how floppy and flexible it was. "Who else do you know that has a neat elephant trunk like me?" Now I had won them over entirely.

I allowed them to play a bit with the strange toy and it became a part of the Christmas festivities for them.

A few days later, the tube came out of my nose, surgically replaced by a permanent one directly implanted into my stomach. The Cantor Tube was forgotten, replaced by other challenges.

Years later, two tall, teen-aged young men approached me at another family gathering. "Remember your elephant trunk, Aunt Linda?" Eric asked. Chris chimed in with his own memories.

"Of course I do," I responded, tears filling my eyes. "You two gave me a special Christmas gift that year. You were so brave to come and talk to me. You helped me feel normal again."

They had just been themselves, but because they had accepted me and we had played together, they showed me that it was possible for me to accept myself.

Despite battling serious health challenges, I will always be grateful for the two little nephews who prompted me to take the first step that Christmas Day toward rebuilding my life.

Christmas Muffins

Deb Kemper

Christmas Eve night my children brushed their teeth and chose which book to read at story time. I prepped our breakfast for Christmas morning. My son is a breakfast eater, the only person I know who has a snack while waiting for me to cook.

By mixing the dry and wet ingredients separately I narrowed my chore to a few easy steps. While we opened presents, our muffins baked and cooled enough to eat immediately after. My son was satisfied he wouldn't starve and I enjoyed my family.

The process became tradition twenty-five years ago. When we're with one of our children for Christmas morning, I still make blueberry muffins.

Dry ingredients
2 cups all-purpose flour
1 Tbsp. baking powder*
1 tsp. salt *
1 cup sugar**
Stir well, cover the bowl, and set aside.

*or use self-rising flour
**may substitute granular Splenda

Wet ingredients;
½ cup oil or ¼ cup oil + ¼ cup applesauce
2 Tbsp. frozen concentrated orange juice
1 egg
1 cup milk
Whisk together in a large measuring cup, cover, and refrigerate.

Additional ingredients: 1½ cups chopped apples or frozen berries

The next morning preheat oven to 400 degrees. Spray muffin tins with nonstick coating. Pour wet ingredients into dry; whisk, add berries, or chopped apples.

Blend with spatula then fill muffin cups. Bake for 15-20 minutes or until muffins feel springy to touch in the center. Makes 18 muffins.

Christmas Company

Virginia Colclasure

The table, it's a settin'
With the crystal and a rose.
The ham smells like heaven
With its cherries and its cloves.

The cat's in the kennel
The 'tater's in the pot.
The turkey, it's all basted,
'n browned, but not a lot.

Oh Lord, the phone's a ringin'
The message brings me woe.
The company that's a comin'
Can't make it through the snow.

"That's too bad," I say sweetly.
I send them all my love.
Then I place the phone down gently
And go to kick the stove.

The Best Pecan Pie in the World

Cona Gregory

Several years ago, my husband, Bill, and I were visiting his brother and family in another state. His brother was active in Jaycees, a charity organization of men who, among other benevolent activities, gather Christmas gifts for needy children. The Jaycees' wives had produced cookbooks, one for each course of the meal. Bill's brother's wife had just purchased a new Jaycees' wives dessert cookbook, and was planning to pitch her old one. It was showing signs of heavy use, and had lost its cover.

I asked for the cookbook which was about to be trashed, brought it home, and began to read some of the recipes. The first recipe I tried was for Southern Pecan Pie. When I served it at our family's annual Christmas Eve gathering, my brother commented that it was the best pecan pie he had ever eaten.

Needless to say, I have never even tried another pecan pie recipe since. It quickly became tradition to have that pecan pie every year at our family's holiday gathering, and I have served it for many other occasions as well. Recently, a group of ladies were meeting in my home and I served pecan pie. One of my friends made the remark, "Faye makes the best pecan pie in the world."

I would feel very selfish if I didn't share this recipe. Some wonderful lady shared it as the Jaycees' wives cookbook was being assembled, my sister-in-law shared the book with me, and now I share the recipe with you, with a few slight modifications of my own.

Southern Pecan Pie

½ cup sugar
¼ cup butter
½ cup light corn syrup
½ cup pure maple syrup
¼ tsp. salt
3 eggs (sm. or med.)
1½ - 2 cups pecans, broken or cut into pieces.
1 pie shell, uncooked

Cream sugar and butter. Add syrups and salt. Beat well. Add eggs, one at a time, beating after each addition. Add pecans. Pour into pie shell [9-inch pan]. Bake at 350 degrees for 1 hour, 10 minutes, or until inserted knife comes out clean.

Tip # 1: Pecans will not become soggy during baking if kept in freezer until just before adding to the mixture.

Tip #2: Crust edges will not become too brown during baking if covered with strips of aluminum foil.

Tip #3: Crust will be flaky if one teaspoon of lard is added to the Crisco in the piecrust recipe.

Tip #4: Pie halves make a pecan pie difficult to slice; hence the broken pieces.

Teddy Bear in the Attic

Suzanne Gene Courtney

There he sits
silent and sad-faced,
unloved, a dusty remnant
of a childhood past.
No one to claim him
to pass him on,
for my son is gone…
taken in his youth.

Tenderly I hold him,
tears of remembering slide
down my sad face.
Cherished once again,
he struggles to smile
as much as I.

Downstairs we go.
Donned in a red cap,
Teddy sits under our tree.
No more tears. Not this
CHRISTMAS.

Orange Blush

Pat Rowland

Each Christmas, as I prepared menus for the holiday season, my daughter would remind me to not forget the Orange Blush for Christmas breakfast. It was a traditional part of our Christmas morning that began when she was a child. I found the recipe in a Southern Living Party Cookbook.

1 6-oz. frozen orange juice, concentrate, thawed
1 cup cranberry juice
4 Tbsp. sugar
1 pt. club soda

Combine undiluted orange juice, cranberry juice, and sugar. Chill thoroughly. Just before serving, stir in club soda and pour over crushed ice in old-fashioned glasses. Makes 6 servings.

Angels in Disguise

Mia Lynn DeBruyne

Twenty-four hours a day, the dimly lit discount department store faithfully supplies shoppers the basic necessities of life, and more. Upon entering, one notices very little changes inside the forty-year-old store besides the people and the items they carry out with them.

Approaching midnight, just days before Christmas, I found my sanctuary in this store among the frosty pink Christmas trees and gift-wrapped electric toothbrushes. My beloved grandmother's funeral was one week ago. My grief lay hidden from my family, friends, and fellow churchgoers who lived absorbed in the practical affairs of daily life. Apparently, Grandma's passing was a blessing. I did not agree.

Two types of shoppers walked the aisles of the department store this night. Some bustled in, selected their purchases, and rushed back out into the cold. Others roamed the night like ghosts gently brushing their fingers against one item, looking up, then wandering over to the next display. Tonight, I was one of the ghost shoppers. I fondly stroked a tan leather purse, recalling shopping sprees with Grandma.

"I have three grown children," said an elderly voice behind me.

I turned to see a woman dressed in a tattered coat, hand-knit red scarf, and faded blue hat. She was smiling at me. "Oh, a fellow ghost shopper," I thought.

"Will you be celebrating the holidays with your children this year?" I asked.

"No, no, I won't be seeing them this Christmas," she said, although she had a sparkle in her eye.

I was intrigued that the loneliness in life could not penetrate her joy. "Do you shop here often?" I asked.

"Oh yes, I come here often," she replied. "I work here part-time as a greeter. I just finished my shift."

Soon, I sensed that my own empty heart was being filled by this midnight moment of communion with the woman in the tattered coat. She recognized my pain and took a moment to reach out to me with the only gift worth receiving—a gentle spirit of loving acceptance.

I learned that community is not always where we expect it should be. Family and friends may disappoint us. Sometimes churches can feel formal and cold, or effusive and filled with well-intended clichés. That night, community came from an angel in disguise who wore a tattered coat with a mismatched scarf and hat.

Whose heart is the gift awaiting your unwrapping this Christmas season? Perhaps you too will be an angel in disguise.

Oatmeal Date Cookies

Kathy Bruins

This recipe for oatmeal date cookies was my grandmother's and she made them every Christmas. I still have her handwritten recipe. She's been gone for some years now, but whenever I see a cookie like hers in a bakery, I purchase it and enjoy it with lovely memories. Sure, I get a little teary, but it so worth having someone like that in my life. Perhaps this year I will actually make the cookies and continue the tradition.

2½ cups flour
1 tsp. baking soda
1 cup brown sugar
1 cup soft shortening
1½ cup water divided
2½ cups oatmeal
8 oz. dates

Cut dates in small pieces. Cook them on low heat with one cup of water, stirring often until very soft. Mix together flour and baking soda. Add brown sugar, shortening and the remaining ½ cup of water. Mix until smooth. Fold in oats. Roll flour mixture out thin. Cut with round cookie cutter. On half of the cookies cut out, make a smaller hole in the center. These will be the top of the cookies. On the cut out cookies without the hole, place a teaspoon of the cooked dates in the center. Cover with the cookie cut out with the hole in the center and pinch around the edges.

Lightly grease cookie sheet. Bake at 350 degrees for 10-12 minutes.

Plum Pudding

Janet Ann Collins

Every Christmas we gather—uncles, aunts, nieces, nephews, cousins, second cousins, cousin's cousins, first cousins once, twice, and thrice removed, parents, grandparents, grandkids and step-neighbors-in-law. We've done it for as long as any of us can remember.

We don't all make it every year, but those of us who are able always come together to share our lives, and to remember Christmases past and stories our parents and grandparents told. Often those family members who must remain far away will phone, and always those who can't come will think of our reunion.

Before we exchange gifts (the adults draw names so nobody goes bankrupt, but everyone gives to the kids), we share the traditional meal of turkey climaxed by the plum pudding one cousin makes from an old family recipe. The lights are dimmed, and the brandy poured over the pudding is set aflame.

While we watch the blue fire, all of us—Christians, Jews, Agnostics, New Age mystics, young, old, men and women—join in singing the traditional Christmas carols just as we have always done.

And every year I think about what a strange thing this is to do.

Why do we set a lump of food on fire and sing songs around it with words only some of us believe?

Because through decades, probably even more than a century of time, through years of good and bad, births and deaths, wars and peace, it's what our family has always done.

Doing it reminds us who we are.

Great Aunt May's Plum Pudding

1 cup bread crumbs
1 cup suet
1 cup seeded raisins
1 cup seedless raisins
1 cup white raisins
1 cup currants
½ cup brown sugar
½ cup citron
½ cup orange peel
½ cup lemon peel
½ cup cherries
1 tsp. baking powder
1 tsp. baking soda
½ tsp. allspice
½ tsp. nutmeg
½ tsp. cloves
1 tsp. cinnamon
3 eggs
1 tsp. salt
½ cup black molasses
1 cup flour
½ cup milk
1 cup brandy, port wine, or cider

Render suet. Refrigerate, cut into small pieces, and mix with bread crumbs. Add all fruit, salt, spices, flour, sugar, baking powder, and soda.

Beat eggs, add milk and molasses, and mix well. Cover and let stand overnight. In the morning add the brandy, wine or cider, and stir very well.

Bring a large pot of water to boil. Place a pie tin or plate in the bottom to keep the pudding from sticking or burning. Have 1 square yard of unbleached muslin or piece of old but strong sheet ready. Dip the center of the cloth (about 8 inches wide) into the boiling water. Open out the cloth into a large bowl or colander and flour well.

Pour pudding mixture into cloth. Pull corners of cloth together and tie with string, forming mixture into tight ball. Allow a little room for expansion.

Lower pudding into boiling water. Let boil for about 1 hour. Reduce flame and let boil slowly for 5 or 6 hours.

(Pudding may be made ahead of time and reheated in colander over boiling water. Leave in cloth until reheated. Use mixing bowl for cover.)

Serve pudding hot. Burn brandy over pudding and serve with hard sauce. (See recipe below.)

Aunt May's Hard Sauce

6 Tbsp. butter
2 cups powdered sugar
¼ cup brandy (or as needed)

Cream together butter and powdered sugar. Add brandy and stir until fluffy. If needed, add more butter and sugar to get consistency about like frosting. Can be made ahead and refrigerated, but bring to room temperature before serving.

Christmas—Ready or Not

Betty Baker

As I removed the sweet smelling pie from the oven, I wondered what my mother would think being served a frozen pie at the Baker Christmas dinner. For goodness sake, I am the baker of homemade pies.

Recovering from the pie reality, I went to work on the traditional mashed potatoes. How did my dad make them so smooth and creamy? Why are mine so sticky? Maybe they need more milk. No; maybe more butter. No; more milk. Uh-oh, too thin. Should I add flour? Finally, I served them camouflaged in a beautiful bowl. We chuckled at its library paste consistency as we enjoyed eating them to honor my recently deceased father. This was not a Martha Stewart Christmas.

This holiday season, I didn't have the time or mental focus to prepare homemade desserts and new recipes. It was a bittersweet year. Both our sons married wonderful women with our blessing; then both my parents passed away rather suddenly two months apart. Parents' lives ending; newlyweds' lives beginning. I was struggling to deal with simultaneous extreme joy and grief. Suppressing the roller coaster of emotions was not working; grief enveloped everybody's face.

Our older son's wedding the day before at Leu Gardens was like a magical fairy tale. The reception seemed to end too soon. We were delighted to welcome our second daughter-in-law into the family. Magic filled the air as we danced and toasted the bride and groom's future.

But it did not feel like Christmas.

I had prepared for the wedding and the holidays, but I hadn't prepared my heart spiritually for the celebration of Christ's birth. While attending church on Christmas Eve, I came down from the wedding "high," entering the sanctuary consumed with guilt. I was not ready for Christmas. Reflecting on the inspiring words of "The Little Drummer Boy," "Joy to the World," and other hymns stirred my soul. Radiant beams revealed the baby Christ Child in the humble manger. I was overcome with peace and joy as I once again acknowledged God's amazing love revealed through the gift of His Son, Jesus Christ. It didn't matter whether I was ready for Christmas; it would come anyway.

Christmas day dawned. Cookie crumbs and wrapped packages under the tree showed signs of Santa's nocturnal visit. The last day of round-the-clock nostalgic music ends tonight, I thought, dreading the meal preparation ahead. Today was the day for me to take the family baton by preparing the family meal. Although it was exciting to imagine creating new family traditions for future generations, I was inexperienced in preparing the entire turkey dinner.

Dinner guests included our younger son and new bride from California and my husband's parents. My dear mother-in-law was confused why she wasn't the cook in the kitchen; dementia had stolen that ability from her.

Our home was soon full of the savory fragrance of apple pie and roast turkey. Afterwards, while struggling to remain awake, we began our gift exchange by reading "One Solitary Life," a story of the effect of Jesus on mankind. Ever so slowly, one at a time, we opened our gifts. Years would pass and the family would grow, but this day would be etched in my memory for years.

A new era was beginning—a changing of the guard in process. Christmas and change comes whether or not you are ready. No matter the age of your parents when they pass, you probably are not ready for that either. Although change and the journey of grief was beginning anew, I rested in the healing joy and peace of Christ's birth.

The Fruitcake Mission:
Three Decades of Giving

Lisa Harris

I perch on the kitchen's wooden stool with a notepad in front of me. The smell of cinnamon, nutmeg, and baking bread fills the kitchen; the scent envelops me like a velvet cloak. Outside the picture window, trees sway in the wind, crimson and gold maple leaves flutter to the ground. Like the damp earth, my counter is also splattered with color: brown sugar, tawny spices, red cranberries, green pistachios. It's fruitcake baking season. A torn page from a magazine leans cockeyed against the window sill. The paper is yellowed and my handwriting noting alterations to the ingredients crawls through butter stains. It doesn't matter; I know the recipe by heart.

"You busy with the cakes?" my friend Margaret asks, weeks before the holidays. "I'm counting on you for dessert."

"Just checking you have one for me," a neighbor inquires while dog walking. "Your cakes are part of my Christmas dinner. Wouldn't be the same without it."

"My mom's sure looking forward to the holidays with your cake," my architect says, years after the house was built. I've never met his mother. The first year I gave him a cake, he called that evening to say it was the best fruitcake his mother had ever eaten. She's received one every year since.

For almost three decades I've made and given fruitcakes as holiday gifts, a festive acknowledgment of fellowship and thanks to my family and friends. I started making them in college, at a time when I couldn't afford to buy gifts. I chose fruitcakes because they symbolized a Dickens Christmas—visions of plump cooks baking while snow gently dusts the village's thatched roofs. The grocery store in my Midwestern hometown sold flavorless fruitcakes filled with day-glow globs masquerading as fruit. Producing a drop-dead delicious fruitcake challenged my creativity. I never thought I was starting a tradition.

Now I make them because my friends and family expect them, and because I get a kick out of contravening people's expectations that all fruitcakes taste like those my grocery store sold when I was growing up—a cloyingly sweet dry mass that stuck to the roof of the mouth. Thirty years past my college apartment stove, I've turned into a missionary on behalf of the fruitcake.

I bake two dozen or so, depending on the names jotted on my notepad. My family always appears—my brother, his wife, my parents, my cousin, my in-laws.

These are a given. Each year, I also give my fruitcakes to friends who have played a significant role in my life: the fourth-grade teacher who put my oldest daughter at ease in a new classroom, the contractor who built my dream house, the midwife who helped with the birth of my second daughter, the neighbor who pampered my pets while I traveled. I give them to friends who have listened to my tales of woe and have celebrated in my successes, to college buddies I haven't seen in 25 years, to never-marrieds who are alone on the holidays, to an old friend who sat with me after my first husband died. A few cakes are held back, like a vintner's reserve, and remain in my freezer for future tasting. I have never sent one to the White House. Nor do I plan to, regardless of who lives there.

The fruitcakes from my childhood were wrapped in candy-apple red cellophane that crinkled loudly when touched, like a swarm of angry bees. I package my fruitcakes in a burgundy box with my initials embossed on the lower right-hand side and tie it with a gold bow—simple, elegant, and silent.

"It's a fruitcake," I say when handing them out.

If my friends have received one previously, or are already fruitcake lovers, they usually respond with "oohs" and "aahs," as they embrace the box with mittened hands. Sometimes, their eyes roll heavenward, reliving the divine taste of Christmas past.

Reactions from recipients who have only experienced fruitcakes from my childhood grocery store, or one similar to it, are expressive. Eyebrows rise, the mouth twists into a grimace, and tentative hands hold the gift as far from the body as possible. Their eyes search for the nearest trashcan and their bodies tense, ready to ditch the hellacious gift once I leave the vicinity.

"Let me know if you like it," I say. "I'm always looking for ways to improve the recipe."

They nod, and now are obliged to try a bite, maybe a slice.

"I loved your cake," some report later. "I never knew fruitcake tasted good. I always thought they were made from fake stuff, you know, those green and red whatevers." Or "I brought it to a last minute potluck and was surprised how many people asked me for the recipe." Bingo—converts.

One friend missed the fluorescent candied fruit globs. She was a pastry chef at a fancy restaurant and her grandfather's family had owned White Swan Candied Fruit Company, the purveyors of day-glow fruit. "It was delicious, but if you want to call it a fruitcake," she said, "add maraschino cherries."

If my cake is snubbed, I'm apt to believe the recipient is not worthy of my friendship. Once, standing at the door of a boyfriend's house, I offered my box. He cautiously stared at my gift, worried it contained a contagious disease called commitment. After some hesitation, he placed the container on a dusty credenza. By the time New Year's came, I'd forgotten his name. In another instance, I spotted my familiar box on the kitchen counter at a friend's holiday potluck dinner, unopened for a week. I suggested the hostess offer it to her guests. Refusing, she said, "Only fruitcakes like fruitcake." I can't say we've spoken much since and the following year, her name did not appear on my list.

 Sitting on my kitchen's wooden stool, I watch steam rise from a batch of golden brown loaves fresh from the oven. Beyond the cooling racks, maple leaves flutter and a squirrel dashes across the crimson-carpeted yard, its cheeks stuffed with winter provisions. I add a new name to my list, a recently acquired friend. I wonder what her reaction will be when I present her with the burgundy box—a smile or a grimace? Either way, I'll keep spreading the news.

Lisa's Fruit Cake

2/3 cup firmly packed dark brown sugar
½ cup (1/4 lb) butter at room temperature
3 lg. eggs
1¼ cups all-purpose flour
½ teaspoon baking powder
½ teaspoon ground cinnamon
¼ teaspoon ground mace
1/8 teaspoon ground cloves

Fruits and nut mixture:
1 cup currents
½ cup golden raisins
½ cup dried blueberries
½ cup dried cranberries
½ cup dried Bing cherries
½ cup unsalted pistachio pieces
½ cup pecan pieces
About ½ cup good quality port

In a large bowl, beat sugar and butter with a mixer until well blended, then beat in eggs, 1 at a time. Stir together flour, baking powder, cinnamon, mace, and cloves. Add to egg mixture; stir, beat to blend. Stir in fruit and nut mix.

Spoon batter equally into 6 greased 2½ -by 4-inch individual loaf pan or 1 regular-sized loaf pan. Spread batter evenly and smooth top.

Bake at 300 degrees until toothpick inserted in center comes out clean and cakes are firm when lightly pressed in center, 45 to 60 minutes for small pans, longer for regular sized loaf pan (1½ hours). Cool in pans on a rack for 10 minutes, invert onto rack to cool completely.

Set the cakes in a single layer in a 9 x 13-inch baking dish or pan, or set each cake on a rectangle of foil large enough to seal the cake airtight. Spoon 2 tablespoons of port onto each cake slowly enough to let it seep in. Repeat until the cake is saturated. Wrap each cake airtight in foil.

Store at room temperature at least 8 hours or up to 2 weeks; freeze and store up to 2 months. Makes 6 mini loaves or 1 regular size loaf.

A Southern Garden of Christmas Gifts

Sandra Fischer

Come now, December, and what do we see?
All kinds of gifts spread under a tree.
Oh, not the kind that at stores do abound,
But those we've been blessed with all the year 'round.

You won't find a bottle of costly perfume,
But a bouquet of fragrance to fill up a room
With velvety petals and colors so bold
Their brilliance and beauty your eyes can behold.

No famous paintings for purchase to pay,
But radiant sunsets are ours every day.
Each one made special with brushstrokes of love,
Wrapped with cloud-ribbons and tied from above.

No jewel-boxed diamonds, so costly and bright,
We're star-struck with billions that light up each night.
And the music we have you won't find on CDs,
But bird, wind, and rain sing unique melodies.

No need to go shopping online or at store
God's garden of gifts is outside the back door.
No need to set out and head for the mall
Look out the window for "one size fits all."

No credit card limits; these gifts are all free—
An abundance of treasures are under each tree.
Nothing man-made can compare in like measure
With what God has made for our joy and our pleasure.

A Husband's Devotion

Rebecca Carpenter

A lopsided, red Santa hat caught my attention. An elderly lady and her husband huddled together on the snack aisle of the Dollar Store. I hurried on to select my items. Later the couple stood ahead of me at the checkout counter.

She seemed a little dazed as she picked up an item and turned towards me—as if to leave the line.

In a quiet, calm voice, the gray-haired gentleman said, "Look at me."

She immediately gazed up into his eyes. "After you open a bag, you can't take it back," he said patiently.

Her head nodded, and she returned the opened bag to the conveyor belt. A chip tumbled out. She picked it up and stuffed it into her mouth. Like a child shopping with a parent, she scanned the display shelf. Then, with a smile, she picked up a candy bar, held it tightly, and looked at her husband for approval.

"No, you can't get it. We have candy at home." Obediently, she placed it back on the rack.

The distinguished-looking man continued talking. "I bought a big candy bar and put it into the refrigerator. Now it's gone. I think Sam took it when he came over. He always looks in there."

His dialogue was one-sided, but he spoke as though she could understand. From a child's conversation to an adult's, he switched back and forth effortlessly though he received little response to either.

"Do you know where kangaroos eat?" he asked the harried cashier.

"At I-Hop," she answered with a grin as the items were rung up.

Despite the obvious difficulties he experienced with his wife, he retained his sense of humor.

What had their lives been like before her dementia? How long had he been her caregiver? Did she even know she had reverted to childlike behaviors? As the questions swirled in my head, sadness covered my heart. Tears came to my eyes.

As difficult as it was to watch their exchange, his devotion and patience filled me with joy and encouragement. He accepted his present life and made the best of it.

When I arrived at my next stop, instead of being annoyed at the long line, I conversed with other shoppers and the cashier. Hopefully, I would enrich someone's day too.

Christmas Wreath

Joyce McCullough

30 marshmallows
½ cup butter or margarine
1 tsp. vanilla
2 tsp. green food coloring
3½ cups cornflakes

In a large pan combine marshmallows, butter, vanilla, and food coloring in top of a double boiler. Heat over water until marshmallows and butter are melted, stirring frequently. Gradually stir in cornflakes.

Drop from spoon onto waxed paper. With hands, shape into a large wreath (about 9"). This can be decorated with red candied cherries, red cinnamon candies, or a white chocolate "bow."

You can also make miniature wreaths or "holly clusters" if you need individual servings.

Pumpkin Bread

Joyce McCullough

½ cup soft butter or margarine
1½ cup sugar
2 eggs
1-2/3 cup self-rising flour
2 tsp. ground ginger
½ tsp. ground cinnamon
½ tsp. ground nutmeg
¼ tsp. ground cloves
1/3 cup water
1 cup canned pumpkin
½ cup toasted pecans, finely chopped
Canned cream cheese icing

Cream butter and sugar together by hand or with electric mixer. Add eggs, one at a time, and beat until mixture is light and fluffy.

Sift together flour and spices, and add to creamed mixture alternately with water.

Beat well after each addition. Add pumpkin and beat until well blended. Stir in chopped pecans.

Spoon mixture into large loaf pan sprayed with cooking spray.

Bake at 350 degrees for approximately 1 hour, or until toothpick inserted in center comes out clean. Cool in pan, and then top with cream cheese icing.

Christmas Haiku

John J. Han

Christmas card...
my old pastor's same old
handwriting

Christmas shopping
even car exhaust fumes
smell agreeable

is Santa real?
my doubting child falls asleep
holding a flashlight

Christmas socks
this year we need one more:
the puppy's

candy cane lights
our puppy pauses
to sniff

slowly, slowly
the neck moves up and down
deer antler light

Christmas intruders:
two deer checking out
the snowy yard

after Christmas
deflated Santa and deer
side by side

Christmas Party Coleslaw

Patti Schieringa

I remember our family of three enjoyed making this special salad even when we didn't have guests. Now, I can take it to potlucks any time of the year and remember when there were no leftovers at our Christmas feasts.

My mother and I would prepare this coleslaw the day before the party. It made the party day less busy and allowed flavors to steep.

¼ cup water
½ cup raisins
2 cups chopped green cabbage
¾ to ½ cup mayonnaise
¼ to ½ cup diced onion
1 tsp. lemon juice
1 Tbsp. sugar, optional
Sprinkle of red paprika

Soak raisins in small cup with water. Combine chopped cabbage in 2-quart serving dish with mayonnaise. Add onion. Mix in raisins and water. Add lemon juice. Mix well. Taste, with clean teaspoon, to decide on more onion or to add sugar. Decorate with paprika sprinkled lightly on top. Cover and store in icebox until serving time.

If we were out of ice, we didn't worry. We just put the covered dish in the unheated back bedroom—not too close to the window though, or it might freeze. Yum.

The Unexpected Christmas Gift

Christine Henderson

As the plane touched down on the tarmac, I anxiously clutched my husband's hands. Was this trip really a good idea? Would it cause more of a rift in my family? Or would it be mended? It had been eighteen months since I had last seen them and I was unsure of how our return would be received.

If only I could go back two years ago and start over. That was when I had stopped talking to my parents; or at least had any serious conversation with them. After that it was just pleasant chatting about the weather, recipes, clothes, and anyone else's life but mine.

The change began when I told my mom I was in love with Joey and we wanted to marry. It was at the end of my first year at college. My mother hugged me and said, "Honey, I'm glad you've found the love of your life. Give it more time. If it's really true love, then it will survive three more years in college."

My dad's response wasn't any better. "You're way too young. Your older siblings waited until they finished college to get married, so can you."

Had they forgotten what love was like after twenty-five years of marriage? Didn't they know the urgency of wanting to be together? No matter what I tried, I kept running into a brick wall with my folks on the subject of marriage.

It was totally different with Joey's family. When he gave me a beautiful sapphire engagement ring at Christmas, they welcomed me into their family with hugs and kisses. Back at my home, I didn't call it an engagement ring. I wasn't up to the argument of once again being considered too young to be getting married.

We made our plans to elope in May. Finally the day to leave arrived. After my parents left for work, I packed up my belongings and wrote a long note telling them about my feelings and how I hoped they would someday understand. I left it on the kitchen table with a vase of roses from the garden as a celebration of my new life with my almost husband. I was both excited and anxious. This step would forever change my life.

We moved across the country, but I didn't have much opportunity to feel homesick. I was too busy with my new job, and learning to budget—which was a new concept to me. I don't know if it was out of guilt or trepidation, but I didn't call or write to my family for the first two months.

I finally made the first phone call to my brother, Bob. I felt he would understand my reasons for leaving. I also hoped he could lend me some money so I could come back for my brother Gary's wedding in August.

I wasn't prepared for his very chilly response as he said, "Mom and Dad are still pretty hurt. Since you didn't want any of the family to be at your wedding, you aren't welcome at this one. You need to give everyone more time to heal."

I was in shock. I had been so excited about eloping that I failed to realize what it did to my family. I must have hurt them very much with my abrupt departure.

I started to call and write letters to my family. But no one mentioned getting together. Another year passed and then at Thanksgiving, Bob called and said, "The whole family is getting together for Christmas at Gary's home in Tennessee. Would you like to come?"

I replied, "We'd like to but can't afford it."

"Don't worry," he said. "I've got frequent flyer miles you can use."

It was to be a secret. Bob assured me the surprise would be a welcome one to my parents. Though we'd been having regular phone calls and letters, my parents never asked when I was coming to visit.

Now we were at the airport's baggage claim area and my brothers were hugging me. Would my parents feel the same once we reached the house? Or would my return bring on arguments and bitterness?

When we drove into the driveway, my brothers had us wait in the car while they set things up inside. Finally they waved for us to come inside quietly. While I was still hidden by the front door Bob said, "Mom and Dad, close your eyes while we bring in your special gift."

My parents quickly complied as my brothers were always full of surprises. I hesitated for a minute until Gary gave me a gentle nudge. I squeezed my husband's hand and then let it go as I tiptoed forward. Mom and Dad were sitting on the couch with their backs to me as I walked in. The house was beautifully decorated for the holidays just like we had always done when I was growing up. The scene was complete with a crackling fireplace and Christmas carols playing. With tears in my eyes I walked up to my folks and put my arms over each of them as I said, "Merry Christmas, I've missed you so much!"

As we took turns hugging everyone, I was happy to be there, yet sad that we had let so much time slip away. We didn't need to let our differences get in the way. We should have continued to talk it out.

That evening at dinner we chatted like we'd been apart for only a few days. When we went to midnight mass later on as a family, it felt like the best Christmas ever. It wasn't about any presents under the tree, but rather the presence of family being altogether once again. From now on I wouldn't let misunderstandings or hurt feelings get in the way of staying in touch with my family. Our love for each other could and would work those problems out.

Apple Crisp

Jewell Johnson

For years I searched for an apple crisp recipe. I've tried many recipes, but this one is the best. Our family likes this better than pie for Christmas Day dinner.

Peel 12 apples (for good flavor use a combination of Granny Smith, Gala, and Winesap)

Slice and place apples in 9 x 12 baking pan.
Mix together and sprinkle on apples:
1½ cup sugar
¼ cup flour
½ tsp. salt
2 Tbsp. lemon juice
1 Tbsp. cinnamon

Topping:

1 cup brown sugar
½ cup butter
1 cup flour
½ cup oatmeal

Mix first 3 ingredients until crumbly. Stir in oatmeal. Sprinkle mixture over apples. Bake at 350 degrees for 1 hour or until bubbly in the middle.

Quilting Memories

Gay Ingram

The special appeal of making patchwork quilts is that you find yourself crafting with your soul. Woven into every quilt we make are bits of imagination, history, and memories. One of my most rewarding projects is a special collection of miniature quilts I recently completed.

Even the materials used had special significance. During her last few months, I had the privilege of caring for my youngest sister who died recently of a brain tumor. We worked together, tying up the loose strands of life's business as she prepared for her homecoming. Also an avid crafter, she gave me permission to pack up anything I wanted to take home with me.

Upon my return, several boxes of material I had shipped confronted me. I gave some thought to what I'd like to do with all this newly acquired supply. Wanting some task that would commemorate my sister's passing and help ease the grief of her loss, I decided to use Jeannette's material to construct miniature quilts for my three remaining sisters and myself. Since we all live in different states, these quilts would be a way to remember one another and the sister who was no longer with us. To make them extra special, I used my sister's accumulation of Christmas prints.

I am a novice quilter, seeking only to create a pleasing finished product. So, my first attempt was a basic Nine Patch quilt, destined for a sister who lived in Connecticut. My next project followed a pattern called the Snail's Trail. I knew the intricacy of the pattern would be appreciated by a sister who also loved to sew. This challenged my skills but after a few false starts, I was satisfied with the results.

By now, creating quilts took up an ever-increasing part of my life. For a third sister's quilt, several patterns appealed to me and I couldn't decide which to do. I solved the problem by making my next quilt a sampler. I made individual blocks of each of those patterns and put them together in a quilt which would go to my sister living in Arizona.

The following Christmas, each quilt was lovingly packaged with an explanatory note and mailed. Not until a year later did I find time to make that last quilt—my own. Now each time the holiday season comes around, I take out my special quilt and display it. It has become a constant reminder of my growing-up years in the midst of a loving family and causes my thoughts to dwell on those I love, both here on earth and gone ahead.

Bread Sauce

Cora Holley

This traditional old English recipe was originally served with roast Christmas goose. The perfect complement to turkey or chicken, bread sauce has been part of my family's Christmas menu for generations. Its creamy melt-in-the-mouth texture keeps my son requesting that I make a "bucket" of it, year after year! It is also my annually sought-after contribution to my husband's office Christmas party.

1 onion (cut in half)
16 whole cloves
6 black peppercorns
1 bay leaf
1½ pt. (3 cups) milk
6 oz. fresh white breadcrumbs (no crusts)
salt and black pepper to taste
1 Tbsp. butter
4 Tbsp. double cream
½ tsp. nutmeg

Stick cloves in onion, and put in medium saucepan with peppercorns, bay leaf, and milk. Warm up slowly, and allow to simmer for about 30 minutes. Bring to a boil, then take off heat. Pour milk through a strainer into bowl, leaving behind onions, peppercorns, cloves, and bay leaf. Return milk to saucepan. Gradually add bread crumbs. Stir constantly on medium heat for 2 to 3 minutes. Reduce heat to low. Add salt, pepper, and nutmeg; stir in butter. Remove from heat. Cover saucepan. Stir in cream just before serving. Serves 12

A Christmas Cinquain: As Years Go By

Cassandra Wessel

First Christmas

Simple,
willowy tree
Christmas, for thee and me.
New home, presents, furniture, thee.
Blissful.

Second Christmas

Wobble,
willowy tree,
Christmas, cat, thee and me.
Bobbles and bangles, free for all.
Topple.

Third Christmas

Lovely,
willowy tree,
Christmas, for thee and me.
Packages, presents, puppy, thee.
Cuddly.

Fourth Christmas

Sleepy,
willowy tree,
Christmas, new family.
Presents, diapers, baby and we.
Happy.
Middle Christmas
Shining,
willowy tree,
Christmas, own family.
Bedlam, children, pets, me and thee.
Busy.

Seniors Christmas

Tiny,
willowy tree,
Christmas, whole family.
Busy, bustling, grands, thee and me.
Noisy.

Last Christmas

Sadly
willowy tree
Christmas, only for me.
No packages, presents or thee.
Lonely.

The Stockings Were Hung

Carin LeRoy

As a little girl, my favorite Christmas tradition in our house was the stockings. My mom made the whole family green stockings decorated with different holiday-themed objects, sewing on sequins and beads and putting our name on each one. Every December, she would hang them on our staircase, and each year I would anticipate the little gifts I'd find. I loved getting up early on Christmas morning and looking in my stocking. I knew I'd find several little treasures hidden inside.

When I married, my mom gave my Christmas stocking to me. I decided I wanted to carry on the tradition in our family, so began to make my husband and children a green felt stocking, complete with holiday-themed figures. I sewed on sequins and beads and wrote their name in glitter glue on each of theirs, just like my mom did. Even when we lived overseas, I carried those stockings with me. Although I was thousands of miles across the ocean, the stockings still reminded me of home.

When my daughter married, she took hers and now carries on the same tradition. The only difference is that I'm sewing the stockings for her family. Every time she has a child, she wants me to create another green felt stocking. Three generations in my family have grown up with homemade stockings lovingly made by someone in the family.

As we move into this Christmas season, let's remember some of the traditions we've grown up with and share them with our children and grandchildren. Christmas isn't all about the gifts, the busyness, or the decorations. It's about family, tradition, and the birth of a Savior. That's why we celebrate!

The Perfect Gift

Joyce McCullough

A flashy golden jewelry box, $20;
the wisdom of an innocent child, Priceless

The children had been rehearsing for the church Christmas pageant since October, and everyone seemed ready to present a great performance of "The Perfect Gift." On the morning of the performance, Jeremy's mom frantically cornered Miss Debbie before Sunday school and told her that she would need to find a substitute wise man. Jeremy had been throwing up since early that morning, and he was also running a low grade fever. He would not be able to play his role as one of the three wise men.

Miss Debbie's brain quickly started searching for a Plan B. Her three-year-old son Jason had attended every rehearsal. It was a stretch, but maybe Jason could play the part. He had actually been singing all the songs for the last month, and the wise man only had to say one line. This might actually work.

That afternoon Miss Debbie shortened Jason's nap and shared with him the good news that he would be playing one of the wise men in the church pageant that night. She called his two older brothers into the den to help with a quick rehearsal. After a short eye-rolling session, they agreed to help.

Debbie handed each of the boys a book from a nearby shelf and told them to pretend that they were carrying gold, frankincense, and myrrh. They were each to walk the length of the den and lay their "gifts" beside the sleeping cat in the kitchen. (The cat served as a pretend baby Jesus.)

Jason not only carried his gift with a regal air, but he also said his line on cue," I bwing you gold." Satisfied that Jason appeared ready to make his acting debut and that the night's performance would go as well as could be expected, Miss Debbie dismissed her two older boys to play in the backyard while Jason continued to practice marching in his bathrobe.

That evening the shortest wise man could not be seen by everyone in the back of the church, but his mom was proud of the fact that he was going to be a good pinch hitter. As the march of the kings' music cued their entrance, the assistant director handed the three kings their gifts and pointed to center stage where they were to face the audience and sing their song.

Jason's gift was actually an old jewelry box that had been spray painted gold and embellished with a few fake jewels. The three-year-old immediately became entranced by the gift he was holding. As the other two wise men sang their song, Jason's attention became totally focused on examining his box and, with great effort, trying to open its clasp. When the song ended, the wise men were supposed to lay their gifts beside the sleeping baby Jesus and then say their lines. Following Miss Debbie's whispered directions, the other two wise men presented their gifts and proclaimed their purposes. Jason, in the meantime, had finally succeeded in opening the clasp on his box, when he proclaimed, "I can't bwing any gold. My box is empty!"

After the laughter died down and the wise men were joined by the rest of the cast to sing their finale, the children received a standing ovation. Many people made comments like, "That's the best program they've done," and "Wasn't that littlest wise man the cutest thing?" Miss Debbie herself couldn't help but be proud of her three-year-old.

Even though Jason was momentarily distracted by the shiny box he was holding and by its jeweled façade, his epiphany was a lesson to us all that we should not focus our attention on the shiny material things in life. If we do, we will find that there is no real gold inside the box. Our lives will be empty if we focus all of our energies on the things that money can buy. On the other hand, if we focus our energies on the love of God and family and friends, then we will discover that the priceless things in life are the most valuable, and they are the perfect gift to ourselves and others.

Cheddar Cheese Logs

Betty Arthurs

I tasted this cheese log at my first job after I got my RN license in 1968. A group of us nurses worked in the tiny town of Adams Basin in the state of New York doing home health visits. A friend made this for our Christmas party. I fell in love with it and have made it every year for our holiday celebration or to give away as gifts.

16 oz. package shredded cheddar cheese
4 3-oz. packages cream cheese
4 oz. blue cheese, crumbled
4 Tbsp. finely chopped onion
chopped walnuts, ¾ cup
sour cream, 1 cup
chopped nuts, 2 cups, for rolling logs in

Whip 3 cheeses together in food processor. Blend in onion, nuts, and sour cream. Chill until firm. Divide chilled mixture in half and place each half on a piece of waxed paper. Shape into log and roll in chopped nuts. Refrigerate several hours. Serve with specialty crackers. This can be made with all low-fat cheeses and sour cream. It can also be frozen, thawed, remixed, formed, and then rolled in nuts. Delicious addition to your Christmas appetizers buffet.

(Yields 2 logs about 15 inches long)

Behold the Sights of Christmas

Debbie Carpenter

Velvet bows, candy canes,
The hat on Santa's head;
Behold the sights of Christmas
In tones of ruby red.

Everywhere Christmas trees
And holly leaves are seen.
Fragrant bayberry candles
Boast shades of deepest green.

Christmas cards of winter scenes,
A snowfall in the night;
Round and robust snowmen
Wearing coats of brilliant white.

Silver bells, silver stars,
Tinsel on a tree;
See the shiny packages
In silver finery.

Golden angels, golden voices,
Golden tales of old;
The gift the Wise Man carried
Was one of purest gold.

Behold the sights of Christmas
In many colors bright,
As we celebrate the Baby
Born for us that night.

Yule Kage

Bruce McLeland

This Christmas bread has been a tradition in both my family and my wife's family as far back as we can remember. When I was a kid my mom let me help her every year. At first I would just do some light mixing, grease pans, and rub butter on the hot loaves. Then as I grew older I was able to knead the bread until it was perfect. Eloise, my wife, now does the kneading work because she has more patience. I then in turn taught my kids to make it. Our daughter makes a great batch of Yule Kage. I am now in the process of teaching one of our granddaughters to make this choice holiday bread.

Every year it seems I get a hankering for this delicacy at a time other than Christmas so I will make a batch in June or July. This bread tastes the best toasted and buttered right out of the toaster. You can use a large Tupperware bowl or another bowl that has a cover; however, you need to grease both the bowl and the cover to prevent the dough from sticking.

1 sm. peeled potato, cooked until soft
1 pkg. yeast dissolved in 1 tsp. sugar and a little (2 Tbsp.) warm water (not hot)
Scald 1½ cups milk
add 2/3 cup Blue Bonnet margarine

Mash potato and add to above mixture. Not the yeast yet. Cool in mixing bowl. Add:

¾ cup sugar
1 tsp. salt
½ tsp. cardamom
2 egg yokes
1 egg beaten

Add yeast mixture, then stir in 1 cup flour. Let sit 1/2 hour. Add:
1-1/3 cup each of raisins and citron fruit.

Then add 6 or more cups of flour to make a soft dough.

Cover and let rise in warm place about 1 hour. It will usually pop the cover when it is ready to continue. If not, it should be pushing against the cover.

Grease hands and punch down and drop the dough in the bowl. Let rise again covered in warm place about another hour. Knead down (key step) and divide into loaves and put in greased loaf pans. Should make 3 medium and 1 small loaf. I am a great believer in making double recipes but I would not advise it with this bread because it becomes too much to handle and knead properly. (I speak from experience.)

Let rise again in warm place. I use the oven that has been pre-warmed (not hot and not on). Cover loafs with damp dish towel. This step will also take about an hour. Before you say, "Wow, all those hours of work," remember, the yeast is doing the work and you are doing something else.

Bake for 45 minutes at 325 degrees until loaves are light brown. Loaves will fall right out of greased pans and into your hand to be put on cooling rack. Rub the tops with a butter or margarine stick. Enjoy the toasted product. Try it with turkey for a leftover sandwich.

I tried this once in a bread machine and it was a dismal failure. It's the kneading that makes this holiday bread. ENJOY.

Our First Christmas

Danielle Mendenhall

The first hopeful kiss
The first gentle hug
The first time I heard the words
You might be in love

The first promising smiles
The first of somber good-byes
The first time I recognized
That look in your eyes

The first of countless moments
The first of longing tears
The first time I knew
Firsts would overwhelm our years

The first of hearts touching
The first of stormy weather
And sweet is the memory
Of our first Christmas together

Red Velvet Cake

Diane Morgan

This dark, red cake with fluffy white frosting has become my go-to Christmas dessert. Whether I make it for my family, a get-together with friends, or take it to the office, people appreciate the beauty, textures, and flavor of this favorite. I have tried or taste-tested many versions of this cake over the years—including cakes baked by pros. This recipe is my top pick.

Preheat oven to 350 degrees (325 if using dark metal cake pans). Grease well bottoms only of two 9" cake pans.

Cream together for 5 minutes:

1½ cups sugar
½ cup butter
2 eggs

Add the following and mix well:

2 oz. red food coloring
1 cup buttermilk
1 tsp. vanilla
1 tsp. vinegar

Combine the following and add to above mixture:

2¼ cups sifted cake flour
2 Tbsp. cocoa powder
1 tsp. salt
1 tsp. baking soda

Pour into prepared pans and bake for 30-35 minutes until toothpick inserted in center comes out clean. Cool cakes for 10 minutes, turn pans upside down to remove cakes onto cooling rack, and cool completely.

Meanwhile combine the following in a saucepan, boil and stir until thick:

2 Tbsp. cornstarch
1 cup water

Remove from heat, place waxed paper directly on top of cooked mixture to avoid forming a thick top layer as mixture cools. Cool completely.

Cream together for approximately 10 minutes:

1 cup butter
1 cup confectioner's sugar

Add 1 tsp. vanilla to butter mixture and mix again. Add the cooled cornstarch mixture and beat further until spreadable. Frost cake and enjoy!

Christmas Forever

Jewell Johnson

Christmas is over,
the tree must come down,
the wreaths and bells put away.
Yet my heart
yearns for the joy to linger,
this wonder to never end.

And it can—as each day
I come to the stable,
gaze into the manger
and search the sky for His star.
As I bring Him my gift—
worship from a humble heart.

Baked Eggs

Ellen Cardwell

When I serve this dish, I can count on people asking for the recipe. It's great because it can be prepared the day before and popped in the oven at the last minute. It's become a permanent part of our Christmas morning menu.

8 eggs, hard-cooked
2 Tbsp. butter
2 Tbsp. flour
1½ cup whole milk
3 oz. sharp cheddar cheese, grated
½ tsp. salt
½ tsp. dry mustard
Pinch cayenne
¼ tsp. paprika

Serves 4. Preparation time: 1 hour

Hard cook 8 eggs and remove shells. Cut eggs into bite-size pieces and place in casserole. Melt butter over low heat and blend in flour. Add milk gradually. Cook and stir until thickened. Add cheese, salt, mustard, and cayenne. Remove from heat. Cover eggs with sauce and sprinkle with paprika. Bake at 350 degrees for 20 minutes. (Overcooking toughens eggs and cheese.)

Returned to Sender

Sherrie Murphree

Ever have a feeling that someone didn't like the gift you gave them? Sometimes you translate this to mean they don't even like you. That's where my feelings stood, and I wondered, Why else are these letters being returned to me?

Indeed my promise gift the previous Christmas had stretched me. I was to share for a whole year daily-living-type things via snail mail. I had clarified to the recipient, my sister Bev, never to feel obligated to answer the letters. Though I meant well, maybe my present didn't measure up to store-bought stuff. Offense tried to sneak in.

I'd given what I call a "drummer boy" gift which I have a fondness for from time to time. This gift is the kind one can't buy; rather, it's made up instead of time, talent, or work. Guess gratefulness would not surface.

But my assumption proved instantly wrong as I opened the front cover of the hunter green album that housed the 26 letters I'd sent that year. It showed Bev had decorated it with great care and trouble. She titled the first page, "A Year in the Life of Sherrie."

My own colors, designs, and sizes of paper filled the pages of the album. I'd written most of them by hand at worked-in moments, telling basically about the activities and well-being of our family.

On this Christmas at Mother's house during gift-opening time, Bev sat watching my reaction as I turned the pages quickly—not wanting to delay our celebration. Then I paused. Written in red on the final page, a surprise note from her shined:

"Dear Sherrie, Your letters throughout the year were a real treat to me. Thank you for giving such a special gift. They are truly a treasure. And that's why I'm returning them to you. They are a valuable history of your family's life—worthy of being preserved. I want them to bring you as much joy in years to come as they brought to me when I received them. I love you, Beverly."

All those returned letters so carefully presented meant she in turn had now given me a drummer boy gift. How I cherish it—and her. This gift will keep on giving and bringing joy as it will land next in the hands of my daughter, Valerie, and on and on for a mini-history of days gone by.

Cathedral Cookies

Carol Dee Meeks

1 12 oz. package chocolate chips
2 beaten eggs
2 Tbsp. butter
1 tsp. vanilla
1 cup finely chopped pecans
1 pkg. colored marshmallows
1 pkg. powdered sugar

Melt chocolate chips in top of a double boiler. Add butter to chocolate chips and stir constantly. When all melted, pour beaten eggs into mixture and the vanilla. Stir until smooth and shiny. Let cool at least 30 minutes.

Put marshmallows into large bowl; add nuts. When mixture is cool, pour over marshmallows and nuts in the large bowl. Stir until marshmallows are covered, then divide them into three balls.

Sprinkle powered sugar onto a sheet of waxed paper. Roll balls into long loaves (your hands will be messy) until mixture is completely covered. (It takes awhile to do this.) Put it all in the middle of the waxed paper and roll it back and forth. Wrap the roll in this paper and place in refrigerator overnight before eating. Continue with each roll of mixture.

Our Family Christmas Eve Soup

Carol Dee Meeks

Buy a frozen package of posole from the store and run water over it in the sink until it is thawed. Put in Crock-Pot and cover with water. Cook on low for several hours, being careful not to let all the water cook out. You may have to add water several times.

While this is cooking, chop up a round beefsteak and a pork steak into small pieces. You can brown the meat in a saucepan as you would a roast, then add the two meats to the posole. Add a dash of GARLIC and ONION SALT, some CELERY SALT to taste. Cover and let this simmer for 45 minutes or so. A red powdered chili sauce may be added here for the color.

While this is simmering, chop, then sauté 1 large ONION in 2 tablespoons of butter. Add 6-inch fresh GREEN CHILI PEPPERS (I string them in pieces lengthwise) or 2 cans of Ortega CHILI and 1 can of STEWED TOMATOES. Let this simmer for 30 minutes. Then add 1 pound of HAMBURGER MEAT you have browned in another pan while this was cooking. Add the hamburger meat to the chili mixture. Season to taste with GARLIC SALT and ONION SALT. This mixture can be added to the posole/meat mixture and cook about 5 minutes, or you can dish up a bowl and fill it with half of the posole mixture and half of the chili mixture.

Serve hot with cornbread, tortillas, or crackers and green enchiladas.

Crystal's Christmas Dove

Ginger B. O'Neill

For years I had promised myself that I would finish my Christmas shopping early but once again I had broken my promise. It seemed no matter how many times I told myself to avoid the Christmas rush and stress, I always had a few last-minute items to buy.

As I pulled into the mall parking lot, I could see that parking was going to be a challenge. I glanced to the left where I always parked. It was full so I turned right to continue my search for a place to park. My stress level increased as I drove and thought of Crystal.

It had only been six months since my youngest sister Crystal had died of cancer. I missed her terribly, especially now, as she and I had had a tradition of meeting at the mall to shop together during the Christmas season. I drove through the busy, overcrowded parking lot fighting the tears with Crystal on my mind.

I finally found a parking place at the far end of the mall. I didn't mind the walk because I knew it would help me to regain my composure and walk off some frustration and emotion.

The minute I walked inside I saw the most beautiful Christmas tree full of beautiful white doves. I was drawn to this tree only to discover that it was the Hospice Christmas Tree. With a small donation you could purchase a dove with a card to place on the tree in memory of a loved one who had died. I was thrilled. Hospice had been wonderful to Crystal so this would not only give me an opportunity to give back to them but to do something for my sister for Christmas. I carefully filled out the card, "To my Beautiful Sister Crystal, I Love You and Miss You, Ginger." I was determined not to cry and mess up my makeup but the tears began to fill my eyes. I quickly dapped them so they wouldn't run down my face. After carefully placing the dove on the tree, I started through the mall feeling much better.

All day people kept commenting on my Christmas spirit. Thinking, I must really be glowing with God's peace and the love I feel for God and the blessing of finding the Hospice Tree, made me smile even more.

A few hours later as I was washing my hands in the ladies room, I looked in the mirror and began to laugh. I had really been glowing! The Hospice dove had had glitter on it and I had dapped it all over my face when I tried to keep the tears from falling. Then I did something I had not done for a while: I laughed out loud.

That day was a gift from the Lord to me at a time I needed a special touch from Him, and it has grown into my own personal Christmas tradition. This season will be my seventeenth year of putting a dove on the Hospice Christmas Tree.

Marshmallow Nut Clusters

Leola R. Ogle

24 oz. pkg. almond bark (chocolate or vanilla—sometimes you can find butterscotch)
1 cup peanut butter (smooth or crunchy)
3 cups Rice Krispies/crisp rice cereal
2 cups salted nuts (peanuts, cashews, almonds)
2 cups mini-marshmallows

Melt almond bark in microwave for 1.45–2 minutes. If not completely melted, do an additional 10-15 seconds, but do not scorch. Stir in 1 cup peanut butter until smooth. Stir in the next 3 ingredients in order given until all ingredients are completely coated. As quickly as possible, drop by spoonfuls onto cookie sheets. Refrigerate until set.

Fast and easy, makes several dozen, and a favorite with everyone all year long. Makes a wonderful gift on a holiday plate or tin for neighbors and co-workers.

Gingerbread Men

Cherry Pedrick

1 cup (2 sticks) butter
1 cup sugar
1 egg
1 cup light or dark molasses (*depending on your taste*)
2 Tbsp. tablespoons vinegar
4½ cups flour
1½ tsp. baking soda

1 Tbsp. ginger
1 tsp. cinnamon
1 tsp. ground cloves
½ tsp. salt

Cream butter; gradually add sugar and beat until light and fluffy. Beat in egg. Blend in molasses and vinegar. Sift together flour, baking soda, ginger, cinnamon, cloves, and salt; gradually add to creamed mixture. Chill at least 3 hours. On well-floured surface roll dough to 1/8-inch thickness. With floured cookie cutters cut into desired shapes. Transfer to baking sheet with wide spatula. Bake 6-7 minutes at 375 degrees. Makes a soft cookie, unlike the firm cookies used in gingerbread houses. Number of servings: Depends on the size of your men!

Note: You're not limited to gingerbread men. You can also make gingerbread women, boys, girls, cats, dogs, etc. I've even made gingerbread turkeys for Thanksgiving. This is a softer gingerbread than that used in gingerbread houses. Roll dough out thicker for chewy cookies, thinner for crisp ones.

These cookies are a Christmas tradition at our house. With our emphasis on health these days, I'm baking less, but at Christmas time, we still have our cookies. I bake several varieties and freeze them in freezer bags. When we need a dish for a potluck or party, I take out my bags and have a ready-made platter of cookies. Another advantage of freezing them is that there are fewer cookies to nibble. Sometimes I'm in a hurry and just want gingerbread cookies without the hassle.

For easy gingerbread cookies that are just as yummy, form dough into rolls, wrap in waxed paper, refrigerate, slice, and bake.

Keep it Simple

Jewell Johnson

It happened again this year at our family's Christmas celebration. Someone said, "Remember the year when Ann made our presents?" We laughed and reminisced of a Christmas thirty years ago.

That December, five-year-old Ann pouted, "I don't have any presents to give." For several weeks, her older brothers and sisters with jobs and salaries had been coming home with packages of mysterious contents. "Don't you dare peek," they admonished as they stashed the bags in closets. Ann felt left out of the holiday excitement.

In an effort to console her, I said, "You could make gifts."

I didn't think Ann would take on the challenge, but I was wrong. She flew to her room and came back armed with a skein of yellow yarn, markers, and a bottle of Elmer's glue. Then she disappeared outside on the Arizona desert landscape. In half an hour she was back and announced, "I've got all my Christmas presents. It's a surprise."

On Christmas Eve, Ann's three brothers, two sisters, her dad, and I opened packages revealing rock people complete with marker faces and yarn hair.

In the years that followed, family members received many gifts from Ann, all more costly than a rock. Yet, at our Christmas gatherings, we talk about the wonderful rock people she gave us that year.

Keep Christmas simple, without frills—like Ann's gifts. Perhaps that's the way God intended the birthday of His Son to be celebrated.

The Making of the Cranberry Sauce

Laurie Barker Copeland

"Who wants to put in the apples?"

Janna shoots her arm into the air.

"Okay, Janna, you get the apples. What about the oranges?"

I assign orange and cranberry responsibilities to eager volunteers as Grandpa finishes his slicing duties. It's Christmas Eve day and time for our family's favorite Christmas tradition: creating the homemade cranberry sauce. This will taste yummy with the turkey for Christmas dinner. Using an old sausage grinder my mom found at a flea market, we all gather around to join the fun.

Soon, the coveted Turning of the Crank begins with the youngest family member. Adults watch for too-close fingers and manage the ratio of the colorful and juicy apple/orange/cranberry blend.

As we take turns adding apple slices, orange segments, and handfuls of cranberries to the grinder, I revel in the feeling of family togetherness. When we finish the blending, the taste test begins. Opinions come from all directions as Nana adds one tablespoon of sugar at a time. Before long, willing hands place the entire concoction in the refrigerator so tart and sweet flavors can blend together overnight.

Tart and sweet—like our blessed family. Combined in just the right way, we make a delightful treat. And that's something I'm thankful for every year.

Cranberry Sauce

3 lg. or 4 sm. apples
(Gala or Granny Smith work well, depending if you want green or red)
3 lg. or 4 sm. oranges (navel oranges work best)
1 lb. bag of cranberries
Sugar to taste

Through the Years

Connie Peters

When the ax
strikes its last blow,
the tree topples
in the woods
to the delight
of the family
immersed
with Christmas spirit,
their voices hoarse
with laughter
their sounds vanishing
with the wind
as they squeeze back
into the station wagon,
the ropes holding
their cumbersome prize
on the roof,
the car engine giving
a little extra effort
for the occasion,
at home, the family dashes
to the basement that holds
boxes of memories
and they decorate
the once slight tree
which, now enormous,
stands in the living room
and they repeat
this performance
year to year
till Grams and Gramps
grow too tired
and purchase
an artificial
for 29.99
at Wal-Mart.

A Memory Locked In Our Hearts

Tammy Pfaff

It was Christmas Eve in 1998 as we filled our gift bags for the E.I. DuPont Children's Hospital. We had filled eighteen bags with dollar store items such as coloring books, crayons, and puzzles for the children who wouldn't make it home for the holidays. Cookies were baked, gifts wrapped, curlers removed, and outfits laid out for the evening. It was time to make our journey to Delaware.

My daughters Jillian, eight and Emily, four, were excited to meet the sick children and hand them the bags they had filled with little trinkets they had handpicked themselves. It was a half hour drive from Philly to the hospital. We arrived, gathered our bags, and headed to the lobby, quite surprised at how empty the hallways appeared.

A friendly nurse greeted us at the nurses' station. "Fortunately, we only have a handful of children who are still with us," she said.

The children were glad to see us since all the visitors had come and gone for the day. Jillian and Emily greeted the children and handed out the Christmas bags. One boy was about the same age as Jillian. We stayed awhile and got to know him. He was full of energy as he ripped the items from his bag; happy the girls were willing to stay a little while and play. He particularly liked the Play-Doh. Before we left he asked if we had a spare bag for his sister who would be visiting him the next morning.

We left several bags to leave at the nurses' station for those who would return. Sharing how happy they felt to make someone else feel special, Jillian and Emily wore ear-to-ear smiles as we headed to the parking lot. They couldn't wait to do it again. What a warm feeling it was to put a smile on another child's face.

As we reached the car, something unexpected happened. I searched for my keys only to realize they were still in the ignition. I went from zero to sixty from feeling good to feeling bad. The only solution was to call my husband Kevin to come bail us out with his spare key.

* * *

Years have passed since we made that particular adventure to the Children's Hospital. But the girls always remind me each Christmas of what a special memory that is for them. Funny thing is, they have long forgotten about the keys being locked in the car, but they look back and remember the excitement in that boy's eyes over a few dollar store items. That Christmas will always be a special memory in our hearts.

Fennel Pistachio Cookies

Peggy Blann Phifer

1 cup (2 sticks) butter, softened
1½ cups sugar
1 egg
2 Tbsp. amaretto or almond extract
1 Tbsp. lemon zest
1½ tsp. fennel seeds
2 cups all-purpose flour
1 tsp. baking powder
½ tsp. salt
¾ cup pistachio nuts, chopped, plus extra for garnish

Preheat oven to 350 degrees. Beat butter with electric mixer until creamy. Add sugar; mix. Add egg; beat. Add amaretto, lemon zest, and fennel seeds; mix. Combine flour, baking powder, and salt; add to butter mixture; beat. Stir in pistachios. Shape dough into 1-inch balls; place 2 inches apart on ungreased baking sheets. Flatten balls slightly and sprinkle with additional chopped pistachios*. Bake 10 minutes or until lightly browned. Cool slightly, then remove to cooling racks; cool completely. Store in airtight container for 1 week. Makes 3 dozen cookies.

*To keep the nuts on the cookies, after rolling the dough into a ball, I dip them in the nuts first, set them on the baking sheet, nut-side up, then flatten slightly. The nuts stay on the dough better.

I stumbled upon this recipe a number of years ago and we loved them so much they've become a once-a-year thing. They are not exactly "Christmassy," but because of the effort involved, I've made it a Christmas tradition. And they are worth the effort. Absolutely to die for.

The Giving Spirit

Annette Rey

I am reminded of the Christmas story of the poor, young woman who had her beautiful hair cut and sold it in order to buy her husband a gift. Meanwhile, he was out selling something precious to him in order to buy an ornate hair comb for his wife's luxurious hair. Romantic.

What about other times of the year when gestures of this type are given not in honor of a holiday, but because caring and empathy pours out as a daily expression?

Many years ago, my ninety-year-old friend, Vera, was passionately in love with her husband who enjoyed riding a motorcycle, even in inclement weather. Red's co-workers made fun of him when he'd arrive at work half-frozen in winter, drenched in the spring, and coughing bugs in the summer. Though he "took it like a man," the teasing bothered Vera. Some of Red's co-workers lived nearby and Vera overheard their chatter.

Without letting him know her plans, one August day she retrieved from the closet the grey "fur" coat he had bought her to keep her warm. (Like the characters in the story, they were poor and the "fur" was fake.) She draped it over the faded bedspread and eyed it. Then, without remorse, she expertly cut it into shapes, pieces of fur flying in the hot, humid air of the room (no air conditioning, either) and slips of fur cloth fell to the bare floor.

She took the shapes and fashioned them into her work of art—a mask that would cover her husband's nose and was long enough to tuck into the top of his cloth coat. Red also needed gloves, but for these she would need a pattern. She sat on the floor and daydreamingly devised another plan. The sun, shining into the room on a slant, caught her attention. It was almost time for Red to return home from work!

Like a demon, she swept at the fur, causing more of it to go airborne. Where to hide the biggest parts of the once-winter-coat? She hadn't thought of that. Dragging a suitcase from the closet (they never traveled), she stuffed everything into it and jammed it back on the shelf.

And just in time too. Red was whistling in the lower hall of their walk-up building. He was surprised she didn't have dinner ready but was not perturbed. Red was easy-going. That's why he could take all the jibing at work.

Vera had her mind on getting Red's handprint so she introduced a game to him. "Did you ever play hand-clapping games when you were a child?"

Red looked at Vera out of the corner of his eye. "No-o-o."

"Well, let me teach you. First . . ."

"Wait, wait, ol' girl. What's with you?"

"Nothin'. Just want to do something different tonight. Just want to be close to you."

"Well, hey, no problem there. I got ideas, too. Let's . . ."

"Let's hold hands!"

Red looked disappointed. "Okay."

"Your hands are so strong, Red. So careworn, it makes me sad." She caressed them and turned them over in her own small hands.

"No matter, ol' girl, I like my work at the foundry. One day you'll have a real house, maybe I'll build it myself—with these same hands."

"Red, hold your hand up against mine. Look how much bigger they are. I bet each finger is two inches longer than mine and your palm is at least that much wider than mine."

"Vera, when I see your eyes all-interested like, I want to hold you forever."

They didn't talk much that evening, just shared their young lives and dreamed of pleasing each other with houses and fur gloves.

Early the next day, Vera made a paper drawing, using her hand as the guideline. She increased the finger size and palm width and seemed satisfied with her final pattern. Using the paper form, she cut more coat material and fashioned gloves. They were a bit bulky but they would keep her husband's hands warm.

Again, she cleaned up the fur remnants before he returned home from work.

The next day, she opened the suitcase to dispose of the cuttings and the rest of the cut-up coat when she realized, she could still have a winter covering—a jacket instead of a coat. She had used the entire lower section of the coat for her project, but the upper portion of the coat down to the waist was still intact so she hemmed it. This was not the style of the day, except maybe in Hollywood. Perhaps Joan Crawford had such a style. She would be proud in her totally different jacket in her neighborhood of old-fashioned people.

The weather began to turn cold and Red was returning home with chapped, red skin not caused by furnaces at the foundry. Vera had kept the secret as long as possible, afraid Red would be mad at her for cutting the coat he had labored so hard to buy for her.

One cold night in late October, Halloween to be exact, Vera had a warm supper waiting for Red when he came home. He ate heartily and they snuggled on the couch while they listened to a radio broadcast of Martians landing on earth, a delightful program that sounded so real, Vera had shivers and Red laughed at her.

Before bed, she unveiled her present to him—wrapped in clean, plain butcher paper from the shop down the street, and decorated with some of her hair ribbons.

"What's this?"

"A present."

"What for? It's not my birthday."

"It doesn't have to be for something, does it? It's just for you!"

He smiled and opened the package. "Vera, what the . . . These gloves are great! Wow! And what is this thing?"

"It's a mask."

"A mask? Am I going to rob something?" He knew he'd never do that.

"It's to keep your face from freezing when you ride on the motorcycle this winter. I'm tired of worrying about you, that's all."

"Sure. And where did all this come from? Did you rob somebody to get this for me?"

Vera raised her chin in the air and squared her shoulders. "I made them myself."

"But, from what? Where did you get the . . .? Vera! You didn't!" Red's eyes grew wide.

"I did! And look, Red!" She ran to the closet, pulled the suitcase off the shelf, opened it, and whipped out the fur jacket. Whirling in a circle, she put it on and modeled it for him in an arrogant and flaunting manner. "I am elegant. I am Joan Crawford." She giggled.

"Vera. You won't be warm. And the neighbors will taunt you as my co-workers do me."

"Then we'll be taunted together and I'll feel better because we'll be sharing that too!" She clamped her lips together and gave a quick nod of her head.

Red held her close. "This feels like Christmas, Vera. I love you."

Red Salad

Anne Grace

When my military husband, Bob, and I were married in 1962, we moved to Mather Air Force Base near Sacramento, California. The only person he knew in that state was his mother's cousin, Virginia Thompson, who lived in Napa. Because Bob and I were alone at Thanksgiving, Virginia invited us to have dinner with her family. The Napa Valley countryside reminded us of where we grew up in southwest Virginia.

Among the many tasty dishes Virginia served that day, the one she called "Red Salad" was especially delicious. She gave us the recipe, which I have prepared each year at Christmas because of the color. I share this with you, hoping you enjoy it as much as our family does.

Red Salad ~ Good at Christmas

2 - 3 oz. pkgs. raspberry Jell-O (or 1 lg. pkg.)
2½ cups hot water
1 #2 can crushed pineapple (15 oz.)
1 lg. can French-style beets, chopped (15 oz.)
½ cup chopped celery may be added, if desired

Combine all ingredients and chill until set.
Serve with mayonnaise or whipped cream and enjoy!

The Old-Fashioned Way

Jane Riley

I developed these cookies and wrote the poem to help parents celebrate Christmas with their children in a simple old-fashioned way. The cookies can be round or cut with a star-shaped cookie cutter.

Star and Moon Cookies

2/3 cup shortening
1½ cups granulated sugar
2 lg. eggs
2 tsp. vanilla extract
2½ cups self-rising flour
Colored sugar

Cream shortening and sugar. Add eggs and beat mixture thoroughly. Add vanilla and flour; mix well. Chill. Preheat oven to 400 degrees. Roll dough thin on lightly floured surface. Cut with lightly floured round and star-shaped cookie cutters. Sprinkle with colored sugar. Bake on ungreased cookie sheets until done, about 5 minutes.

Notes:

1. You may enjoy trying other seasonings instead of vanilla—almond flavor, lemon zest, orange zest.
2. Cookie dough can be shaped into balls and pressed flat with a glass that has a pretty bottom and has been dipped in sugar.

Brother Star, Sister Moon

STAR: Listen to me, Sister Moon.
Can you hear me, Sister Moon?
MOON: Yes, I hear you, Brother Star,
But you're talking from afar.
STAR: Will you help me, little one,
With a big job to be done?
MOON: You know I will. Just tell me
What to do. Won't you tell me?
STAR: Help me brighten up the sky.
Three wise kings are passing by.
I have led them from the East—
Three wise men on camel beasts.
They are wearing rings of gold
On their hands. Their crowns are old.
Golden, glowing Sister Moon,
They'll be riding by you soon.
Please help me fill the dark sky
With pretty light from up high.
Shine bright in the night, Sister Moon,
While the angels sing a tune.
MOON: You know I'll help you, Brother Star.
Tell me why they've traveled far.
STAR: They are bringing precious things
To the little King of kings.
Spices and perfume and gold—
These are the gifts I was told.
For the greatest king of all.
A baby in a cattle stall.
Shine your sweet light from on high.
Soon the three kings will ride by.
MOON: See my light, see how I shine.
Both of us are looking fine.
STAR: We will celebrate the birth
Of God's Son sent to the earth.
MOON: Shine bright, shine bright, Brother Star,
As you travel near from far.
STAR: I'll shine on the baby boy,
Who will fill our hearts with joy.
I will shine my brightest light
On the new king boy tonight.
MOON: Glitter, shine, sparkle, and glow
From up above to down below.

Angels, Roaches, and a Christmas Child

Lorilyn Roberts

I never thought roach droppings would become one of my favorite Christmas stories. But stories have a way of writing themselves on our hearts.

Each year my sister Paige invites all of us to her house. We sit around the dining room table where she has transformed odd knickknacks into lovely Christmas decorations. Paige is an artist, and it's a good thing for my daughters. Most of my art projects never go as planned. I always miss an important step and my results are memorable, but for all the wrong reasons.

Last year all the cousins created angels to hang on our Christmas trees. The ornaments were dressed in white lace, with feathery wings, and a red rose dotting the front collar. Instead of halos, the kids crowned the angels with macaroni noodles.

Joy, my youngest daughter, proudly hung her angel on our tree. Christmas came and went. January rolled around, and I packed the ornaments away in our attic for another year.

The next December I climbed up into the attic to pull out the Christmas decorations. Joy set up the tree and I opened up the first container. When I unlatched it, dozens of roach droppings littered the bottom of the box. A few tumbled out onto the living room floor. Several ornaments had brown pellets clinging to them. I was quite repulsed, only slightly less than I would have been if live ones had scampered out.

I fetched the vacuum and cleaned up all the droppings. Visions popped in my head of hundreds of roaches crawling over my beautiful ornaments. How many roaches would it take to make that many pellets? I cringed. Living in Florida has its dark side.

Then Joy cried out, "Mommy, my angel has no hair."

"What happened to it?"

"I think the roaches ate it," Joy said.

We broke out laughing. The roaches had spent the summer feasting on the macaroni hair of my daughter's angel.

As I think back to my fondest Christmas memories, many of them are also quite eclectic. There was the Christmas in downtown New York when we got trapped inside a car on fire. The electric windows were stuck and my grandfather smashed the driver's side window with a suitcase. Mother pulled me out through shards of broken glass. Sirens blared and emergency lights flickered in the cold night air. We never did get to see the lighting of the tree; instead we spent the evening in a fancy hotel.

Later Mother told me a Hollywood director was there for a children's beauty pageant and had pleaded with her to let him take me to Hollywood. Sometimes I wonder if I missed my chance to be the next Hayley Mills (who I was often compared to when I was young).

My most vivid memory from that snowy winter was Christmas Eve when I heard Santa's reindeer pounding on the rooftop of the apartment building. It was a loud swishing sound followed by gallops. I didn't believe in Santa Claus until that night. Lying in my warm bed imagining what Santa and his reindeer looked like, I wanted to jump up and peek out the window, but I was afraid if I saw them, he wouldn't leave me presents.

The next morning I ran to the window and looked below. To my surprise, there were large sleigh marks in the snow. I stared out the window for a long time.

I've thought about that more this past Christmas because of a strange conversation over Thanksgiving dinner. I asked my brother's wife if their children still believed in Santa Claus. I shared my experience at my grandparents' apartment when I was young, but mentioned only the part about the sleigh tracks in the snow.

Mother said, "I saw them, too, and heard Santa land on the roof."

"You did?" I asked surprised. "I also heard the reindeer hoofs pounding on the roof. The swishing sound woke me up," I added.

Silence followed as we thought about the strange coincidence. Sometimes I wonder if God allows fanciful moments to bring comfort to children. Maybe that's what I needed at that time—to have something to believe in.

Many years later I was in Vietnam on Christmas Eve to adopt Joy. Christmas music wafted through the streets of Hanoi, the beautiful lyrics filling the nighttime air. I rejoiced, so far from home, realizing nothing can silence what God proclaims from the mountaintops—or loud speakers hoisted on poles in a communist country.

* * *

Joy's hairless angel hangs on our tree this Christmas. All the gifts will be opened Christmas morning. I will eat far too much chocolate and then bemoan the five pounds I will gain. I will make my usual promise to start exercising on January 1, which I will probably break by the middle of the month. We will enjoy all the traditions that this wonderful season brings, full of joy, giving, and love. Then the ornaments will be taken down and packed away until next year. Hopefully, the roaches will find something else to eat besides angel hair. Life will resume its regular course, and I will be glad for the start of a new year.

But for now, during this joyous Christmas season, I will pause to reflect on the gift of the Baby, wrapped in swaddling clothes, lying in a manger, knowing someday, too, I will bow before the newborn King. And, just maybe, there won't be any roach droppings there.

Chinese Rice

Natalie Kim Rodriguez

3 cups day-old cold cooked white rice
¼ cup soy sauce
1 tsp. garlic power
1 tsp. onion powder
1 white or yellow onion, finely chopped
1 can sprouts
½ pkg. cooked, cold, crumbled bacon
1 cup chopped ham
2 cups bean sprouts
1 sm. can bamboo
½ can chopped baby corn
1/8 cup oil or melted butter

Combine garlic powder, onion powder, and soy sauce in a bowl. Set aside. On medium heat setting, heat 1 teaspoon oil in large rice pan, or wok. Sauté onion, bacon, and ham. Set aside with juices in a bowl. Increase temperature to medium high heat. Add rest of oil to pan. Once heated, add in rice and stir to begin warming cold rice. Stir in meat and onion mixture until evenly distributed. Then add in corn, sprouts, and bamboo. Once blended, drizzle soy sauce mixture over rice and stir until rice is completely coated with sauce. Heat thoroughly. Serve hot.

Makes 12 servings.

Christmas Chinese Rice

Natalie Kim Rodriguez

My family members are traditionalists. The Christmas tree goes up the day after Thanksgiving; lights stream around the house the last weekend of November. Santa gets homemade sugar cookies and a glass of cold milk on a special plate with a side order of carrot sticks for his reindeer on Christmas Eve. And everyone gets a new set of pajamas, so we have nice looking Christmas morning pictures. Anyone who was naughty gets a coal in the stocking. Sleepyheads wake up to a cinnamon breakfast on Christmas morning. Fresh baked hot bread covered in butter, and decadent, oozing sticky buns, with steaming coffee or hot cocoa. Sugar high and happy, we head off to a late Christmas service followed by football and family dinner.

We gather around a decorated table with all the trimmings of turkey, mashed potatoes, and gravy. Grace is said. Eyes open, hands reach out, and someone asks, "Could you please pass the Chinese rice?"

Yes, I said, "Chinese rice."

We have practiced this unusual family tradition for over twenty years. It's one strange habit that I can blame my father for starting in my childhood. When I was a girl, my mother could burn boiling water, so Father was the designated cook. After a summer trip to visit his sister in Miai, he learned to make Chinese rice from a friend. While preparing Christmas dinner one year, he remembered the recipe. Our family loves Chinese food, so he decided to surprise and impress us with his newfound culinary skills. We loved the change and it has become a family tradition ever since.

In fact, now that we are all grown with families of our own, Chinese rice is the leftover to take home after Christmas dinner. Now that Father isn't with us anymore, Mother has overcome her fear of cooking to make the treasured mealtime favorite. When my youngest sister calls from New York with her travel itinerary, she always asks if Mom is making the Chinese rice. When my brother is running late from work to the family get-together, he asks for a bowl of rice to be put aside for him so he doesn't miss out. The picky children who won't eat any turkey for dinner on Christmas day will gladly eat a plate of the brown pile of salty heaven. Perhaps, the C in Chinese really stands for Christmas?

Picture Perfect

Janet Roller

Each year after the combination of turkey, stuffing, football, family, and cylinder-shaped cranberry sauce with can ridges still in place, the countdown to Christmas begins with all the busyness of the season. Although every year I vow to focus on the "true meaning" of the season, I inevitably get caught up in the whirlwind of presents, parties, special services, and traditions. One of the simplest stresses of the season is the family Christmas card picture.

After decorating our tree with every ornament it can hold without tipping over, my husband, children, and I dress in our most festive attire to pose for our annual picture. Somewhere along the way it became important to "put on a good face" to show my extended family how happy we are, at least once a year. The Christmas card seems like the perfect opportunity to celebrate our Savior's birth and subtly brag about our beautiful brown-eyed babies.

One year stands out. My children were two and three. We were still in the days of film cameras…pre-digital when you didn't know immediately if the last shot was a "keeper." I placed the piano bench in front of the beautifully decorated Christmas tree and my husband began balancing the camera at just the right height to capture our little group. With the four of us dressed in coordinating colors and appropriate amounts of red gingham, we set the timer.

Two rolls of film and two exhausted parents later, I hurried to the one-hour photo developer to check out the results. Although my husband and I looked exactly the same in every take, no picture contained a moment when both children were looking at the camera and smiling. Obsessed and distressed, I did what I had to do. Taking the best shot of my son and the best shot of my daughter, I spliced, scanned, and copied my way to the picture perfect family.

We received so many compliments on our picture that year! I did it. No one had to know the effort involved in crafting this grinning group. I knew. Each time I see that picture now I think of my senseless attempt to appear unflawed and "together" as a mother. My effort to send out the best smiles on paper was more than just about showing my friends and family how much my kids had grown. It was a 4x6 glossy representation of my heart's desire for approval. By sending out a "perfect picture" I was really asking, "When you look at our home, our marriage, and our children, am I enough?" After all, what would they think if I couldn't capture one moment of happiness during the holiday? A simple gesture of joyous greeting became a fixation to prove to myself we were, well, happy.

Honestly, I wasn't happy. I was stressed. Christmas shouldn't be stressful. I lost the focus of the reason we celebrate. The holiday season is filled with traditions for most families. However, the endless pursuit of finding the perfect gift, tying the perfect bow, or sending the perfect card can distract us from the Perfect Gift.

Now my children are much older. Many Christmases have come and gone, some with pictures in cards, some without. Sifting through the years of shots, we love the shots with missing teeth and cowlicks more than the plastic poised people. Go figure.

Looking Forward to Aunt Teddy's Snicker Doodles

Joanne Sandlin

Cinnamon and gingerbread! Sweet, marshmallow-topped cocoa and snicker doodles! All of these good smells tell me Christmas is coming. And that means baking!

This all started when I was a little girl who loved to help my Aunt Teddy bake what seemed like mountains of cookies. She was my only aunt and had no children so I got to play that role—and what fun it was. Since this was the 1940s and 50s we donned our starched, colorful, cotton print aprons and went to work measuring and sifting, cutting, rolling, and decorating every kind of cookie imaginable to share with her co-workers, neighbors, family friends, and even the milkman and paperboy!

People looked forward to her annual cookie gifts and started talking about them weeks ahead. Of course, I got to taste every kind, but the one I will always remember that wore the label "the best Christmas cookie ever" was the snicker doodle.

To this day snicker doodles are made early on and several times throughout the anticipated holiday season as "Queen of the Cookies." I passed this tradition on to my own children and my son, Steve, is now the official family snicker doodle eating champion (a title he practices annually!).

This recipe was one of the inspirations behind the fulfillment of my lifelong dream of publishing my own cookbook in 1993 in honor of my special aunt and all those wonderful hours we spent baking cookies anticipating the joy of sharing with others each Christmas season. There on page 95 I become a little girl in a plaid apron dropping snicker doodles on a baking pan and smiling as my aunt and I share a wonderful memory kept alive every year.

Aunt Teddy's Snicker Doodles

Mix thoroughly:

1 cup shortening (part butter)
1½ cup sugar
2 eggs

Sift together and stir in:

2¾ cups sifted flour
2 tsp. cream of tartar
1 tsp. baking soda
¼ tsp. salt

Roll into balls the size of small walnuts. Roll in mixture of 2 tablespoons sugar and 2 teaspoons cinnamon. Place 2 inches apart on ungreased baking sheet. Bake until lightly browned, but still soft. (They puff up at first, then flatten out.) Bake in a moderately hot oven—400 degrees—about 8-10 minutes. Cool completely on wire racks after removing from oven and waiting 2 minutes to set up for easier handling. Makes about 5 dozen 2-inch cookies.

Surprise Christmas

Verna Simms

How clearly I recall the day—December 1986. I can almost smell the pine needles from our beautiful large tree placed in front of the picture window. It's the day before Christmas and everything is won-der-ful. There's snow for the children, sleigh bells ringing. Do I hear angels singing? No, it's all a big lie. I'm so blue, I could cry!

Two letters arrived last week and now lay facedown in the living room, where I had carelessly tossed them on the coffee table. I snatched one in my hand to read once more.

"Dear Grams," the first letter had been scribbled in black ink. "I've decided to stay in Columbia for Christmas. Teri and I have plans to celebrate with friends. Love, Larry."

Larry, my firstborn grandson, was a senior in college. I sighed, thinking to myself, Who can blame him for spending the holiday with his girlfriend and classmates? Not me. I reprimanded myself for thinking otherwise. I jammed the letter back into the envelope.

Then, my second grandson wrote, "Dear Grams, Hi? It's Mark here. Our company is cruising in the Persian Gulf on the Destroyer U.S.S Waddell. I don't know how long I'll be here, but definitely over Christmas. Do me a favor, will ya, and mail something nice to Cathi and my three girls. They are still in California and will be lonesome Christmas. I can't buy anything as the navy sends her my paycheck, but it only covers essentials. Hope you have a nice holiday. Tell everyone hi from me. Love ya, Mark"

I sat devastated. Fifteen hundred miles away. Poor babies. Shopping the stores, much as a zombie, was no fun. To me, Christmas is about people, not presents. Almost half of my extended family would not be attending our yearly celebration.

Somehow the holidays passed, and I did my best to show happiness for the sake of other family members. I don't remember Christmas day clearly, but I do recall the next day.

"Honey," I asked my husband Howard, "will you carry the tree to the basement for me?"

He agreed.

Gingerly, we removed the most fragile decorations from our seven-foot artificial blue spruce. I opened the door for him to carry the tree safely to our rumpus room in the basement. Howard placed the tree on a table in the far corner of our family room and I replaced the few decorations, and then covered the fully decorated tree with a sheet.

"That should keep the tree safe until next Christmas," my husband said, and left to go back upstairs.

Telling no one, I made my plans.

No one really knows the exact date of the Christ Child's birth. This year I chose to celebrate His birthday a second time on the day our young sailor, serving in the Persian Gulf, returned safely home.

I shopped in secret. What a joy after the busy season. All prices were reduced and I could afford more. Home each day, I wrapped the gifts in pretty paper and slid them under the sheet below the tree.

The long, cold winter months dragged. One day the phone jangled. I snatched it on the third ring.

"Hello, Grams."

I squealed, recognizing the voice. "Mark! Where are you?"

The excited voice came over the line loud and clear. "Guess what, Grams. I'm getting leave. The girls and I are flying home. We'll be at your house Saturday. Think you could call Larr and see if he can come. I've already talked to Mom and Dad and they said okay to all meet at your house. It'll be nice to see all of you guys at the same time. Okay? Gotta go now, Cathi wants me for something."

I heard a hearty laugh before the line went dead.

Finally, one hot day in July, our family gathered together to welcome our sailor home; even Larry's girlfriend came. I had rented a video camera and prepared a huge meal. All was ready.

Mark arrived with his family. What a pleasure to see three little girls dressed in red and white. So precious and, unknown to them, appropriate for what I had planned!

Turkey, browned to perfection, not a lump in the mashed potatoes, fresh green beans, and red-ripe tomatoes, both fresh from my garden and picked that morning, raw baby carrots, a heaping plate of my famous sourdough biscuits and two homemade pies topped with vanilla ice cream for dessert. A feast fit for a king! If I do say so myself, the aroma that came from my kitchen was tantalizing.

Seated at the table, I suggested we hold hands. We lowered our heads and listened to my husband's solemn voice, "Dear Lord, We thank You for Your bounty—this delicious meal my wife has prepared. Most of all we thank You for protecting our grandson Mark as he sailed the dangerous waters." Silently, we waited for him to finish. Then in a voice heavy with emotion, he continued, "Stay by his side as he returns to duty and hold him in the safety of Your loving arms. We ask these blessings in Jesus' name. Amen."

The only casualty was a spill on the sparkling white sailor's uniform, but modern washer and dryer soon solved that small mishap.

When everyone was properly stuffed, I rose from the table and announced, "Help me store the leftovers. Then we'll leave the dishes for later. I have a surprise. Follow me."

Leading the way down the basement steps, I glanced around the corner at the tree. It didn't disappoint me. Everything met with my approval and I loved the way the fully lit tree glowed in the darkened corner of the room.

"MERRY CHRISTMAS everyone!" I shouted. They were stunned. Christmas in July?

The oldest girl, four, asked to play Santa and hand out the presents. We were pleased to let her. Each and every one opened their gift and displayed it for the video camera.

Afterwards we adults dragged ourselves outside and rested while the younger ones romped and played in the warm sunshiny backyard. Someone took advantage of the movie camera and recorded our every move.

Back in the house we transferred the film to a larger VCR tape, and viewing began. How odd to be able to see yourself on television. My favorite is watching Natalie crawl up on her daddy's lap and share The Monster at the End of the Book (by Jon Stone and illustrated by Mike Smollin). His laughter and happiness, her expressions caught on film and in my memory, are priceless gifts.

Don't tell me I didn't have my entire family together for Christmas that year. I have pictures to prove that I did!

Loss Brings Poignant Holiday Memories

Deb Wuethrich

One of the things about celebrating holidays is that remembrances can come to us like soft footsteps meandering down memory's road, sometimes catching us unaware. Such times can be especially poignant for those who have lost loved ones, and hasn't everyone lost someone along life's journey?

Parents whose children have grown and moved away or noncustodial parents know such emotions, as do troops serving in foreign lands that will not be able to see their families this Christmas. Seniors may get friendly visits from local groups but might not have family members in the area and they miss them.

A few Christmases after our daughter's death in 1982 from spinal muscular atrophy (SMA), a form of muscular dystrophy, I knew such a time. It's the kind of nostalgia that others who are missing important people in their lives may also be recalling as they draw from their own rich wells of memory during the holidays.

I'd been feeling a little like Scrooge that Christmas. "Bah, humbug!" was not my usual style, but I found myself thinking that year, "So what?" about all the holiday happenings. I dutifully put up a tree right after Thanksgiving to try to capture some holiday spirit—but my heart just wasn't in it.

Then, the ghost of Christmas past paid a visit as I found myself remembering the previous year's tree. It was the second such holiday without Michele. We took a tentative step that year. We bought a tree after a couple of treeless seasons, so it was the first since her death. It wasn't a big one. In fact, it was a tiny, fragile tree that we set up on our living room floor. It was the cutest little thing, more on the line of a Charlie Brown tree. I kept hearing what sounded like echoes of Michele's sweet voice trilling, "A little baby tweee," whenever I looked at it.

But the next season when I was feeling down again, I looked at a larger tree, one more like those under which Santa had once left gifts labeled "Michele," and I thought of the scrawny specimen from the previous year and how it had gradually brought a little of the season's spirit back into our lives in spite of our grief.

About that time, I rediscovered a collection of holiday writings from a second grade class. The year was 1978. One story went like this: "Once there was a mommy Christmas tree who was going to have a baby. A boy planted the tree one summer. The mommy named the little tree Sinthya. Someone chopped her down when she was three. Sinthya went to a tree sale. No one wanted to buy her. Then Michele came and bought the tree."

The seven-year-old author was, of course, Michele. The story carried some symbolism for us, and the author's fictional willingness to accept what no one else wanted demonstrated her own gift of self—something that seemed to come quite naturally to our daughter. It's a gift worth passing on for it embodies the true spirit of Christmas. As the poet Kahlil Gibran said, "It is when you give of yourself that you truly give."

The ghost of Christmas present then tapped softly on my shoulder the year I was feeling depressed and I was pulled from my reverie rereading my daughter's writings. Gifts of self. What can I do? There is cruelty, hunger, and despair! I'm just one person. I can't save the whole world. Then I wondered, what would Michele do? I didn't really have to think about it. She may have had SMA, but she'd say a kind word to someone, write a sunny note (like the early one that said, "Mom: Don't be bad. I love you," written, by the way, on one of my moodier days). Or she'd smile at someone from her wheelchair. She'd start with just one person. Like a ripple in a pond, her influence would spread and upon reflection I could see how it continues circling out, even now, as I am yet blessed to be able to share Michele through writing about her. Perhaps I, too, could start with just one person by speaking one kind word or offering a gesture—one small gift of self.

The ghost of Christmas future? I now let him in before he knocks for my sight becomes clearer with each passing year, even as I have encountered other losses, including Michele's dad, who now celebrates Christmas with her in heaven. Michele only had eleven of these earth seasons we call the Christmas holidays and her daddy had fewer than I might have hoped, but when I sift and sort the materials of Christmas past, I find that memories provide abundant gifts that can lift spirits, even years later. Influence like that extends far into future seasons, even as we are still touched by the love of a Savior born in a lowly stable. My duty is to find the courage to keep those ripples going, touching lives and remembering the joy of living, the way my loved ones did, so the memories of their kindnesses—and the spirit of Christmas—will continue on in the lives of those who remember them.

Christmas Cake

Jane Riley

Nonstick cooking spray
½ cup self-rising flour
1 cup grated fresh apples
1 cup grated fresh carrots
1 cup finely chopped frozen collards
2 Tbsp. lemon juice
2 cups candied red cherries
1 cup candied green cherries
½ cup chopped candied pineapple
1 yellow cake mix with pudding
3 eggs
1/3 cup cooking oil
½ cup gold rum
1 can coconut pecan frosting

Preheat oven to 350 degrees. Prepare 9 x 13 x 2 cake pan by spraying it and lightly dusting flour on it.

Pour the lemon juice on the apples, carrots, and collards. Set aside. Coat cherries and pineapple in remaining flour. Set aside. In large bowl combine cake mix, eggs, oil, and rum. Beat until smooth. Add apples, carrots, and collards. Continue to stir. Add candied fruit. Stir lightly. Pour batter into prepared pan. Bake 1 hour or until knife inserted into middle of cake comes out clean and edges of cake pull away from sides of pan. Remove cake and cool it on rack in pan. Spread frosting on top.

Memories of Mother
(and Mothers-in-Law)

Hundreds of dewdrops to greet the dawn,
Hundreds of bees in the purple clover,
Hundreds of butterflies on the lawn,
But only one mother the wide world over.
—George Cooper

Love What Is Before It Isn't

Carol Mottinger Ramirez

Dorothy closed her eyes and smiled. Except for the discomfort of having x-rays taken, it had been a good Christmas Eve. Even the x-ray provided a good laugh when it revealed an unusual darkened area in the shape of a Christmas tree. Technicians failed to remove her one piece of Christmas jewelry that her husband, Bill, had attached to her hospital gown. Her dimpled smile grew more pronounced as she recalled her family's reaction to the image.

Family meant everything to her. She thought of them, and praised God for the Thanksgiving week when they gathered together to share a Caribbean cruise. Bill and Dorothy offered this vacation as a gift to all their children and grandchildren.

When travel plans unveiled in April, Dorothy found her children's responses surprising. "I have a new job." "My company will never let me travel that week." "There is a professional conference I must attend because I'm presenting a paper." "We can't take the kids out of school."

"God, I know there will never be a perfect time for busy people to drop everything," Dorothy said looking toward the heavens. "It's in Your hands now. I give up!"

A few weeks later, the middle child, a son, called to say that he and his family could go. "It's a busy time, but we can swing it."

The eldest child, also a son, called a few weeks after that. "Someone else can present the paper this year. And, we'll resolve taking the kids out of school when the time comes."

The youngest, a daughter, still insisted she could not go.

"I'm sorely disappointed that she can't work this out," Dorothy wrote in her journal dated May 2, 1990. However, by May 7, a happier entry noted, "we're all going!"

Thanksgiving week finally arrived and the first few days were glorious. Taking advantage of time together, they snorkeled in the crystal-clear water, climbed waterfalls, and toured cities by day; evenings focused on dining and reminiscing over family memories together.

Thanksgiving evening, Dorothy turned in early. "I'm so tired," she said as she excused herself. Friday, she took part in a tour, but soon found herself out of breath and quite weak. She spent Saturday resting. By Sunday, she needed assistance in returning home to Texas.

The next week she attempted preparations for the Christmas season, completely ignoring the fatigue and pain. She baked her special chocolate chip cookies to go with the homemade peppermint ice cream, then set up the folding table in the guest bedroom and began addressing Christmas cards. Her husband brought down Christmas decorations from the attic. Propped up on the den sofa and unable to participate in one of her favorite seasonal activities, Dorothy supervised while Bill trimmed the tree. The next day she succumbed to reality and entered the hospital. Cancer consumed her body, but not her feisty spirit.

Alone in her hospital bed as Christmas Day dawned, Dorothy drifted off to sleep and thought to herself, "I am truly blessed."

* * *

As I sat with Dorothy (my mom) in ICU a few weeks later, she turned and looked at me. She mouthed the words, "I want to go home." The next day she did indeed "go Home."

Dad, now in his nineties, still hosts his children and grandchildren for the holidays; we still use Mom's recipe for chocolate chip cookies and for peppermint ice cream; stories—many wonderful familial tales—are still shared; and I still wear Mom's Christmas tree pin. Her Christmas tree x-ray lies buried somewhere in Dad's garage.

Famous Aunt Hallie

Barbara Boothe Loyd

My great aunt Hallie lived in Gonzalez, Texas, in a Victorian-style house with a deep front porch. Summer visits there were special; my sister, brother, and I had fun sleeping in daybeds on the porch. Aunt Hallie was famous for her delicious desserts. The following recipe is for one of her special cakes which she passed down to my mother. We anticipate eating it at Christmas time. It not only tastes delicious, it is a pretty cake.

Great Aunt Hallie's Luscious Cake

Make a white or yellow cake in round or square pans. Add the following filling and topping when cool.
1 cup sugar
3/4 cup butter
4 egg yolks
1 cup chopped pecans
1 pkg. pitted dates, chopped
1 sm. pkg. sweetened, shredded coconut
grated rind and juice from one orange

Cook sugar, butter, and egg yolks in double boiler until thick. Add remaining ingredients, stir well, then let mixture rest off heat until it thickens. Put half between the cake layers, then add the remainder atop the cake.

Mom's Extreme Holiday Baking Project

Emily M. Akin

The holidays always bring back memories of Christmas back home. The one thing that I remember most was my mother's annual Christmas cookie and candy baking—and baking and baking. Lots of people bake for the holidays, but she took it a level higher than anyone else—and she had a full-time job, a husband and two kids, a large extended family, and an active social life including church and community activities.

When it came time for the Christmas baking, it was "all hands on deck and no complaining," or you wouldn't get any of the goodies. Although Mom didn't like anyone in the kitchen while she was cooking, the holiday baking sessions were desperate times, so I was allowed to measure, mix, roll, cut out, and especially clean up. My brother was the trash-can taker-outer, and he made extra trips during the holidays. Also, he was conveniently present whenever a bowl needed licking.

Besides the regular baking sessions, Mom would often get up early and make a batch before work. Goodies were stashed in airtight tins and plastic containers all over the house—under the kitchen sink, in the utility closet, in the freezer. And we knew better than to try to sneak a bite.

Now, you might be thinking that we were some hefty family if we ate all that ourselves. But the Christmas goodies were not for US! They were for everybody ELSE in town.

The goodie gifts were her edible Christmas card to people in the community, especially the people that might not be remembered by anyone else. Let's see, we had the neighborhood kids (numerous), the bag boys at the grocery store, co-workers, the custodian at the courthouse, shut-in friends, and the pastor's family, to name just a few. Each gift was personalized for the individual recipient, because Mom knew each person's favorite treat and adjusted the gift contents accordingly. The boys at the grocery were more than happy to carry out all the flour, sugar, nuts, and other ingredients, all the while knowing that they would see those plates of goodies with their names on them come Christmas week.

We made chocolate chip, orange slice, pecan cookies, and thumb prints. Some years, we'd do fruitcake cookies or butterscotch brownies or lemon squares or coconut balls. For the kids, we made each child a personalized Christmas tree-shaped sugar cookie, decorated with red and green sugar, red-hots, or sprinkles.

And then there was the candy. Old-fashioned Hershey fudge (with nuts and without), pecan divinity, and sometimes peanut butter fudge.

Once the baking was done, the gift packages were assembled as needed so that they would be fresh when delivered. Using a sturdy paper plate (red, green, or a festive print) as the foundation, we'd fill it with cookies and candies, and that "name" cookie went right on top. Last, the plastic wrap and some tape to hold it steady, a bit of ribbon, and it was ready to go.

Now my father was a rural mail carrier, so the holiday season wasn't exactly a slow time for him. After driving and delivering mail all day and working at a local business for a few hours after that, he was subject to cookie delivery runs at night and on weekends. Of course, Mom would take the gifts herself if she had time, but she made so many that we all had to pitch in.

The Extreme Baking Project made our holidays hectic, but it was worth it to see the smiles on the faces of those who received the gifts. Besides, we were never at a loss for goodies at home. Some of Dad's mail route customers would meet him at the mailbox with a box of their homemade goodies on Christmas Eve.

What Mothers Do

Bill Butler

As a five-year-old, I didn't know how poor we were. We had just moved to Manhattan and knew no one in that city. My father would not be home that Christmas Eve; he was in the army serving overseas. My mother, then in her twenties, and I worked all afternoon making tree decorations. The kitchen table was crowded with stars, globes, and animals made of shiny paper. There was at least a dozen feet of a chain made of colored paper loops.

She explained that we would get a Christmas tree later in the evening, when the prices usually dropped. Just after sunset, we bundled up against the chilly Manhattan night and walked four blocks to a Christmas tree lot.

"How much is your cheapest tree?" my mother asked the man standing at the lot entrance.

He held his gloved hands over the fire in a steel barrel. His brown skin glowed in the flickering. "Thirty dollars, Miss."

Her smile disappeared. "Nothing for less?"

The man picked up a small tree branch and dropped it into the fire. "I just work here, miss. I can't change the price."

The sudden melancholy in my mother's face made me sad.

The man looked down at me for what felt like a long time, although it probably was only moments. He pointed at a mound of branches, the size of a car, in the corner of the lot. "See that pile of cuttings? Behind it is a tree that we can't sell. You can have it for free."

"Thank you," my mother said. She nudged my shoulder.

"Thank you, sir," I said.

We hurried to the back of the mound. There it was, a scrawny thing just a little taller than me leaning against the wire fence. Having only a few branches, it was almost a ghost of a tree.

My mother shouted to the man, "Can we take some of these branches too?"

He waved his arm. "Take it all if you want to, miss."

I hauled the tree and she carried a bundle of branches. Back home we set the tree in the corner of the living room, away from the radiator. I couldn't imagine how we could hang many decorations on something so sparse.

She was smiling again. "Go to sleep now. Santa will decorate the tree for us."

I woke at dawn and rushed into the living room. To my amazement, the tree had filled out. I couldn't even see the trunk anymore. And, it had a beautiful natural shape. The decorations glistened in the morning light. The chain of blue, red, white, and green paper draped gracefully around the tree. I almost didn't notice the presents wrapped in shiny paper under the tree.

Days later, curiosity made me examine the tree closely, and I found that my mother had used wire from clothes hangers to somehow attach the discarded branches to the almost nude tree trunk. Then she had carefully trimmed it with scissors to get its perfect shape.

A few weeks later, my father returned from overseas. When I told him about the tree, something happened that I didn't understand at the time. Tears filled the eyes of that burly soldier.

Since then, I have seen many wonderful holidays—but that Christmas remains as my favorite.

My Mother's Gingerbread Recipe

Paige Carpenter

I spent my childhood roaming the New Hampshire woods. Northern winters are dark. Clouds hang heavy in the sky for weeks without a sight of the sun, and the gloomy daylight fades into twilight in mid-afternoon.

During these dark winters, my family would kindle lights inside: a fire in the hearth, scented candles, strings of Christmas lights. And my mother would make gingerbread to warm us inside and out. There is no gingerbread as good as my mother's: soft as velvet, with a gingery bite.

Now I live in Florida, where winters are short and sun-drenched. But every year for Christmas I bake loaves of my mother's gingerbread, and I remember the cold, haunting darkness of New England winters.

Mother's Gingerbread

Preheat oven to 350 degrees and grease 9 x 13 cake pan. Take out a stick of butter to warm to room temperature.

1 stick unsalted butter
½ cup brown sugar (tightly packed)
1 cup molasses
Cream butter, brown sugar, and molasses together until smooth. (If starting with frozen butter, chop it into cubes and stick it in the microwave for about a minute on very low power until it is soft but not melted.)

2 eggs
1/2 cup sour cream

Beat in the eggs and sour cream.
2½ cups flour
¼ tsp. kosher salt
1 tsp. cinnamon
1 tsp. crystallized ginger (packed)
3 tsp. ginger
½ tsp. nutmeg
½ tsp. allspice
2½ tsp. baking powder
½ tsp. baking soda

In another bowl, whisk dry ingredients together. It's always a good idea to cream wet ingredients together in one bowl, and mix dry ingredients in another. Then, while stirring, gradually add dry ingredients into wet ingredients until they form a rich, dark batter.

1 cup boiling water
While adding dry ingredients to wet ingredients, start a pot of water boiling. By the time you finish mixing the wet and dry together, the water should be boiling. While stirring, SLOWLY pour the water into the bowl. But be careful as boiling water will slosh everywhere.

Mix it up nicely. The bowl will be hot, so wrap a towel around it while pouring batter into the baking pan. Bake for 35 minutes.

Wait. While waiting, lick the bowl and the beaters and the spatula. Then clean up the mess.

Now open the oven and stick a toothpick into the center, the thickest part of the gingerbread. If it comes out clean, it's done!

Mama's Magnificent Meatless Mincemeat

Rebecca Bruner

Because Christmas Day is usually full of activities with our extended family, I have tried to create a special annual tradition for just my husband and our children. Every Christmas Eve, we break out our prettiest tablecloth and set the table with china and silver. Then we have an intimate, candlelit supper before heading to church for the Christmas Eve service at midnight. The pièce de résistance of our little feast is always my homemade mincemeat pie served warm and topped with a generous scoop of ice cream.

Meatless Mincemeat

1 lg. navel orange, peeled and sectioned
1 sm. lemon, peeled, seeded and sectioned
2-2/3 cup raisins
3 lbs. (8 med.) unpeeled Granny Smith apples, cored and sliced
1½ cups apple juice
3 cups firmly packed dark brown sugar
1½ tsp. salt
1½ teaspoon each of powdered cinnamon, nutmeg and cloves

Using a coarse blade, chop orange, lemon, raisins, and unpeeled apples together in a food processor. The resulting mixture should be well mixed together and chopped, but not pureed (closer to the consistency of crushed pineapple than to applesauce). Put apple juice in a large saucepan. Stir in chopped fruit and raisin mixture and bring to a boil. Simmer, uncovered, for 15 minutes. Add remaining ingredients and simmer for 20 minutes longer, or until thick. Makes enough filling for three 9-inch pies. Filling may be frozen.

Piecrust (makes enough for one 9-inch pie with lattice top)
½ cup margarine or shortening
2 cups flour
dash of salt
6 Tbsp. + cold water

Use pastry cutter to cut together margarine and flour until they are a uniform substance resembling coarse corn meal. Add salt.

As you stir with a fork, add water a little at a time, until dough sticks to itself readily. (Push dough into itself in the center of bowl as you stir. Stop adding liquid as soon as dough holds together. The varying humidity will affect the amount of liquid needed.)

Divide dough in half. Roll out one half of dough and line a 9-inch pie plate with it. Pour in mincemeat filling. Roll out remaining dough and cut into strips. Lay strips across the pie in two opposite directions to form lattice top. Crimp edges of top and bottom piecrusts together with fork, then trim off excess dough. Heat oven to 425 degrees and bake for about 30 minutes. The crust should be golden, and the filling should be bubbly.

Lil's Sugar and Spice Cookies

Lynn Hartke

In my kitchen cupboard next to the peanut butter is a small, tan pottery jar. The sides are worn and the cork is stained a darker brown from years of holding cinnamon and sugar. Before it came to my kitchen, it resided on the shelf of my mother-in-law, Lil.

I think that little jar holds magical powers.

With just a light sprinkling of cinnamon and sugar, I am transported back into Lil's bright blue kitchen with patchwork curtains over the windows. The years fall away and I can see Lil standing over the stove frying bacon or over the sink deboning shrimp for her famous shrimp cocktail. Over the holidays, she would also grab the pottery jar when she was mixing up her famous Sugar and Spice Cookies. As the cookies baked, the smell of molasses and cinnamon would fill the small kitchen, drawing family members from all corners of the house to sample the cookies' warm goodness right out of the oven.

My memories of that little jar are sweet, but those memories have nothing to do with the sugar in the mixture. The sweetness is mixed with memories of loss and happy times and thoughts of being a new bride and spending time with my husband's mother.

I didn't always appreciate her.

When I was newly married, someone told me that a man usually marries a woman like his mother. I looked at Lil with shallow eyes and laughed, knowing I was nothing like her. She struggled with her addition to cigarettes. She never lived outside of St. Louis, spending most of her life in the tiny house on Starboad Street where she and her husband raised their three boys. I saw her as a small woman living in a small world.

I was wrong.

Through the years I watched her love and care for her husband as he struggled with the lingering effects of a stroke. We vacationed together and she taught me the gift of truly relaxing as we would face the day with nothing organized or planned. Later when the guys were busy golfing, she and I discovered the joy of boutique shopping. And in her later years, I observed her courage and tenacity while battling cancer.

With wiser eyes, I remember her, and realize she was content with her family, her faith, and an intimate circle of friends. We should all be so fortunate.

At different times I have been in conversations with young brides who are struggling with their mother-in-laws. I tell them to give it time. To look for things they can appreciate. To not focus on the differences, but on how they are the same as women. That sometimes small worlds and small things can contain a lot of sweetness.

Like my jar of cinnamon and sugar.

Lil's Sugar and Spice Cookies

3/4 cup shortening
1 cup brown sugar
1 egg
¼ cup molasses
¼ tsp. salt
2 cups flour
2 tsp. baking soda
½ tsp. cloves
1 tsp. cinnamon
1 tsp. ginger

Cinnamon/sugar mixture:
4 Tbsp. white sugar
1 tsp. cinnamon

Cream shortening, brown sugar, egg, and molasses. Add dry ingredients and stir until thoroughly mixed. Roll batter into round balls. Roll balls in cinnamon/sugar mixture until coated. Bake at 375 degrees for 10-12 minutes.

The Unexpected Gift Exchange

Carol Moncado

There's nothing worse than showing up at a Christmas party with no present and seeing a table full of gifts.

In 1985, my parents, Mike and Linda Gammel, had nothing in hand for the annual faculty/staff gift exchange at the Northwest Christian Academy (NWCA). There had been no sign-up sheet in the teacher workroom and no one had told them about it. They knew why, even understood why, but it had the potential to be awkward at best. Why hadn't anyone told them? Because that was the year Mom had cancer. She had worked only a couple weeks at the beginning of the school year. Medical bills were piling up. And the health insurance—well, it was a fiasco.

And everyone knew it.

For my birthday the month before, I'd received a gift that is still among my most treasured. Ten envelopes with ten pennies, ten chocolate chips, ten peanuts, and so on (it was my tenth birthday, after all). Treasured? Yes. An example of how strapped things were? Also yes, though it wasn't until years later that I truly realized that.

A few weeks later at the Christmas party, my parents rationalized no one had told them about the gift exchange because they wouldn't have the funds to participate. If they didn't know about it, there would be no unnecessary pressure to spend money we didn't have.

They were about to discover the reality was far different.

Everyone in the tight-knit community did know how tough things were for our family and decided to do something about it. That year, instead of a gift exchange, the faculty and staff drew names. Not each other's names for a Secret Santa, but my family's names.

All of the gifts piled in the library that day were for us.

To make sure two little girls didn't face an empty Christmas tree.

The irony was in the form of an unexpected financial blessing received a few days earlier. My parents were going Christmas shopping for me and my sister that afternoon. Between it all, there were well over eighty presents under the tree that year. For four of us. Yes, Dad had us wrap each pair of socks separately (doesn't everyone get socks under the Christmas tree?), but we still ran out of room.

The outpouring of love from our NWCA family brings tears to my eyes over twenty-five years later. I still have several of the gifts I received that year. The little mouse planter-turned-pencil-and-pen-holder from my first grade teacher—appropriately named Mrs. Love. The Care Bear notebook from someone whose name I no longer remember. A teddy bear my children now sleep with.

Mom fought the good fight for a couple more months, but ultimately the cancer claimed her life.

I miss Mom. I always will. I've never forgotten my tenth birthday present, and I still have the envelopes. But that year, a group of teachers and staff at a small school at 43rd Avenue and Thunderbird in Phoenix, Arizona, showed me the true meaning of Christmas.

And that's something else I'll never forget.

Ma's German Christmas Bread

translated from German by Florentine Hardt,
modern mixing steps by Elaine Hardt

2 cups Real Idaho potato buds
2 cups milk
3 pkg. dry yeast
1 tsp. salt
2 eggs
2 cups sugar
1 cup butter
1 rounded tsp. nutmeg
1 lb. citron
1 heaping cup of nuts, chopped
1 cup coconut powdered sugar to coat loaves
Flour

In large saucepan boil 4 cups of water, then add 2 cups of Real Idaho brand dried potato buds. Add milk and stir. Mix together yeast and 1 cup of flour, then stir into mixture. Add salt, eggs, sugar. Beat with mixer on low speed. While mixing, add butter, nutmeg, and 3 cups of flour.

As soon as too stiff for the beaters, mix with wooden spoon. Transfer dough to large bowl (I use my roaster pan). Add 2 cups more flour, but before stirring in add citron and nuts. (When the citron and nuts are lightly coated with flour, they are less likely to sink to the bottom of the dough.) Continue stirring and adding flour until consistency to knead. Knead lightly.

Cover pan with waxed paper, let rise approximately 1 hour. When double in size cut into 8 equal pieces, knead and shape into small loaves. (My loaves are about 7 inches long at this point.) Place on parchment-lined cookie pans and 9 x 13 inch baking dish. (If not using parchment paper, be sure to grease bottoms of pans.) Let rise till light. Bake at 350 degrees.

Check on loaves after 20 minutes. Remove from oven when a dark golden brown. Set on racks to cool. While still hot, coat the tops of loaves with butter, then pat generously with powdered sugar. Let cool before slicing. Makes 8 loaves.

***

Can you guess how my version is different from Florentine Hardt's recipe? Yes, she peeled real potatoes. And in the early years she mixed it all by hand. Women in the kitchen were strong back in the early 1900s! Florentine Pufahl Hardt lived from 1896 to 1984 and Don and I married in 1954, so you see I had many years to enjoy her wonderful German Christmas bread the way she made it. Later, I adapted it and made it myself. Don agrees it's delicious.

Cranberry-Orange Relish

Rhonda Brown

There's nothing exotic about this recipe. It is in both of my wedding-gift cookbooks from nearly 40 years ago, and I find variations in several other recipe collections residing on my shelves. But to me, the Christmas table would be incomplete without it. The radiant jewel-tones of the cranberries and oranges are a feast for the eyes, and the tart-sweet flavor combination is a refreshing counterpoint to meats and vegetables. And yes, my mother made it too, so it is part of holiday memories.

4 cups fresh cranberries
2 oranges, quartered and seeded, but with rind included

Put the fruit through a food chopper or grinder on coarse setting. Stir together with 1½ to 2 cups of sugar, to taste. Store in the refrigerator—it will keep for weeks.

Mother's Large Custard

Frances E. Luymes
(*by my mother, Vera Crystal Kuehner*)

This is my mother's custard recipe that she often baked for my dad. He had stomach problems and could eat almost all of the large custard himself. She was a teacher and married a farmer in 1925 and was almost instantly consumed by cooking for ranch hands and my dad's brothers. Her delicate white hands turned to hard work.

She raised three girls in eastern Washington State. I am the first one and I think sometimes she lost patience with me as I liked to color and draw or make homemade mud pies with my sisters. When I walked home from school, about two miles, she always had cinnamon rolls or hot bread ready.

At 83, I now live in Trenton, Ontario, and still use her recipe. All my children have made the recipe many times, and also my grandchildren, one of whom lives in Italy where she makes my mom's custard recipe, along with pizza and spaghetti.

10 Egg Large Custard

10 eggs, beaten well
1 cup sugar
¼ tsp. salt
1 tsp. vanilla
6 cups milk

Beat all ingredients together thoroughly, and bake at 350 degrees in a shallow pan approx. 8 x 11 x 2 for 30 to 40 minutes, or until thick in center and all the way through. Cinnamon may be added. For smaller amount, cut ingredients in half.

Mother's Magic

Barbara Russell Chesser

The best and most beautiful things in life cannot be seen or even touched…they must be felt with the heart. (Helen Keller).

The worst Christmas of my childhood turned out to be one of the most memorable. My mother and grandmother anticipated that the two days before Christmas would be extra busy in my grandmother's café. So some relatives took my two brothers and me home with them until late Christmas Eve.

Spending time away from home with cousins was fun during the summer, but the prospect of leaving home only a few days before Christmas did not sound like fun to me or to my brothers. We were ages six, seven, and eight, and we treasured time with our mother. Our father had been killed in an auto accident six years prior, and we were a close-knit family of four.

Our home was small—three rooms and a tiny bathroom. My brothers and I often hovered over the radio in the living room to listen to our favorite programs until Mother came home from work. She usually joined us; her laughing with us made the programs even more delightful. At bedtime, we all piled onto one of the twin beds in our bedroom for her to read to us. In really wintry weather, to combat the shock of the cold sheets, we all cuddled down under the covers of one bed for reading time. Mother and I slept in one bed while my brothers slept in the other one. For breakfast Mother made us hot buttery cinnamon toast. Warm, cozy times in our small home made me want to be there and not with relatives—especially on Christmas Day.

All hopes for our being home for Christmas morning were dashed to pieces when my aunt told us that we would be taken home later that afternoon. Watching our relatives open their presents wasn't the most agonizing aspect of this revised plan. The big problem was that my brothers and I had not bought Mother any gifts! Not knowing that we would be sent home with relatives, we had planned on buying her gifts a day or so before Christmas Day.

When we arrived back at our own home, the adults had their conversation while we eyed our packages under the scrawny Christmas tree. (The decorations were even scrawnier; we had hurriedly made them after we learned that we were going to be whisked away before Christmas.) As soon as the relatives left, we jubilantly opened our presents. Our jubilance was short-lived, for we soon remembered again that we had no gifts for our mother. Curious as to why our mood had suddenly turned so somber, she asked, "Why are you so sad? Don't you like your presents?"

All wailing at the same time, my two brothers and I tried to convince Mother how badly we felt that we had no gifts for her. In her usual loving way, her face revealed a million dollar smile as she put her arms around us and, one by one, placed us under our Christmas tree. "Listen closely," she said softly, "you have given me the best presents you can ever imagine." Puzzled by her words, we gave her our full attention as she continued, "You are my gifts!"

That scraggly tree suddenly became the most beautiful Christmas tree in the world. Looking at each of us crouched awkwardly under it, Mother repeated, "You are my gifts!"

What magical words! Spoken more than sixty years ago, Mother's words have only become more precious to me. They are a powerful reminder that the best gifts are not particularly those bought in a store and beautifully wrapped. The best gifts are those felt in the heart.

Reprinted with permission from *Keeping Christmas: Stories to Warm Your Heart Throughout the Year*, Legacy Publishing, 2011 (Compiled by Barbara Russell Chesser).

Lost Tradition

Linda Rose Etter

Cinnamon, ginger, molasses, and walnut—the smells of Betty Etter's kitchen just before Christmas are etched in my memory forever. Mom never failed to touch the lives of those she loved and did business with all year. From family, friends, and neighbors to pastors, doctors, and the people she visited monthly to pay bills, all were blessed at Christmas with Mom's cookies.

To Mom this was a tradition; it was what you do at Christmas. You give a homemade gift to others. It was a law written in her heart. Year after year, she never failed to put a smile on people's faces (and probably a pound or two on their waists).

I remember the look of surprise on her friends' faces when they stopped to receive these "tasty treats." Mouths flew open as they walked into the dining room and gazed at the stacks of beautifully hand decorated delicacies.

"Oh, look at all of them! How many did you make?"

Mom loved to showcase her labor of love. The answer would vary from 72 to 86 dozen in 13 to 15 varieties, all unique and one of Betty's favorites.

Dad enjoyed watching the joy it brought my mom and never said a word about the large grocery bills.

I remember one special Christmas when my sister and I each received another homemade gift. Mom had sat for days handwriting 197 pages of her favorite recipes on three-hole paper which she displayed in a binder. The second page said, "This Cookbook Written for You with Lots of Love from Nov. 6 to 26, 1988. Your Mom Betty Etter." The contents listed these section titles: "Poems, Beverages, Doughnuts and Quick Breads, Breads, Cakes and Frostings, Cookies, Pies and Salads." As I looked through the 59 cookie recipes, I recognized all the Christmas ones!

She had lovingly tucked another surprise in the midst of the cake section. The title said it was for a wedding cake but as I read, I choked back the tears. Under ingredients it listed all the wisdom for a happy marriage, ending with "then bake gently forever." Using a familiar approach, a recipe, she was passing knowledge down to us.

Now years later both parents are gone and the tradition has ended. Not many people join in a labor of love with homemade blessings any more. However, I think Mom knew we would find the wedding cake words of love. And the smell of those cookies, no one can remove!

Santa's Whiskers
from Betty Etter's cookbook

1 cup sugar
1 cup oleo
2½ cups flour
1 tsp. baking powder
1 tsp. vanilla
2 Tbsp. milk or cherry juice
¾ cup red or green candied cherries—chopped
½ cup nuts—chopped
¾ cup coconut

Cream sugar, oleo, and vanilla. Add flour, milk or juice, baking powder, candied cherries, and nuts. Form into 2 rolls 2 inches in diameter and roll in coconut. Wrap in waxed paper and chill overnight. Slice into ¼ inch-thick pieces. Bake at 350 degrees for 10–12 minutes.

Makes 4 dozen.

Christmas Brunch

Ashleen O'Gaea

The year I got married and moved from Oregon to Arizona was my parents' first Christmas on their own in almost 25 years. Now that I lived too far away to visit more than once or twice a year, Mom and Dad were lonely—even with my friend keeping her promise to look in on them now and again.

What you need to know to really appreciate what happened is that my mother's name was Martha, but her last name was nothing like Stewart. She aspired to be a sterling hostess, and yet….They say the devil's in the details; I don't know about that, but the details of successful entertaining sure did bedevil my mother.

For that first empty-nest Christmas, they decided to invite a few friends over for brunch. The plan was to have a relaxed mid-morning meal, and then open a few presents. But my parents were stressed. For the last several years they'd left it to me to get a tree and decorate it, and to wrap most of the presents. This year, they had to do all that themselves. And fix brunch.

"They're out of practice," my friend told me. "I offered to help them with the tree, but they wanted to do it on their own. I didn't even take a picture." That was astounding, because my friend was (and still is) the Scrapbook Queen of the World, and takes pictures of everything. Celebrating my first Christmas as a married woman, with a very nice tree in my rented living room, I could only imagine what my parents' holiday was like.

"I'm going to their house for the brunch," my friend said. I thought I heard a little shudder in her voice. Given the cooking skills my parents had demonstrated over the course of my lifetime, that was perfectly understandable. Did I mention that my mother was Martha, but not Martha Stewart?

I should say that although as cooks my parents thought solidly inside the box (as in, boxes of potato flakes and other imitation foods), they were both enthusiastic and intuitively talented gardeners. They grew herbs and vegetables that people actually looked forward to sharing. So it was unconventional, but not surprising or completely alarming, when they announced that for Christmas brunch they'd be serving tomato juice—made from their own hot-house tomatoes.

Nor, with their reliance on packaged food and their lack of baking skills, did it disturb my friend when she arrived a bit early to see if she could help and noticed two or three packages of pineapple Danish on the kitchen counter? My parents' eccentricities were well-established, so she wasn't worried that my leaving had been too much for them to bear, and made them kitchen-crazy.

Maybe this Christmas brunch wouldn't be too bad after all. My friend tucked a few brightly wrapped gifts under the tree, and greeted other guests as they came in, leaving my parents free to finish their preparations in the kitchen and dining room. By quarter to eleven or so, an assortment of in-laws, garden-club friends, church friends, and my like-another-daughter friend were seated with Mom and Dad. Brunch smelled great!

"It's a good thing it smelled wonderful," my friend told me by phone a couple of days later. "I think that was all that got us through."

I'm sure they were expecting a buffet. Some eggs, maybe some hash browns, bacon or maybe ham, perhaps some fruit, and those Danish. What they got was the Danish—still cold from the 'fridge, and still in the Styrofoam packaging, albeit with most of the plastic wrap removed—and tomato juice. Hot. Blended with skins and leaves.

"It was dead silent," my friend reported, and for a few seconds we recreated that reaction over the phone. "Somebody raised their glass of juice and made a Christmas toast. When he was done coughing up the bits of leaf, he had to peel tomato skin off his teeth."

I believe I credibly disguised my laughter as a sympathetic moan.

"I went out and got a pitcher of water and some paper cups left over from Halloween because the rest of the glasses were in the dishwasher," she said.

(My parents had lots of glasses, but they ate mostly from paper plates, so it took a long time to fill the dishwasher. They didn't run it till it was full, and they didn't wash anything by hand because they had a dishwasher.)

"When I got back, everyone was nibbling bits of Danish and licking their fingers. I went back in the kitchen and brought out some napkins. The only ones I could find were leftover paper ones from Thanksgiving."

I offered another moan, this one sincere.

"So then we all talked about what a wonderful Thanksgiving dinner your mom made last year, and nobody touched the juice or the Danish again."

"How did opening the presents go?"

"In the time it took one of your mother's friends to go out to her car and get a box of cookies she was taking to another party, I checked all the packages and got all the price tags off," my friend said. "Everybody relaxed when your grandmother explained that your parents were giving all gag gifts this year. Then your dad said, 'No we aren't,' and everybody thought that was part of the joke.

Your mother was still eating her pineapple Danish, so I said I'd get her some upholstery cleaner in a couple of days.

"All in all," she said, with only the hint of a sigh, "I think it went pretty well."

* * *

I miss my parents, Bob and Martha Not-Stewart. But—with apologies to my friend—I'm not sorry I missed that Christmas brunch…and I haven't handed the recipes down.

Magical Windows of Christmas

Nancy Julien Kopp

At least once during the Christmas seasons of my childhood, my mother and I rode the elevated train from our suburban home to downtown Chicago, exiting at the Marshall Field's station. Pigeons strutted on the wooden walkway and railings, flapping soft gray wings now and then, drawing my attention, but Mother pulled me toward a long flight of steps to the street, leaving the pigeons far above us.

We headed to a special, magical place—the big department store's Christmas windows. Often, the wind and cold air stung our cheeks and snowflakes floated lazily over us, but it didn't matter. A crowd formed close to the windows of Marshall Field's, and Mother and I wiggled into the center, moving closer and closer to the front until we stood before Christmas Window #1.

There before us was a wonderland that brought oohs and aahs from the crowd. "Look, Mommy!" could be heard as excited children pointed out the obvious to their mothers.

Marshall Fields initiated the Christmas window display in 1897. During November, the windows were covered with brown paper and not unveiled until the day after Thanksgiving. For weeks, designers and their staff worked long hours to create a story told in eleven successive windows, using a fairy tale or child's book theme. Animation came in later years, and the designs grew more and more lifelike. Piles of snow and frost-covered trees looked real enough to touch, and a tray of gingerbread men appeared so perfect, I could almost smell the spicy aroma. A scroll or some other unique prop told part of the story, and the rest came with our imagination.

The earlier windows were toy displays, a marketing scheme that drew thousands of shoppers. Later, in the mid-40s, the story windows began, and Uncle Mistletoe and Aunt Holly were introduced.

We moved from window to window enjoying the continuing tale. Stories like Snow White and Pinocchio came to life behind the giant windows. They were probably more exciting in these days prior to television, for we had nothing like this anywhere but the movie theaters. By the time we'd walked the entire route, our feet tingled with the cold, and we headed into the store to warm up.

What better place to thaw out than in the line that ended with a short sit on Santa's lap. By the time we reached his throne, we'd shed gloves and hats and unbuttoned our heavy coats. I told him my dearest wishes, never doubting that he'd remember and bring at least one of the items I'd requested.

When I grew older and could make the trip downtown to Marshall Field's with my girlfriends, my excitement stayed at a high pitch. I noticed more details then, and my friends and I giggled and chatted and pointed things out to one another. With rosy cheeks and numbing toes by the time we'd gotten to the end, we headed into the store—not to see Santa but to savor a cup of hot chocolate and then spend some time wandering through the massive place looking for Christmas gifts for our family members. We might finish the day with a Frango Mint, the candy made famous by Marshall Field's.

Today, Field's is no more. The sign in front now says Macy's. It was a sad day for me when that happened. A piece of my childhood crumbled, never to be the same. But the memory of the Christmas windows and my visits to Santa remain even many decades later.

Mother's Cinnamon Rolls

Kris Lindsey

My mother makes the best cinnamon rolls in the world. Whenever I catch a whiff of the delicious aroma from those mall bakeries, memories overtake me. But I have to hold myself back, because if I succumb and buy one I know I'll be disappointed. Yes, they smell like Mom's, but taste dry and bland by comparison.

Christmas at our house kicked off with a warm home-cooked breakfast. On Christmas Eve morning, I awoke to the smell of bacon, fried potatoes, and eggs cooking on the stove. My sleepy eyes found the table adorned with a red tablecloth, our good dishes and silverware, a juice glass and a water glass, and holiday decorations. But the centerpiece we all anticipated was yet to come.

As I took my usual seat, steaming platters of breakfast food appeared, filling the empty spots around the table. Then Mother stepped toward the oven to retrieve the final dish. As she opened the door, the sweet perfume of warm cinnamon escaped and filled the room. Oven-mitt clad hands held the coveted pan high, and then lowered it carefully onto the table. Satisfaction settled in. Our special treat was at hand.

We said a prayer, and then passed the serving dishes. Each person politely took only one cinnamon roll. When my turn came, I made sure to scoop up my fair share of brown goo and pecan halves with the serving spatula. I eyed the pan as it made its rounds to see how many were left, and where it would land. If it stopped by Dad I'd better keep watch and make sure it passed by me again before it was too late.

I developed my own technique of eating my roll. I tore off one piece of the spiral at a time, revealing the pecan treasures imbedded in the cinnamon-covered insides. That way, each bite also included a mouthful of syrupy pleasure from the pan bottom. I made sure to slowly savor each morsel.

The years passed and my sister and I both married. Our new husbands were more than happy to adopt this tasty tradition. My wise mother adapted to the increased numbers by making two pans of rolls—one for each end of the table. At last I could eat in peace, knowing there was more than enough seconds for everyone.

Eventually we had children of our own, and moved most of the Christmas festivities to my house. My sister and her husband, who live close by, hosted Christmas breakfast. But Mother still made and brought her cinnamon rolls. It wouldn't be Christmas without them.

One year, my sister decided to hold Christmas breakfast at a nearby restaurant that had a great brunch buffet. She reserved a cute little room just the right size for our family, which now included our daughters' fiancés.

"But what about Mom's cinnamon rolls?" I asked. "We all know they're one of the main reasons we keep this breakfast tradition going."

"I'll call the restaurant and ask if we can bring them in with us."

Sure enough, they not only let us bring our family specialty, they offered to warm them too.

Mother grew up in the Midwest in an era where cooking was quite an art, and taught high school home economics until she had us kids. She always made her rolls from scratch, spending all day mixing, rising, and punching the dough. Since I'm not that patient, and the sugary goo and nuts are the real yummy parts, I shortcut the bread and dress it up with Mother's fixings. I hope you enjoy this scrumptious delight.

Sweet Goo

1½ cup brown sugar
½ cup water
3 Tbsp. margarine
1 tsp. vanilla
1/8 tsp. salt
½ cup pecan halves

Combine sugar and water in a small pan and boil 4 minutes. Add margarine, vanilla, and salt. Pour into two 9 x 13-inch cake pans. Arrange pecan halves evenly on the pan bottoms.

Scrumptious Cinnamon Rolls

2 loaves pre-made frozen white bread dough
¼ cup melted margarine
¾ cup brown sugar
1½ Tbsp. cinnamon
½ cup chopped pecans

Thaw bread per package directions. On lightly floured board, roll dough out into two 12" x 10" rectangles. Using half of the remaining ingredients on each rectangle, brush with melted margarine, distribute sugar evenly over the entire surface, sprinkle generously with cinnamon, and scatter the nuts at equal intervals. Roll up tightly, jelly roll style, into two 12-inch-long rolls. Cut each roll into 12 1-inch slices. Arrange pieces in the pans with the goo sauce. Cover and let rise until doubled in bulk—about 1 hour. Bake at 375 degrees for 15-20 minutes, or until golden brown. Brush lightly with melted margarine before serving. Makes 24 rolls.

Christmas Eve Buffet

Diane Morgan

After my parents retired and relocated to Arizona where I lived with my young family, Mom began the tradition of a Christmas Eve buffet which included several appetizer-type dishes, along with cookies and punch. Every Christmas Eve, after my brother and his wife arrived from wherever the Marine Corp had stationed him that year, we would dig into this scrumptious buffet, jiggling the plates on our laps while we sat together around the Christmas tree. After we were semi-full, we began our annual exchange of gifts. Following the opening of gifts, someone usually wandered out to the kitchen, refilled their plate—and the eating would start all over again while the kids played with their new toys.

Initially Mom spent days making all of the dishes ahead of the big event. As she aged, however, she began finding that many of the same dishes could be purchased in the freezer or deli sections of the grocery store. This simplified everything for her while allowing her to continue the tradition without too much stress. As her grandchildren grew older, they also enjoyed going early in the day and helping her prepare the buffet.

A few years ago, Mom had a major surgery in December, and her place of residence on Christmas Eve was a rehab care facility. All of her grandchildren (now grown and married) divided up the buffet items and we had a carry-in buffet in Grandma's room that Christmas Eve. It was quite the spread! (I think the other residents may have been a little jealous.)

The fun of everyone contributing to the buffet has allowed our tradition to morph into a good fit for our family today. Last year we had the buffet and gift exchange at my son and daughter-in-law's home. The kitchen counters almost sagged with the weight of our old stand-by favorites, along with new creations vying for their place on the table.

My children have now invested themselves in this tradition, and it will be a joy for me to watch it continue to grow year after year. Sometimes the best traditions are the flexible ones.

Spritz Cookies

Rhonda Brown

The Christmas tree, star, and snowflake are not the only patterns on the disks in my cookie press. But, typically, Christmas is the only time of year the cookie press makes its way out of the highest cupboard and sees active service. I have several recipes for Spritz cookie dough, and can't even remember from year to year whether I favor the one with powdered sugar or with granulated. My mother also brought out the cookie press at Christmas time, so again it's part of memory and tradition, one of the special pleasures of Christmas.

Since the powdered sugar recipe is the one with a separate card in the recipe box, that's the one I'll include!

Sift together into bowl and reserve:

2½ cups unsifted all-purpose flour
¼ tsp. salt

Put 1 cup soft butter or margarine in large bowl.

Sift into small bowl enough confectioner's sugar to make 1¼ cups. Measure into bowl with butter. Beat with mixer or wooden spoon until mixture is light and fluffy.

Beat in:

2 egg yolks
½ tsp. almond extract
1 tsp. vanilla

Add flour mixture. Beat until blended. Shape with cookie press. Bake at 375 degrees for 10 to 12 minutes. Do not brown. Store airtight; can be frozen. Makes about 5 dozen.

The Perfect Gift

Deborah G. Onderdonk

Beverly read once that only in northeast Florida were there days when you needed your heater in the morning and your air conditioner in the afternoon. And so it was today. It was thirty-seven degrees when she walked the dog this morning, and now, in late afternoon, it was seventy-six degrees—just three days before Christmas. She was lucky. She had completed most of her shopping, except for the candy for the stockings. The longer candy stayed out of the house, the better. And she still needed a gift for her mother.

Why was it the same every year? Her mother's gift was the one she wanted to stash away first and it always eluded her till the last. It was the one gift she most wanted to be perfect and was the least likely purchase to put her mind at ease.

Early in the season Bev thought she had the best idea ever: a trash composter. True, it was a little out of the ordinary, but not for a gardener going through her "think green" phase. It would have been a winner. But do you think she could find one anywhere? Not even on line.

So here she was again: three days and counting. What is a daughter to do?

"Lord, please do not make me have to go into Wal-Mart one more time. Six trips are enough for any one holiday season. I cannot go in there on December 22nd and expect to keep my sanity, much less find the perfect gift."

But she knew the superstore would have the best prices on Christmas candy. So, as if with a mind of its own and knowing the garden center entrance would be less crowded, the six-year-old CRV pulled into the second entrance.

Bev gave herself a little pep talk. "Okay. Take a deep breath. It won't be so bad. Keep your head down till you reach the candy in the big cardboard boxes. By now they'll be practically giving that stuff away. A couple of quick glances to the right and left won't be so bad. You may get lucky."

As Beverly gave the greeter a "Merry Christmas," in response to his "Happy Holidays," she saw it. There on a lower shelf, just to the left as she entered the double doors, sitting beside the most pitiful poinsettia she had ever seen, was a solid white amaryllis in full bloom!

How could this be? Her mother had tried for years to find such a solid white bloom. The bulbs she nurtured always seemed to force a blossom with a tinge of pink here or a tip of red there.

Yet here, in the least likely of hothouses, was a snow-white bloom. Beverly didn't even look at the price and the candy was completely forgotten. The line at the checkout was the sweetest time of thanksgiving prayer she had had since the fourth Thursday in November. She actually hummed "White Christmas" all the way to the car.

And there, when she finally had the white flower nestled in the front seat beside her, she reached for the plastic tab identifying the name of the plant...this most perfect gift. It was called "Immanuel."

Christmas Brunch

Debbie Schmid

Which was more important, opening gifts or making breakfast for a family of six? It all depended on who you asked. If you asked the children, hands down, it was opening gifts! If you asked Mom, feeding four hungry children ranked number one. So how do you solve this Christmas morning dilemma? Make Mom's Delicious Egg Soufflé!

Once this recipe was discovered, it became a win/win Christmas morning family tradition. Prepared the night before, and set to rest in the refrigerator for 14–20 hours before baking, this delicious recipe baked in the oven while my three brothers and I examined the goodies in our stockings and tore open our Christmas gifts. Then, mmm…mmm. By the time we realized we were hungry, the buzzer on the stove went off and breakfast was served.

Now that my brothers and I are adults with families of our own, Mom's Delicious Egg Soufflé still makes it to the breakfast table every Christmas morning; an old tradition now mixed with the new. To all who try it, enjoy the simplicity of Christmas morning brunch.

Mom's Delicious Egg Soufflé Recipe
from the kitchen of Adrienne Etters Brouk

Prepare 14–20 hours in advance.

8 slices of white bread (remove crusts and butter both sides)
1 lb. bacon, fried and crumbled
1 (8 oz. pkg.) shredded cheddar cheese
2 cups milk
1 doz. eggs, beaten
Salt and pepper (optional)

Line a 9 x 13 greased pan with buttered slices of bread. Mix all other ingredients together in a large bowl and pour slowly over bread. Cover pan with aluminum foil and refrigerate overnight. In the morning, bake at 350 degrees for 45 minutes in foil-covered pan. Remove foil and bake for about 15 minutes longer. This egg soufflé served with warm muffins and fresh fruit makes a great holiday brunch.

A Sweet, Rich Tradition

Liane Williams

My mouth savors the sweet, rich taste of Braided Cardamom Bread. When I was a baby, my mother asked her friends for a good recipe for Christmas bread and received this one. Christmas would not be complete for our family without this annual tradition.

Braided Cardamom Bread always baked in the oven at Christmastime when I was growing up. When we were old enough, my sister and I stood at the cupboard and helped roll out the strands of bread for the braids. My mother would divide the bread dough she had made into twelve equal balls. We would each take a dough ball and begin to roll it between our hands making long snakes, just a little longer than the baking sheets we put the bread on. I can remember the warm, prickly feeling in my hands as the dough twisted back and forth, getting thinner and thinner.

Sometimes we would roll it with our hands on the countertop. Mom would check and smooth the strands to make sure they were fairly even in size and shape. Then she would take three strands at a time, laying them on a greased baking sheet, pinching the ends together, and begin to braid, tucking the ends in and under with another pinch at the end. My sister and I would help brush the melted butter over the loaves and then Mom would sprinkle them with sugar. Soon the house would fill with the rich, tantalizing aroma of cardamom as the four loaves baked in the oven.

Year by year, my mother baked. When I had my own home, I began making the bread for my family. My participation as a child made it natural and my mother's example passed on an unquestioned confidence. I learned about yeast. It wasn't hard to check the warmth of the water on my wrist like you would for a baby bottle. I learned about mixing the dough, adding just enough flour until it wasn't sticky. It was easy to set the covered dough and then the braided bread in a slightly warm oven to rise until plump. Soon my own children were helping roll the strands at our kitchen table. Enjoying the scent of baking bread and pulling out golden bread fresh from the oven were the easy parts. Savoring the bread as it melts in our mouths is the best part.

After it cools, each loaf is wrapped in tinfoil. When I am going to serve it with a meal, I warm it in the oven before serving just as my mother does. My family of five cannot eat four loaves at one time so I often take two loaves along when I visit my husband's family. At other times, I wrap an extra loaf for a special taste at New Years or Easter.

Braided Cardamom Bread was a part of Christmas. It was a part of my life. Now it has become a part of my own family traditions.

Braided Cardamom Bread

2 cups milk
½ cup margarine
½ cup lukewarm water
1 pkg. yeast (1 Tbsp.)
2 tsp. cardamom
5 cups flour, plus approx. 5 cups additional
1-1/3 cup sugar
1 tsp. salt
1 beaten egg

Melt oleo and milk on low. Cool. Add egg. Dissolve yeast in water. Add ½ teaspoon sugar. Leave until foamy. Put flour in a large bowl and mix in sugar, salt, cardamom.

Add milk and yeast mixtures. Beat well. Add 2-3 cups more flour. Knead on a board with more flour. Add just enough flour until it's not sticky. Place lightly greased dough ball in greased bowl, cover, and let rise till double in a warm place. Divide dough into 4 equal parts. Divide those into 3 equal parts. Roll into ropes, just longer than the cookie sheet to be used. Take 3 ropes, pinch ends together, braid, then pinch bottom ends together.

Brush with melted butter and sprinkle with sugar. Cover, let set for ½ hour. Bake at 375 degrees for 15-20 minutes till lightly browned.

Makes 4 loaves. Wrap each loaf in tin foil. Can be warmed in the oven before serving, or frozen.

Memories of Father

Any man can be a father. It takes someone special to be a dad.
—Author Unknown

Christmas Lights

Kelly Combs

Each year when I was young, my dad would excitedly ask us, "Are we going to look at the lights?" My siblings and I would all pile into the paneled station wagon as my dad drove all over Richmond looking at what has affectionately become known as the "Tacky Light Tour." My dad loved it, and the bigger and brighter the display the more he loved it.

As a matter of fact, my dad loves everything about Christmas, and did everything to make it special for us growing up. He still does today. Whether it is his famous homemade dressing (never stuffing!) that we all clamor for on Christmas Day, or his absolute conviction that he does in fact believe in Santa Claus, my dad always makes Christmas extra special.

Even now that I am 42 years old and married, every year my dad asks, "Are we going to look at the lights?" Now I am the one driving, and it's not a paneled station wagon but a minivan. My dad rides shotgun directing me to the best lights, and it's my kids who are in the backseat. Going to look at the lights is special not only to my dad and me, but to my kids now as well. But it's not the lights that make our Christmas tradition special. It's my dad.

Daddy's Christmas Box

Connie Coppings

When does your Christmas spirit begin? When the first snowflakes fly in the crisp November air? When decorations appear in the stores? Perhaps it's when carols ring out on the church bells that you're moved toward thoughts of Christmas. As a child, the twinkle in my daddy's eyes told me all I needed to know. The closer Christmas got, the bluer the twinkle became.

In the weeks before Christmas it was hard to keep my mind on schoolwork. Perhaps you think I was dreaming about what gifts I'd find under the cedar tree cut on our farm. Or, what I'd receive from aunts and uncles. No, it was something more important.

Actually, I had one question, "When will 'the box' appear?" Each year a box appeared under our tree. I'd hurry up the gravel road every afternoon to see if "the box" had arrived while I was at school. Sometimes it wouldn't appear until Christmas Eve. It might be there before bedtime, and then, it might not be there until Christmas morning.

Not knowing when the box would appear was nerve-wracking. With great glee my daddy built the excitement by putting no name on the box. If he really wanted to pique interest, he'd announce the arrival of the box with a jubilant "Ho! Ho! Ho!" that would send shivers up my spine.

My sisters and I would engage in whispered bedtime discussions about the contents and potential recipient of the box. Daddy's voice would boom, "Okay girls, we need to get some sleep." We'd ask for hints, but Daddy's hints only increased the anticipation. The "who" and "what" always remained a secret till Christmas morning.

The size and shape of the box gave no clue to its contents. It was always a gift that would result in "oohs" and "aahs" from the receiver. The gift might be a doll or a stuffed animal for one of my sisters. Sometimes the box contained jewelry, a kitchen appliance, or a sweater for my mother. Never something we expected. Daddy's gift always surprised the person receiving it.

The box made its final appearance during Christmas of my college freshman year. We'd opened all our gifts and then I noticed it, sitting in a corner behind the marble-topped table. I looked at my daddy. The blue twinkle appeared in his eyes; he nodded and suggested I go see what the box contained. With trembling fingers, I opened it. A big, brown teddy bear tumbled into my arms. I heard my daddy quietly say, "Just thought you might need him to keep you company at college."

My mother later told me the bear didn't come from a toy store. It seems Daddy looked until he found just the right one. This bear sat in a rocking chair in an antique store, but it wasn't for sale. However, my daddy convinced the owner he really needed that teddy bear for his daughter. (I wonder if Daddy told him his daughter was 18 years old!)

It was my daddy's delight, searching for just the right gift to bring joy to someone. Unfortunately, he died a short time later and Christmas changed forever. Over the years as the first signs of Christmas appear, memories stir anew and I am reminded of Daddy's "Christmas box."

Please Don't Sing

Don Cunningham

The church I attended as a young child encouraged us to participate in its musical program. At a young age, I joined the choir. As a mischievous young boy, I enjoyed playing pranks. I sat behind Dottie, a short female soloist, and noted that when she reached for high notes she popped up on her toes. Dick, one of the men in the choir, had also observed her heels leave the floor. He handed me a hymnal and pointed to Dorothy's heel. The next time she hit a high note I slipped the hymnal under the heel of her shoes. The next word squealed into eternity. From then on I was not allowed to sit behind Dottie. Many years later, when I visited her in a nursing home, she laughed about the incident.

As I was growing into adolescence, the choir director gave me a solo in our Christmas cantata. I was to sing the part of the slave in the carol "Good King Wenceslas." Dick had the role of the king. We were to sing our parts while walking down one aisle, across the raised pulpit area, then back down the other aisle.

During rehearsals the lights were on, but the night of the cantata the church was dimly lit. Dick, who was somewhat forgetful, left his glasses at home. While the choir started the first part of the hymn, we started down the first aisle. We were about three quarters down the aisle when Dick was to sing "Hither page and stand by me." In the dim light he couldn't read the words. Almost running down the aisle we moved onto the platform. He held the sheet music under a small lamp and sang his part.

Then, as we moved across the platform, I began my first—and final—solo. "Sir, he lives a goo-oo-d dea-eal hee-heence…." In that eternity of time my voice decided to change, I was becoming a bass-bara-tenor. Our serious carol turned into a Christmas comedy. Fortunately, the laughter drowned out the rest of our singing. My adolescent voice change finalized my singing in church choirs. My brother, and a cousin who attended church with me, asked me to please not sing while standing next to them. I think my family would have purchased a soundproof shower if they existed.

Years later, similar requests were made. Louise, the music director at the church I pastored, was a music teacher at a large local school. She played an electronic organ while directing the choir in our small storefront church. She also was a concert violinist.

The choir was to go Christmas caroling and invited members to go with them to homes in the community. Following that the group was to sing at a local radio station.

Though singing was not my forte, I decided to go along. Shortly before we were to leave the church parking lot, Louise asked if she could speak to me privately. We walked down the driveway. Obviously uncomfortable, she hesitantly and humbly asked, "Pastor, I don't want to hurt your feelings and you are welcome to sing at the homes we visit, but would you please not sing at the radio station?" Chuckling inside I smilingly agreed.

After the choir finished singing at the radio station the manager asked if I would give a five-minute Christmas message. The gifts of Christmas music and message went out over the airwaves that night.

I have learned over the years to use the gifts God gives us and not to cause disharmony by trying to invent ones that clearly have not been given to us. While melodies continue in my heart, I paraphrase the apostle Paul, "Let Don be silent during the singing in the churches!"

Memories of Grandparents

*Grandparents make the world...a little softer,
a little kinder, a little warmer.*

—Author Unknown

Oh Tannenbaum

Diane Ellenwood

Grandma's house was a busy place during the holidays. Mom would play the piano in the dining room and we would sing Christmas carols. Children giggled while reciting "'Twas the Night Before Christmas" together. The smell of fudge cooking and cookies baking from the kitchen added excitement to the anticipation of Christmas morning. The Christmas tree with its fresh smell of pine decorated with strings of popcorn and handmade paper chains lit up the living room.

Not long before, there was another Christmas scene that didn't seem to be as joyful; a miracle needed to take place. In the fall our family moved home to Michigan after living in Indiana. Dad hired a company to move our belongings for us. They never arrived. Everything we owned—all personal items, clothes, pictures, toys, furniture—gone.

Dad managed to get a job and began to pick up the pieces, replacing the household items, but December was approaching fast.

We spent Christmas Eve stringing popcorn and making our decorations. Later we snuggled into bed with no tree and no presents—only the assurance in our spirits that in the morning a miracle tree would appear with presents under it.

Dad worked all day, hustled to the bank at closing time to cash his check, and then went shopping, carefully selecting presents for each of his five children. It was late when he finished and there was no money left for a tree. As he walked home, a truck hauling Christmas trees turned a corner in front of him. One of those trees fell off the truck and rolled in front of my dad; the truck kept right on going. Looking at the truck that kept on going, then down at the tree, Dad picked it up by the trunk and walked home.

In the morning we awoke to our presents wrapped and under our Christmas tree, decorated with popcorn strings and handmade ornaments.

For me, Christmas just isn't Christmas without the fresh smell of pine! And that year our childlike faith had produced our miracle tree!

The following is my grandmother's recipe for fudge, the old fashioned way, enjoy!

Grandmother's Fudge

2 cups sugar
¾ cup milk
½ stick of butter
1/3 cup dry cocoa
1 cup peanut butter

Combine sugar, milk, cocoa, and butter in a saucepan, stirring until all ingredients are thoroughly mixed and mixture is boiling. Cook on medium heat until a drop of mixture in cool water comes to a soft ball stage.

Remove from heat, stirring continuously while scraping the sides of the pan. Add peanut butter and stir until mixture becomes thickened. Pour into greased 8 x 8 pan.

If needed, you can add more peanut butter which will help thicken the fudge.

The Best Christmas Present Ever

April Smith Carpenter

When I was 29 years old and pregnant with my first child, I visited Mamaw in her assisted living complex. It was about four weeks before Christmas and Mamaw was feeling blue. She was 94 years old and missing her home. A few years earlier my father moved Mamaw to Memphis from Knoxville to be closer to the only family she had left. She lived in East Tennessee all of her life; it was the only life she knew. Pressing matters at the time of her move were declining eyesight and the imminent decision to remove car keys from her. Mamaw drove her 1967 Chevy Malibu, 2-door hardtop, on the wrong side of the road, and also ran a motorcyclist off the road—without a clue that it had even happened.

On the way to my visit with her, I decided it was time for me to start gathering some family history from her, starting with something that she once really enjoyed doing—cooking. I entered her small apartment that day with a notebook and pen in hand, and a mission. I would compile recipes of some of Mamaw's favorite dishes and neatly type them so she could give copies to everyone that Christmas.

In talking that day about how to cook a ham, green beans, and biscuits, her advice was "forget the biscuits from scratch, use the ones in the cans. You have too many other things to worry about than to fool with homemade biscuits."

After discussing the recipes, how the table should be set, and how she missed her vegetable garden, we discussed the ins and outs of being a mother. Being pregnant I thought, "Hey, this is good, I can always use advice and Mamaw raised two very successful boys."

Mamaw's life was difficult from the beginning. She was born Ethel Householder in the year 1902, the oldest of eleven children. Her mother died when she was seven years old, and she cared for her younger brothers and sisters, as well as doing all the cleaning and cooking. Her father remarried, she claimed, only to have someone raise the children. "You couldn't blame him; he had to work in the tobacco fields in the middle of summer. He didn't have time to tend to us children."

The most interesting bit of parental advice Mamaw shared with me that day was "Do not purchase a lot for the baby, not until after he gets here."

"Why do you say that, Mamaw?" I asked curiously.

"Because you need to wait and see if the baby lives or not," she replied.

"Some babies die, you know, after they are born." Needless to say I was speechless.

All I could think was that Mamaw's intentions were good. She was telling me this because she cared, and this was the life she grew up in; it was really all she knew. She grew up in a society where the death of a newborn infant was more prevalent than it is today. I remember thinking how difficult life must have been for her growing up, and even as an adult as her husband, my Papaw, died the year before I was born.

I left full of mixed emotions, memories flooding my mind. Growing up, I always lived at least eight hours away so we only visited her at Christmas and during summers, or sometimes she took a Trailways bus from Knoxville to Memphis for a summer visit. Visits to her house consisted of sleeping with her in her bed with a hot water bottle at our feet, trips to the cemetery to leave flowers on Papaw's grave, and picking fresh vegetables from her garden. When she visited our home, I specifically remember her helping me learn the Apostles Creed and the 23rd Psalm.

Mamaw loved to crochet, so for Christmas every year my older sister and I would get a new pair of crocheted house shoes. As an adult I realize that those house shoes were made with lots of love.

As for the recipes that she shared during that memorable visit in December of 1997, a quaint cookbook was formed. Recipes were neatly typed, pasted onto index cards, and bound together with curly ribbon. An introduction letter told the family how the project came about. This was her special present to all of us that Christmas.

Mamaw went home to be with the Lord around Mother's Day of 1999 at the age of 96. Looking back, I wished that I had shared my appreciation to her more than I did. But most of all, I wished I had shared with my Mamaw that the best Christmas gift she ever gave me was moving to Memphis and sharing the last few years of her life with us.

The Memories of Sugar Cream Pie

Diane Morgan

Over the years, I have noticed that only Hoosiers seem to understand Sugar Cream Pie. It is a treasure! Unfortunately, most of America is not familiar with this pie and its delicious, yet humble, roots. The ingredients were readily available to farm cooks who could make any meal special with this dessert. I grew up in an Indiana city where Sugar Cream Pie was appreciated by local patrons of many restaurants.

When it came time for dessert following Christmas dinner at Grandma's house, it HAD to be pie—usually several different selections, including this Sugar Cream Pie.

Sugar Cream Pie

Unbaked pie crust (homemade or packaged)
1 cup white sugar
2/3 cup brown sugar
½ cup all-purpose flour
1 cup boiling water
1 cup heavy cream
1½ tsp. vanilla
Nutmeg

Preheat oven to 450 degrees and place piecrust in 9-inch pie plate. In a bowl, mix together sugars and flour. Pour in boiling water and stir until dissolved. Add cream (no need to whip), stir, add vanilla, and stir again. Pour into crust and sprinkle with nutmeg. Bake for 12 minutes, then lower oven temperature to 350 degrees and continue baking for 35 minutes.

The Perfect Duet

Rebecca Carpenter

A tiny Christmas tree blinked at the head of Ashlyn's bed as we prepared her for sleep. I tucked her in and said a prayer.

"Grandma, you didn't sing me a song. Sing one I don't know," she implored.

It was getting harder and harder to find songs she didn't know. "I can't think of any."

"That's okay. Sing something you sang at church tonight."

"How about 'Silent Night'?" I asked.

"I love that one."

That special carol always touches my heart. I have sung it in many churches, schools, and in groups over the years—often with tears streaming down my cheeks. It was the perfect song for us to end Ashlyn's day.

As I began singing "Silent night! Holy night! All is calm, all is bright," Ashlyn's sweet voice joined mine. Decades separated us in age, but the beautiful song joined us in spirit. From her bed she reached up, put her arm around my neck, and pulled my head to hers. We finished singing our duet cheek to cheek. When the song ended, I kissed her and wished her a good-night. What a glorious way to end the day.

Grandchildren's Christmas Delight

Willow Dressel

Before starting, preheat house with crackling fire in hearth, approximately to 80 degrees Fahrenheit

Amount
- 2 grandchildren, any gender will do
- Increase ingredients as necessary

Ingredients
- 2 warm coats, hoods attached
- 4 fuzzy mittens, warmed by the fireplace
- 2 pairs fur-lined, waterproof boots
- 2 long wool scarves, any color will do
- 1 long leash

Stir gently with
- 2 grandchildren
- 1 dog
- 1 horse open sleigh

Frost with
- Freshly fallen snow and
- 30 minute drive to Christmas tree farm, bells a-jingling

Mix with
- Many rows of Christmas evergreens
- 1 long walk to find the perfect tree
- A pinch of cooperation
- 1 large dollop of grandparents' patience

To prepare
- Cut perfect Christmas tree 2 inches from ground
- Wrap tree carefully and place in sleigh
- Trot horse briskly home
- Christmas carols optional

Drop
- Frozen grandchildren, dog, and tree into pre-warmed house
- Frozen horse into barn

Warm
    Above ingredients, uncovered, by the hearth

Fill
    Children with hot cocoa and cookies
    Dog optional

Decorate
    Tree with tinsel, twinkle lights, and handmade ornaments
    Top with star

Sprinkle
    With lots of love, laughter, and a prayer!

Memories in the Making

Phyllis Qualls Freeman

"I have a surprise for you, Amanda," I told my granddaughter one night as we prepared to retire. "Go see who is tucked into our bed."

Amanda ran to the guest room, clopping along in her too-big high heels. She took one glance at the Raggedy Ann in the bed and gave her a big hug. "I love her, I love her, I love her," she crooned and fell back onto the bed with Ann hugged to her little chest.

Because seven-year-old Amanda had a hard time staying away from home overnight, I hoped I'd discovered something special to help her focus positively on bedtime at Mamaw's house.

Years before, my husband Bill watched me peek at the Raggedy Ann and Andy dolls through a glass case in the lobby of a retirement home. They were hand sewn and stuffed by an elderly lady. I made such a fuss over the dolls' red yarn hair and red and white outfits, that Bill surprised me with them as a Christmas gift. Years passed, and I stored them away in the attic of our new home when we moved to Tennessee.

That night, I told Amanda she was the first grandchild to see these dolls. Then I read her the story of Ann and Andy from a library book to lull her to sleep. Gratefully, it worked; we were able to drift off with Andy tucked gently under the green and yellow quilt, and Ann held tightly in Amanda's arms.

When we met her mom and dad on Sunday, Amanda could hardly wait to say, "I'm the first grandchild to see them, Dad."

"See what, squirt?" her dad asked.

"Mamaw's Ann and Andy dolls, I'm the first one."

It was a wonderful weekend and I knew we'd made a memory for Amanda.

That year, after Amanda visited, I knew what I would do to make our family Christmas special for the three smaller grandchildren. I'll have a Raggedy Ann Christmas, I thought.

I located a booth at the Sweetwater Flea Market where two ladies made beautiful Ann and Andy dolls. Two sets of the dolls would be enough for Amanda to have a set, and then Beth, another granddaughter, would have an Ann doll, and her brother William an Andy.

At Christmastime, we had our family's traditional lasagna dinner during which our son-in-law, David, set up his tripod and took pictures of Mamaw and

Papaw with the grandchildren. Next he snapped pictures of each of the three families, then the complete Freeman family. Kara, our oldest grandchild read the Christmas story in her sweet voice from St. Luke and we had a family prayer before turning to the gifts.

The grandchildren were ready. They pulled presents from homemade gift bags Aunt Sherry had made, all the while laughing, squealing, and jumping up and down. Then I brought out yet another gift for them.

Ripping the red and green Christmas paper from the gifts, they discovered the Raggedy Ann and Andy dolls. Amanda squealed. Beth and William giggled. More paper fluttered to the floor as they ripped the wrapping paper from the storybooks relating adventures of the dolls. We made another memory for them, I thought as I breathed a sigh of satisfaction.

* * *

I never wanted to compete for the grandchildren's attention by what I'd buy them, but I wanted to make memories with them. Snap…snap…I couldn't get enough photos whenever they came no matter what project we concocted.

At Christmas, or on short trips to the zoo, a ride on a train, or to see an air show, we documented the events with photographs. Several years later, I made memory books for each of the grandchildren. There were pages and pages showing our special times, including pictures of when William and I sprayed the car with the power washer. Though he was only eight, he deposited the quarters in the slots and proudly helped scrub and rinse Mamaw's car. He especially loved the power rinse. There were also pages called "Papaw and me" from Bill's projects with him. William loved wearing his farmer overalls if Papaw did too. I thought, He will enjoy the pictures and remember those times for years.

Beth's book portrayed our baking projects as we created bunny cakes, salted pretzels, and chocolate chip cookies on a stick. There were pictures of her climbing trees and hanging upside down on the jungle gym at the park.

Our Amanda had a heart condition when she was little and later said she didn't remember a lot from before the surgery at thirteen. But when I gave her the memory book, she turned page after page. When she spied the photos of our Raggedy Ann Christmas, her eyes became as bright as a kitten's when the sun hits them. She said softly, "Oh, now I remember and I remember that, and that, pointing to other pictures." I was so pleased that the book had jogged Amanda's recall.

I had that intent of making memories the year I made the crayon-decorated, cardboard box playhouse for the oldest grandchild, Kara. There were tales of our adventures near most of the pictures.

Certainly all these projects did build memories for our grandchildren. With their books full of pictures and stories to recount our fun times, I knew they would never forget us.

And as I thought of the hope that the book would keep alive our times together, I came to realize that each event we shared with them was stored as memories for us as well.

Perhaps memories created for others are memories returned.

Struggling with the Season

Linda Gillis

On my way through the mall, I walked past a dozen or more stores suggesting something to buy as a Christmas present—a warm robe, pj's, sparkling dresses, scarves, red shoes. My Christmas gifts were already wrapped and ready to be mailed or delivered. I wanted nothing more to do with Christmas—just let me get in and out of the Eye Master store to get my glasses to fit my face, and out of the mall before I heard "Deck the Halls" over the speaker system one more time.

Shortly after Thanksgiving I had begun to ask myself, "Do I put up the same old fake tree, or do I just use the two-foot artificial one designed to hang on the wall and light up a corner?" In the forty years of having my own home, I'd never missed a year putting up a Christmas tree. Many years ago I started to collect angel ornaments. My first one-foot tree held about a dozen angels, and now the six-foot tree I usually put up has barely enough space for each angel to shine with all their glory. But this Christmas we would be visiting our daughter and her husband in California, and no one would be around to see my angel ornaments—except for my husband, Glen, and he didn't have much interest in my collection.

I knew the history of the hundred-plus angels in crates waiting to be displayed again this year—the feathering ones made by a dear friend every year, the pounded tin gem I found in Germany, the hand-carved one I picked up for a quarter at a garage sale. Glen probably didn't realize that every time I got a new angel, she took her place at the top of the tree right below the tall glorious treetop angel with her arms spread out wide to protect the rest of the angels. Any new angel I get this year will just have to wait until next year, I thought.

About a week later we took our six-year old granddaughter, Mikaila, to the holiday electric light parade and brought her home with us for the night. Even the extravagant two-hour parade of lights didn't budge my Scrooge heart.

The next morning Mikaila jumped into bed with us to cuddle. She lay quietly for a while and then said, "I know what we can do today, Grandma Linda. We can put up the Christmas tree! And then we can go to church!"

Half asleep, I moaned and was about ready to say, "We're not putting up the tree…" but when I looked at the pair of sparkling blue eyes, I knew I had lost this battle. With this cuddly little angel of hope bringing good cheer to me first thing in the morning, I figured I'd better give my Christmas angels the chance to shine, too, until we go to California.

Grandpa got the tree out from a shelf in the garage, and together Mikaila and he matched red branches to red holes, green to green, brown to brown, etc., until the six-foot tree took the shape of the finest fir in the forest. Mikaila oohed and aahed over each angel as she carefully attached one to a low branch. I took a nostalgic trip with each angel I placed on the upper branches of the tree, carefully placing the newest feathery beauty high on the tree. After hanging the last angel, we stood back and looked at our creation.

"Isn't the tree beautiful, Grandma?"

The white lights on the branches highlighted each angel, and the tree—and something in my heart came alive again. "Yes, Mikaila, it is just perfect. Now, let's get ready for church."

Grandma's Peanut Butter Divinity— a Christmas Tradition

Joyce Komar

With the whole family still asleep on Saturday morning, I knew I had the quiet kitchen to myself. It would be a perfect time to try the old recipe that had been scratched out on a faded scrap of paper. For years we all heard Grandma insist that the Peanut Butter Divinity recipe was a family Christmas tradition and very simple to make. Even though I could not remember ever eating it, I could easily imagine the light tan peanut butter candy on the large green Christmas platter which would be set out beside all the other Christmas goodies.

Cook sugar, syrup, and water. That seemed simple enough for anyone, even me, a terrible cook. But the words "hard ball stage" presented the first complication. I recalled the test for hardness was to put a spoon of syrup in cold water. When I tried it, lovely delicate threads appeared, but I knew that was not hard ball stage. As the candy boiled away, I dug out the old used cookbook that had long since lost its cover. Finding the right page I read that threads appear at 230 degrees, soft balls at 235, firm balls at 245, and hard ball at 255 degrees. Then it said soft crack appeared at 280 degrees, hard crack at 300, and finally the hottest was caramelized sugar at the maximum of 340 degrees.

As the mixture boiled on, I looked for the candy thermometer in the gadget drawer. My son poked his head into the kitchen to see if any breakfast was cooking and to chat with his mom. Trying not to get distracted, I put two pieces of raisin bread into the toaster and pointed to the orange juice container.

Retrieving the thermometer from the drawer, I discovered the candy mixture was light brown instead of the clear color I expected. Quickly putting the metal tip of the thermometer into the syrup, I watched the needle move up to 230 degrees. An alert cook probably would have taken the pot off the stove or at least turned off the burner, but silly me was so engrossed in watching the temperature rise to 240 degrees that I just stood and stared at the mixture. Very quickly the needle moved past hard ball stage and up to 270 degrees. That could not be good for Peanut Butter Divinity.

My son looked over my shoulder and inquired if the needle could go all the way to the top at 400 degrees. Scoffing at the idea, my eyes opened wide as I watched the temperature quickly rise to 320. A recipe for custard with caramelized sugar topping flashed through my mind, but I wondered how I could get the custard made fast enough to use this syrup. It was a wasted thought as the temperature went up to 350 degrees. Discouraged, I turned off the burner and took the thermometer out, plopping it on the counter.

As my son left the room, I gave in to curiosity and—knowing I could not salvage the sugar mixture—I promptly put the thermometer back into the pot to see if the mixture really would go up to 400 degrees. That was exactly what it did.

The dark brown mixture had no redeeming value as far as I could see and disposal seemed to be the best option. Eliminating the idea of dumping it into the sink, the garbage disposal, the toilet, and the plastic-lined kitchen garbage bin, I knew none of these would be acceptable because it would harden as it cooled. I figured that an old coffee can from the garage was a better option. I listened as it sizzled when the hot sugar and water mixture hit a residue of water left in the can. Apparently, my attempt at Peanut Butter Divinity had sizzled also.

Using soapy hot water and plenty of elbow grease to clean the pot, I began to think about the divinity being a family tradition. If Grandma made this simple recipe, I surely thought I should be able to make it too. Taking up the gauntlet, I measured out the sugar and water to try again. Relying on my recent experience, I easily brought the syrup to hard ball stage. Next the recipe said "Beat egg whites to stiff peaks, gradually pouring hot syrup mixture into eggs." I managed that also and it looked good.

I glanced back at the recipe and read the instructions to "Beat at high speed and add peanut butter. Beat until it holds shape, but not dry." Now that called for a value judgment. What was not too dry? I had to be careful as I checked to see if the mixture would mound and not flatten. Too late!

Instead of the smooth silky look I expected, I watched my spoon sink into a hole in the mixture as the candy crumbled into pieces. It did not mold and it did not flatten. It really did nothing at all except crumble and certainly did not look how I imagined Grandma's Peanut Butter Divinity would look. Putting a piece in my mouth I discovered it did not taste bad; in fact, it was quite good.

If it could be salvaged, the entire day wouldn't be wasted, so I rolled the crumbly mixture into balls, pressing them tight, and then heated chocolate to make a coating. By 3:30 in the afternoon a pile of homemade chocolate candies with peanut butter divinity centers was waiting on the special green Christmas plate for the family to admire and taste. I smiled and proudly informed the family that this candy was a Christmas tradition passed on from Grandma. My personal spin on the old family recipe would not be mentioned.

Peanut Butter Divinity

2½ cups sugar
½ cup corn syrup
½ cup water
2 egg whites
½ cup chunky peanut butter

Cook water, sugar, and syrup to hard ball stage, stirring only until sugar dissolves. Beat egg whites to stiff peaks, gradually pouring hot syrup mixture into eggs. Beat at high speed and add peanut butter. Beat until it holds shape, but not dry (3-4 minutes).

Mixture should mound and not flatten when tested on waxed paper. Drop by teaspoon on buttered platter.

The Christmas Sideboard

Jerri Clark Legler

In the early 1920s, Grama and Grandpa ("Papa") Bruno's big, two-story house, with the long porch that stretched across the front, sat along a dirt street up the hill from the ocean. It was to this home that the bustling Italian family gathered on Christmas Day—sons and daughters, aunts and uncles, brothers and sisters, cousins and grandchildren.

The event was always one of my favorite times of the year. I remember the living and dining room that faced the front of the house. I can still hear the rinky-dink sound coming from the player piano, as we kids took turns choosing from one of the various rolls of music that made us feel like we were overnight virtuosos. I remember the scent of the pine, and the lovely old ornaments on the Christmas tree that stretched almost to the top of the high ceiling.

But most of all I remember the anticipation as I ran up the steps and into the dining room—heading straight for the sideboard where Grama's delicious chocolate pies and strufolli were waiting in pretty dishes and ready for eager guests to devour.

The pies were handmade turnovers filled with a special homemade blend of chocolate pudding mixed with pears and then deep-fried. The edge of the dough was turned back and forth across the curve of the half circle. We would break the little ears of crust off and eat them one at a time, eventually devouring the thick, creamy homemade pudding inside. The tiny deep-fried dough balls called strufolli were complemented with a tasty syrup of honey and spices. We poured it over the little pieces that are similar to today's popcorn balls, only without the popcorn.

For Christmas dinner we had the traditional turkey with all of the trimmings, but our special time also included Italian dishes—spaghetti and meatballs and gnocchi. There was never a dull moment, and certainly never a silent one as any number of people talked all at once—yet each seemed to know what was being said by the other. It was only years later that I came to appreciate the many long hours Grama must have spent lovingly making all of these treats one delicious morsel at a time. While there were some gifts under the tree they were few, and weren't the most important part of my memories.

That dirt road I remember as a child is today a section of Pacific Coast Highway and runs through what is now a bustling coastal town in Southern

California. Long after Grama and Papa were gone, I went to see that house. I rather wish I had not, for it had shrunk over the decades. In fact, everything was smaller than I remembered from this little girl's larger-than-life eyes. But while the house may have been a little smaller than I remembered, I am confident to this day that the sideboard was full and running over with tasty treats produced by my hardworking grandmother's tender loving hands. In fact, if I allow myself to think very long on it, I can almost taste the chocolate pies now.

Head Cook at Junior High

Diane Morgan

My grandmother was the head cook at a junior high school in our city, during a time when all of the cooks arrived early each morning to make the entire lunch from scratch for 300 to 400 hungry seventh, eighth, and ninth graders. Grandma took great delight in feeding those kids every day. Because she never wanted lunch to be boring, she was on a never-ending search for new recipes, often found at church potlucks and neighborhood gatherings. She would tweak these in her own kitchen until she was satisfied with the result. Then she would convert and multiply the recipe to feed "her kids."

Neither my mother nor I remember the exact source of the original recipe for Festive Christmas Jell-O, but it most likely came through the process I described sometime in the 1950s or early 1960s. Both our family and the kids at Harrison Hill Junior High enjoyed it every Christmas.

This beautiful dish is cut in squares to highlight the festive red, white, and green layers. Three generations of cooks have now ensured that it is always on our family's Christmas dinner table. Grandma understood that we taste with our eyes first, that attractiveness affects taste. Although by today's standards this "salad" won't pack a huge punch nutritionally, I can attest that it is light, refreshing, and most definitely good for you!

Festive Christmas Jell-O

3 oz. cherry gelatin
3 oz. lemon gelatin
3 oz. lime gelatin
4 cups boiling water, divided
3 oz. cream cheese (I use Neufchatel), room temperature
4 oz. crushed pineapple, drained
¼ mayonnaise
8 oz. heavy cream, whipped

Dissolve cherry gelatin in 1½ cups boiling water. Pour into 10 x 6 glass baking dish and place on shelf in refrigerator where it will be level. Let it set approximately 1 hour.

Meanwhile, cut softened cream cheese into small pieces. Dissolve lemon gelatin in 1 cup boiling water. Add cream cheese and stir until nearly dissolved. Allow mixture to cool and whisk in pineapple and mayonnaise. Fold in whipped cream. Pour over hardened red gelatin layer and return to refrigerator for at least 2 hours.

Dissolve lime gelatin in 1½ cups of boiling water. Allow to cool slightly, and gently pour over lemon layer. Return to refrigerator for a minimum of 1 hour.

This is a perfect make-ahead dish, and can be cut into any size squares to vary the number or size of servings. With all of the other goodies on our Christmas table today, I find that 1½ inch squares of this dish served on a pretty plate makes the table look festive and is a good serving size.

A Thrill and Miracle

Loreen Kollmorgen

What a thrill and miracle it was to watch my grandson Matthew come into the world on July 28, 1993. With the cord wrapped around his neck and his turning blue, his father, nurses, and I were very worried that the doctor was not going to get there in time. My daughter was told to pant and not to push. I thought back to the labor and delivery of both of my children and started to pray for her, as I knew how hard it was not to push. But in came the doctor and Matthew was brought into the world with a hardy cry at 7 lbs. 9 oz. and 19 inches long.

With my daughter going back to work and my son-in-law working, they asked me to watch Matthew for them, to which I happily agreed. For the most part he was a happy baby, but could throw a tantrum once in a while that would keep him from going to sleep for a nap. This really caused a problem for me as I was running a beauty salon inside a senior citizens apartment complex four days a week.

I have always loved to write poetry, songs, and stories, so the idea came to me to write *Pretty Birdie*, a poem and put it to a melody to sing to Matthew. The first time I sang the song to him, I was amazed that he went right to sleep and it continued to work for every nap time, especially while I was busy in the beauty shop.

The real test came at Christmas when Matthew was five months old when his grandparents from Michigan came to visit. My daughter and son-in-law took them for a ride to see the Christmas lights in the neighborhood and out to eat. This is when Matthew started his fussing and throwing a tantrum. My daughter said to her mother-in-law, "Watch this," and she started to sing the song I wrote. Immediately he fell to sleep. Both the mother and father-in-law said that it couldn't be the song that put him to sleep, but the very next day, she sang it again to get him to take his nap.

I was able to use this song for naptime until Matthew was about two years old. When I sang the song to him one particular day, he put his hands on his hips, looked me straight in the eyes, and said, "Nana, don't sing that song, I am not tired." My little grandson was now a grown-up toddler.

Pretty Birdie

Loreen Kollmorgen

Pretty birdie in the tree,
Sing your special song for me.
High note, low note,
Anything you choose,
Pretty birdie, I love you.
Pretty birdie in the tree,
God made you for children like me,
In the spring sing your song and
I will love you all year long.

My Grandmother's Noodles

Andrea Arthur Owan

My grandmother was a simple woman. She dressed simply and practically; she kept a simply decorated, warm and tidy home; and she possessed a simple, deep faith in God.

Born Wilhelmina Derian in Odessa, Russia in 1899, "Minnie" was a descendant of the Germans who were brought from Prussia by Catherine the Great to farm the fertile Black Sea region. In school, she went as far as the third grade. To escape foreseeable persecution, her family walked from Russia to Germany just before the Russian Revolution. From Europe, they sailed to America, where they disembarked at Ellis Island and proceeded into the Dakotas to start a new life in a free land.

Somehow she managed to learn to read and write English, although her cursive was always shaky and her English grammar poor. The only items I ever saw her read were the newspaper and the Bible, both of which she read daily. As her eyesight waned in later years, she labored to read them, squinting through a large magnifying glass.

She began working at the age of fourteen, and met my grandfather in Chicago while she was washing dishes in a restaurant. They were married when she was eighteen and he was twenty-seven, and raised five children—my dad being the second born and oldest of four boys. She gave birth to her last child at the age of forty when my dad was eighteen.

While my grandfather was a kids-should-be-seen-and-not-heard kind of man, my grandmother solidified the family through love, selfless devotion, and unwavering faith until her death. I can still see that radiant smile of love and devotion light up her eyes and plain face when I walked in the door to visit.

Minnie never learned to drive and, when my grandfather was unavailable to drive her, she walked everywhere she needed to go—to the grocery store to buy food, to church, or to the utility office to pay her bill with cash. Never a check or credit card; always cash.

At the age of fifty-two, she was hit by a bus while walking to the store and spent three days in a coma. It took more than two years for her to recover and learn to walk again with a steel plate in her leg. And forever after that accident, she was confined to wearing orthopedic shoes—those heavy, black, clunky shoes that you used to see old women wear. Before her feet hit the ground in the morning, she had to put on those shoes, or she couldn't walk. But walking for my grandmother—even with those shoes on—was more of an awkward and painful, side-to-side-listing gait. You always knew where she was in the house; you could hear that loud, characteristic clump. Those ugly shoes used to embarrass me when I was younger; now I recall them with tender feelings and sadness.

And those hands that—aside from her two years of recovery—had engaged in hard labor every day since she began working as a young teen grew knotted and stiff. Those hands that washed and ironed other families' clothing during the Great Depression to help avoid having more than the couch repossessed. Those loving, hands that tenderly touched and gently stroked a grandchild's cheek, that faithfully clasped in prayer before bed each night—and that made those great noodles.

For special holidays, like Christmas and Thanksgiving, my grandmother pulled out the flour, eggs, milk, and water, floured the kitchen counters, dampened scores of kitchen towels, and went about the laborious task of making noodles. She never used a written recipe or cookbook for cooking; everything was made from scratch and from memory. These noodles were no exception.

Minnie would measure out as much flour as she thought necessary for the number of people eating and sift that into a mound on the floured counter. Into a well in the middle of the mound that she created with her hands, she cracked as many eggs as she thought she needed to make the flour stick together. A little salt was added, and maybe a small amount of milk or water as she kneaded to work the ball of dough into the right consistency. Then out came the rolling pin, and she would roll vigorously until the flattened pancake of dough attained the desired thickness for hearty noodles.

Following this vigorous task, my grandmother would cut the noodles into four to six-inch long, half-inch wide strips. More supremely clean kitchen towels would be laid out around the kitchen, and the strips would be carefully positioned on them to dry. In the parched Mojave Desert region of Lancaster, California, the drying process occurred rather quickly—within four to six hours—but if Minnie really needed to speed up the process, the large oscillating fan would be strategically placed and called into action. On special summer days, you could find towel-bearing noodles draped over the back porch railings and, on occasion, the backyard glider. If a large crowd was expected, the kitchen and porch were both coated with noodles.

My grandmother seemed fulfilled when she was cooking or feeding others her abundant, handcrafted meals. Joy reigned supreme in her heart and eyes when large numbers of family gathered in her home to enjoy her Christmas banquets—with abundant turkey, fresh green beans, potatoes, stuffing, pies, and those stick-to-your-ribs noodles. With limited monetary resources or options, it was the one gift she could always give that provided such contentment for us. Showing appreciation for her delicious labors was the priceless gift we could give her. The family matriarch asked for nothing more.

There are many things I remember about my grandmother, but the four things that stand out are her simple unshakable faith, that unconditional love, the orthopedic shoes, and the noodles decorating the back porch.

She and those noodles were Christmas treasures.

A Transformation

Donna Collins Tinsley

Every year I try to have my annual Christmas sleepover for my grandchildren. It is before Christmas of course, as they want to be at home on Christmas Eve.

When they were little, the money I had for gifts seemed to go pretty far and it really looked like a Christmas morning as they opened numerous gifts. The older ones knew the younger one's gifts were less expensive so they didn't mind that they might have fewer to open. But when my husband's business nearly caved in with the economy, I wondered how I was going to make our Christmas sleepover special.

We used to have a family dinner with their parents coming also, but now the sleepover night gives parents a night to themselves to shop, or whatever needs to be done before Christmas Day.

It all comes down to revolving around food and eating, it seems. So I ask them to bring food to give to the needy and then we make and eat way too much. When asked for requests for the next morning, my grandson, Austin said, "You can make pancakes and bacon and then Aubrey and I will make a peach dump cake and homemade caramels!" His sweet tooth was aching to be filled.

"How can you even want anything else after all the chocolate covered pretzels and 'Death by Chocolate' we had tonight?"

"Oh, MeMa! It's Christmas!"

Christmas it is, so Death by Chocolate has turned into Red Velvet Christmas Delight as the former name just doesn't fit into the Christmas spirit. We have food and we share food and that is part of what makes Christmas fun at our house.

Red Velvet Christmas Delight

1 box Red Velvet Cake mix prepared as directed and baked in a 13 x 9 inch pan.
2 boxes chocolate instant pudding prepared as directed
1 lg. container Cool Whip
1 lg. Symphony bar crumbled into pieces
Butter brickle bits

In a large bowl (a pretty punch bowl is perfect), layer:

Cubes of cake
Pudding
Pieces of candy and brickle bits
Cool Whip

Shave chocolate on top for a decadent look.

For a different effect you can use vanilla pudding and white chocolate chips. You can color the Cool Whip green for a more Christmassy look.

Grandma Fran's Christmas Rolls

Cassandra Wessel

When the children were small, we traveled over the state line to visit Grandma and Grandpa Barto in Ohio. Grandpa made sure to shovel the driveway and decorate the house and tree with Christmas lights. The children helped by adding tinsel and ornaments to the tree—either saved from years gone by, or freshly handmade.

Grandma made a huge amount of food for the Christmas holidays. Tray upon tray overflowed with sweet treats, nut rolls, butter cookies, and butterballs. Potato salad, heaped high in bowls, nestled in the refrigerator. Great covered trays of cold cuts, ham, and turkey graced tables in the cool basement. When company arrived, everything migrated upstairs to the table.

Throughout the holidays, relatives and friends feasted upon treats. Gifts were exchanged only among the closest relatives, but homemade treats and gifts were shared among friends. Grandma Barto's Nut Rolls remained our favorite. Now that she is no longer with us, her Nut Rolls keep her memory alive, especially at Christmas.

Sweet Dough

1 cup hot potato water
½ cup shortening
½ cup granulated sugar
4 cups flour
1 cake yeast
2 eggs

Take ½ cup of the hot potato water. Let it cool to lukewarm. Add yeast and stir gently. Set aside to rise until double in bulk (about 1 cup).

In a bowl, mix remaining ½ hot potato water, shortening, granulated sugar, and salt. When cool, beat in eggs. Mix in the flour. The dough will be sticky. Refrigerate a minimum of 4 hours, but overnight is best.
Next day, divide dough into 4 portions. On parchment paper or pastry sheet, dusted with flour, roll out until thin (less than 1/16 inch). Spread fillings on

dough and roll tightly. Transfer to cookie sheets. Brush with egg mixture. Cover and let rise for 30 minutes.

Bake at 350 degrees about 30 minutes or until golden brown.

Egg and Water mixture:

2 Tbsp. water
1 egg

Blend together until spreading consistency. Apply with pastry brush.

Nut Fillings:

½ lb. walnuts*
½ cup granulated sugar
½ cup warm milk

* Other varieties of nuts may be substituted. For other fillings, substitute poppy seeds, prunes, apricots, or raisins.

In blender or food processor, add sugar and warm milk to walnuts. Blend until a paste is formed. Spread with pastry knife over dough.

Peppernut Memories

Christy Williams

Grandma Anna said "I love you" with flour, sugar, and Crisco. As a mother to a farmhouse filled with hungry boys and hired hands, she made sure they never doubted her motherly affection, filling them with kraut bierock and apple streusel.

Whenever we came to Kansas for a visit, she would wink at me from across the table. "I made the noodle casserole just for you, Christy," she would say, pushing her Pyrex casserole dish towards me. "Surely you can eat more than that." Surely you could eat more than that was German Grandma for I love you.

Some years Grandma spent the holiday season with us in sunny Arizona. The dishwasher roared and the rolling pin spun as Grandma Anna worked on hand-cut noodles, warm, glazed cinnamon rolls and, best of all, tiny gumdrop peppernuts.

Gumdrop peppernuts taste like Christmas. These little crunchy, gooey cookies are absolutely amazing. They require days of hand chopping gumdrops with scissors; mixing, rolling, cutting and placing hundreds of thumb-sized cookies onto baking pans; and then catching them before they burn. Even into her 80s Grandma Anna made heaps of gumdrops every year. On years that she stayed in Kansas for Christmas, she sent us brown wrapped packages with homemade scarves, Christmas decorations, and, of course, peppernut cookies. The year I got braces I received my own bag of peppernuts with no nuts or gumdrops. Although gumdrop peppernuts with no gumdrops and no nuts tasted fairly pointless, I'll never forget her thoughtfulness.

Grandma left Kansas for heaven in 1993. For a while, the women in our family divided up the task of making the Christmas peppernuts. We gathered in my sister's kitchen, rolling and cutting in an assembly line. But, as our lives became busier, the peppernut tradition became less and less frequent. My first Christmas as a married women in my very own kitchen, I decided I could take on the responsibility of the peppernuts. Full of energy and optimism I tied on my vintage poinsettia apron and set to work. By Christmas Eve, I had cramps in my fingers, aching in my back, and sores on my feet. Flour and Crisco covered my face and my countertops. But, I had piles and piles of peppernuts.

On Christmas Eve I watched my family devour my hard work like it was movie popcorn. I slowly savored each chewy bite. That year, I missed and respected my Grandma more than ever before. And, most importantly, I learned the meaning of the word "appreciation."

Grandma Anna's Gumdrop Peppernuts

¾ cup shortening or oleo
1½ cup brown sugar
½ cup cream
½ tsp. salt
¾ tsp. baking soda
1 cup nuts
1½ cup white sugar
3 eggs beaten
1 tsp. vanilla
¾ tsp. cream of tartar
5 cups flour
1 cup gumdrops, cut into tiny pieces

Sift dry ingredients together. Cream shortening and sugars. Add beaten eggs and cream. Cut gumdrops into small pieces and chop nuts fine. Add flour to creamed mixture and mix well.

Keep in refrigerator until ready to bake (about a day). Roll into long strips and cut. Bake at 350 degrees for 8-10 minutes.

Oh, Christmas Tree

*The best of all gifts around any Christmas tree: the
presence of a happy family all wrapped up in each other.
—Burton Hillis*

The Beginning of Traditions

Liane Williams

A little blue Mazda sedan, a length of rope, a handsaw, and two newlyweds at Christmas time. It was our first Christmas together in our small, three-room apartment. We were headed out into the cold Michigan winter with newspaper ads in hand and high hopes of a tree.

Soon we stood on the edge of a field of cut-your-own Christmas trees with pines of all sizes stretching in front of us under a gray, dreary sky. To my chagrin, my own family had given up real trees years ago. I grinned and my eyes sparkled in anticipation as we stepped forward.

This tree is too tall,
that one too small.
This one has a hole on that side,
and that one on the other.

The air was cold as we tromped on through the snow, discussing various trees as we went. Finally, we found the tree. In the back of the lot. Farthest from the car. Never thinking about the long drag back.

It's funny how trees don't look as big when they are sitting amidst other trees in the great outdoors. When we got it home and set it up, the width of that tree filled the corner and spilled into the walkway to the kitchen. I can still see it in my mind's eye.

Year by year, we have tended to choose short, fat trees. I always say I like short and dumpy, though they are always a little taller than my five foot nine husband. It has been twenty years and year by year the trees we find are closer and closer to where we park the car. Funny how that goes.

Every Good and Perfect Gift

Nanette Thorsen-Snipes

Several years ago, my husband, Jim, brought in another scrawny Christmas tree, and put it in a base in the living room.

Not again, I thought. I slumped in my chair.

With four children to feed, our finances sat perilously at rock bottom. I gazed out our picture window, imagining what it would be like next year. I'll get a tree like the one in Macy's. It'll have delicate pink bows and pink balls peeking from the branches and slender ribbons cascading like a waterfall down all sides.

My preteen children, Jamie and Jon, lugged boxes of ornaments from the basement. Although it didn't seem to matter to them, I dreaded taking out faded chains of construction paper and the odd assortment of ornaments we'd collected through the years. Soon, the kids began chattering and hanging bright red, green, and blue balls.

"Come on, Mom," Jamie said, urging me from the melancholy that threatened to envelop me. "Let's hang the ornaments."

I stood up and plucked an ornament from the box. "Look, Jamie, this ornament says 'Baby's First Christmas'."

"It has my name on it." Jamie's blue eyes sparkled, and she grinned. It was the first ornament she hung every year. She placed the ornament in front where everyone could see it. My only girl among three boys, she had been special from the time she was born. Not long after her birth, I cradled her against my body, touching her soft, sweet-smelling fingers and kissing each one.

In the still of the moment another birth came to mind. That Baby was special too. I'm sure His mother counted His toes and fingers and kissed each one. When I tilt my head just right, I can almost hear her voice as she cooed to Him. And I can imagine her kissing His forehead and whispering His name—Jesus.

Jon's voice broke through my reverie. "Mom, this is my star!" I smiled, taking the tin star. It was not so long ago when his father patiently helped him hammer his name across the front. When I hung it, I visualized the star of Bethlehem—a star of rejoicing—that led the wise men to the birthplace of the Son of God. I could scarcely imagine the brilliance of this star announcing the greatest birth the world has ever known.

Next, Jim crowded in front of the tree and handed me an angel with lace wings. "Who gave you this?"

"Barbara," I said softly. My thoughts raced back to another year when my friend and I exchanged gifts after a disagreement. We had sat across from each other in the restaurant the week before Christmas, while I made uneasy small talk. As we had for many years, we exchanged gifts. Just before I left, my friend hugged me as though no cross words had ever been spoken.

An inner joy spread through me as I drove home. I smiled, realizing what we really exchanged that day was the gift of forgiveness. What greater gift could friends give?

I placed the angel ornament near the top of the slender tree. Long ago, an angel appeared to an unassuming group of shepherds, bringing news of great joy—the birth of Jesus—to all people. Ironically, this baby in His humility would one day die a cruel death on a tree, and He would say, "Father, forgive them, for they do not know what they are doing."

I sat there on the floor with my children, the pitiful little tree decked out with ornaments that made up our very lives. My breath caught in my throat—for almost every ornament on that tree, there was an equally important event in my life. My life was literally suspended on that scrawny Christmas tree. Funny how I'd never noticed how precious the timeworn ornaments had become.

Looking back, I felt unsurpassing joy knowing how much God's love was embodied in a simple ornament given to a baby, an angel given in love by a friend, and a tin star made by a child and his father.

The Christmas Angel

Connie Poole Wesala

For most of us, the Christmas season evokes common images: snow-covered Christmas card scenes, candles glowing in church, an old cardboard crèche, sugary smells from the kitchen, the crisp hard jingles of the street corner Salvation Army bells, and everywhere, the mischievous smile of Santa Claus, from the department stores to the Coca Cola bottles.

For each of us, however, those images soften and spread into personal memories of Christmases past. A treasured gift, a special person, a particular tree, a prayer answered. They glow brightly on a dark Christmas morning in a candlelit room, as you sit surrounded by soft holiday music, close your eyes, and think of the people you love and cherish.

As I close my eyes, I turn to a page in our heavily creased family photo album. Each black- and-white glossy is held in place with four white corner tabs. I am six years old, in my one-piece pajamas, curly hair surrounding a face full of awe and anticipation, listening raptly to my father read the Christmas story from Luke. My mother sits beside us beneath the Christmas tree.

Dad probably had to top the tree again that year. He always chose a tree too tall for the room. It was as if he could never remember the ceiling height as he stood in the grocery store lot and picked out the thickest cedar tree he could find. He would cut the trunk as far as possible, although he was limited by our old handmade wooden tree stand. He then began to trim from the top, as Mother loudly admonished, "Leave some branches for the star." Next he would find the "holes" in the imperfect tree. He would take the branches he had cut from the bottom, and with string, he attached some here and there to fill in the empty spaces. At last he would step back and nod his head in acceptance of the now perfect Christmas tree.

The nod gave Mother permission to haul out the large box of multicolored light strands, the aluminum garland, and the thick strings of silver tinsel. I loved the candle-shaped lights filled with liquid that made the flame flicker up and down.

When the tree was fully decorated, Mother placed our slightly crinkled tin star on top of the tree, but just before the star, came my ornament—a flesh-colored ceramic cherub with gold foil wings hung by a satin ribbon. Her hair was carved and unpainted and her small childlike face consisted of two small black dots above a Mona Lisa smile. She was purchased when I was five weeks old. Dad had returned from his post in Europe in time for my birth. Glass was unavailable during World War II, so the ceramic angel became a part of our family tradition and is still among my treasures.

Each Christmas when we took down the tree, we carefully wrapped her in layers of tissue paper and placed her gently back into the ornament box until the following December. I have carried her with me from city to city, house to house, and tree to tree throughout my lifetime. Each year when I unwrap the tissue, her eyes gleam with recognition, and I position her on the highest bough in a place of honor.

I didn't put up a tree this year. We were celebrating at my daughter's house, and it seemed a hassle I didn't need for once. But the day before Christmas, I went to the garage and pushed and pulled and rearranged until I could reach the box of ornaments. Lifting the lid from the plastic storage bin, I patiently sorted through paper and trimmings and ribbons until I found what I was looking for.

There she was, sixty-five years old. She has a few hairline cracks around her face and torso, not unlike the fine-lined wrinkles appearing on my own. There are some creases and tears on her gold foil wings, and her white satin ribbon is faded yellow. But the old girl is in pretty good shape for her age and has outlived many broken ornaments in her lifetime.

I couldn't help but think of all we've been through together during those many years: the moves, the changes, the loss of parents, the births of children, the happiness and grief. Her presence reminded me that I am simply a composite of all the people I've known, all the love I've shared, and all the experiences God has provided. And I feel so fortunate and humbly blessed.

I found an ornament hook and carefully slid her ribbon through it, wrapped her once again in her protective paper, and put her with the brightly wrapped packages I would take across town the next morning. She will, no doubt, outlive me but I know that she will be delicately placed on future Christmas trees, and I also know, without a doubt, that she and I will become a cherished memory for someone sitting in a candlelit room with soft holiday music playing on a dark Christmas morning.

The Stolen Tree

Cassandra Wessel

The children tore into the kitchen yelling at the top of their lungs. "Mommy, the tree is gone!"

I whirled around, suds dripping from my hands. "What? The tree is gone?"

My daughter answered. "Yes. Somebody cut it off with a knife."

"Are you sure?"

She bored the floor with her angry gaze. Defiant, she said, "You got to believe me. It's gone. Somebody took it."

"I'm coming. Let's go." I doffed my apron, donned my coat, mittens, and boots. Off we went slogging through knee-deep drifts along the path previously laid by my children. When we got to the place where we had carefully been pruning our tree for Christmas, all that remained was the telltale stump. It did look as if someone had patiently whittled away our tree with a knife.

No other white pine had been as perfect as this one. We had nothing else on the hillside except scrawny excuses for trees. Dejected, we trudged back toward the house. My six-year-old piped up. "Mommy, maybe God will get us a tree."

Her childish faith pulled me up short. Would God "get us a tree"? My recently downsized husband and I certain could not afford to buy one. This Christmas promised to be truly slim. Homemade or recycled gifts from yard sales had kept me busy while the children were in school. I sighed and threw up a prayer. We hiked back to the house.

That Sunday at church my children told everyone about our stolen tree. The following week, when the choir went caroling, they showed up at our place. In their hands they bore a well-shaped pine tree, and chorused, "We wish you a merry Christmas." My young son's faith had indeed been seconded by a God who cared enough to "get us a tree."

The Abandoned Christmas Tree

Cherry Pedrick

As Christmas neared, I looked forward to shopping for a Christmas tree with my new husband, or perhaps cutting our own. Then he delivered his speech defending the millions of pine and fir trees, a speech I have heard many times since.

"What do you mean, 'You don't believe in cutting down Christmas trees?' What am I supposed to do with the Christmas ornaments we bought?" I asked Jim.

The year before, we had bought a set of five Christmas ornaments on sale after the holidays. I had looked forward to hanging them on our first Christmas tree, but now it looked as if we would not have one.

I looked out the window, beyond the yard, to the field behind our house. No trees there. We lived in a high desert in Idaho surrounded by sagebrush. "Well, it might not be green, but it will hold the ornaments," I said to the empty room.

After Jim got home from work that evening, he saw the ornaments hanging from my "tree." Well, it wasn't really a tree. It was a tall sprig of sagebrush stuck in a coffee can filled with dirt.

"That'll do, and no one will ever miss that sagebrush," Jim said.

I thought this would be our only Christmas tree until I found one at the Salvation Army. A new artificial tree was out of the question, but this one was only five dollars.

"That's the ugliest tree I've ever seen!" Jim said when I brought it home.

"Wait until you see it decorated, it will be beautiful," I assured him calmly.

"What's this?" he asked, as he picked at the wrinkled tinsel hanging from the branches.

"It's tinsel," I told him. "Whoever owned the tree before put tinsel on it. It doesn't come off easily. That's probably why they gave it away. With a little time, I think we can get it all off."

I went to work on my Christmas tree. After several minutes of picking at the tinsel, I gave up and put it together. Then I hung my five ornaments on it.

"It looks better," Jim admitted reluctantly, "but it still has a lot of that silver stuff on it."

Every year we picked more tinsel off that tree and decorated it with our growing collection of ornaments, lights, and garland. To others, it may not have been as attractive as some trees, but to me it was beautiful. It was a part of our Christmas celebration for two decades. Every year we considered getting a new tree. At first we could never afford one, and then when we could, it was still hard to part with it. A friend suggested I buy a new tree and put the old tree in the yard. It could still be a part of our Christmas celebration.

One year I faced the choice again: Get a new artificial tree or talk my husband into a live one? Decorate my old tree and place it outside to weather the storm? That year, we broke tradition and bought a new artificial tree, and returned the old tree to its home at the Salvation Army. I just know someone has decorated it and put it in a place of honor in their house. Each year they'll pick a bit more tinsel from its worn branches and add more ornaments and garland. I'm sure my tree is now more beautiful than ever.

A Fresh Pine Memory

Betty Ost-Everley

"Look what my mom is doing!" yelled my five-year-old son at the top of his lungs.

Concentrating on the task at hand, I tried to ignore the stares of others. The tree saw kept binding as I tried to draw it along a cut I'd made in the bark.

After my divorce three years earlier, my two children and I decided that we would make "new" Christmas traditions. Some of these traditions centered around making cookies to give away to neighbors, or buying a new ornament each year, which I easily dated or personalized with a quick flip of a paintbrush.

The best new tradition was cutting down our own tree. We chose a Saturday about two weeks before Christmas to drive to the country in search of the perfect tree. We'd then decorate it to the strains of Handel's "Messiah."

This particular year, the morning was very cold with snow expected. I got down on my hands and knees to begin the tree-cutting process, the trunk hidden by pine boughs. I drew the saw back and forth, becoming concerned because this tree seemed to be much more difficult to cut down than those previously.

"Why is this taking so long?" my daughter asked.

"I guess the saw is duller than I thought."

The saw finally began to glide and the tree fell with a whoosh. I hauled it through the tree farm where it was shaken, netted, and hoisted on top of my minivan for the drive back home.

That turned out to be the easy part. I pulled and pulled, finally squeezing through the door. Ready to put the white pine in the stand, I realized why it had taken me so long to cut it down. My saw wasn't dull…the tree trunk was huge!

Standing it upright, I carefully cut the netting that had bound the tree. Whoosh! It violently erupted into our living room, filling almost half of it! The children helped me move furniture around, and we gingerly crammed it into a corner.

We decided to decorate only the half that was easily reachable. Even at that, it took every strand of lights and nearly every ornament we owned. It was big and beautiful, although its grand scale was much too big for our house.

Traditions are memory-makers. That tree twenty years ago is still one of our favorites…a fresh pine memory.

Oh, Christmas Tree

Cona Gregory

A
very
unusual
holiday happen-
ing took place at our
house on Christmas Eve.
It was enough to cause anger
it was enough to make us grieve.
We waited until the last minute to buy
a special Christmas tree. It was a precise
size, with perfect symmetry. On Christmas Eve,
we pulled it inside to trim. As we carried it through
the house, we discovered something grim. The tree was
still green, but dead as a doornail. As we brought it into the
house, pine needles rained down like hail. It was too late to find
another tree, the problem to rectify. How could we have Christmas
without a tree, I wanted to cry. Long gone were the days when we could
trek into the woods and chop one down. I wanted to stamp my foot-I wanted
someone to crown. Not only did we have no tree, We vacuumed piles of needles.
Honey, we need an artificial tree, I wheedled. "After Christmas sales" gave us a great
opportunity. Now I decorate the tree each year, with impunity. No worry about droop-
ing, no watering to do. I like the convenience. I like the look of it too. After all, it's not the
tree
that
counts
It's what's under
it. Don't you agree?

The Christmas Tree Parade

Annette Geroy

What is that? The question echoed around us as we gawked in astonishment! Up the winding mountain road trudged a yellow VW Beetle with a huge blue spruce strapped to the roof, tip and tail dragging along the pavement. The driver, wide-eyed with anxiety as he peeked around the branches blocking his view, threw a weak smile our way as he passed.

Seconds later a miniature blue pickup slung its way around the next curve, the butt of a Douglas fir braced against the tailgate. The tip of the tree hung over the cab, flouncing and threatening to take flight at any moment. Terror-driven thoughts of death-by-tree-in-flight drove us toward the precarious drop-off at the shoulder of the pavement. Whew! We maneuvered safely past that one!

Our racing hearts were just beginning to quiet when a station wagon whizzed by with a small fir bouncing out the back window. In its wake came a Suburban with a huge Ponderosa pine, almost as wide as the road, latched to its roof. Where were they going to put that thing? Next in line was a white Cadillac with a tiny tree, neatly wrapped in a blanket and nestled across the trunk. Unlike the monster trees, I could envision it sitting primly on a table, decorated with proper red balls and silver icicles.

We watched in amazement as the string of Christmas-tree-carrying vehicles extended, bumper to bumper, for miles. We were enthralled—flatlanders from southern Louisiana witnessing a parade of snow-kissed Christmas trees.

It was our first winter in Colorado and snow was a novelty. We were mesmerized as the fat, puffy flakes changed into small sticky ones that went "splat" on the windshield. The quietness that accompanied freshly fallen snow evoked a moment of solemn gratitude. But the frenetic frenzy of collecting Christmas trees defied the silence.

Areas of the forest were designated for cutting Christmas trees each year. You could purchase a limited number of permits for a very reasonable price. The process was monitored closely by forest rangers as crowded young trees were thinned out in an area undergoing reforestation after a fire. Unlike the familiar sap-laden pines of Louisiana, these mountain-hardy trees had firm branches that would support almost any ornamentation. All you had to do was figure out a way to transport your tree from the forest to your living room!

The practical creativity of mankind was expressed to its fullest in the

Christmas Tree Parade. Some vehicles had sheets or blankets wrapped around their precious cargo. Others had ropes snaked through open windows and across the roof, leaving the passengers shivering in the frigid air that poured through the car. Bungee cords, duct tape, newspaper, netting, and even human bodies played a role. At one point we were gripped with fear as a rusty old rattletrap trudged by with a burly teenager in the back. Bouncing precariously, he struggled to hold down a huge pine. The arrangement looked none too safe but the teen waved, grinning from ear to ear, when he saw our shocked faces.

Spotting a quiet side road in the area designated for tree harvesting, we pulled in and parked. Breathless from wading through hip-deep snow, I spotted a stately blue spruce. The flat branches, covered with short gray-green needles, were perfectly shaped and promised to fill our vaulted living room with its distinctive fragrance and beauty. What a joy to bring home a freshly-cut symbol of new life and hope as we prepared to celebrate the Christmas season.

My husband secured the beautiful evergreen into a tree stand and we began the arduous task of stringing white twinkling lights onto a fourteen-foot tree. The hours spent decorating waxed bittersweet because we were away from our family that Christmas. The handprint hearts the kids made in kindergarten, the red Popsicle-stick sleds we bought at a crafts fair, the button-covered wreaths I made from the treasures in my grandmother's button jar, quilted hearts with crocheted edges, clothespin Rudolphs, resin figurines, glittery stars, and cherubic angels invoked memories of special times and Christmases past. Tears flowed as I remembered the special person or event represented by each ornament. My heart ached with the missing. Wiping away my tears and stepping back to admire the memory laden tree, I was overcome with a sense of great blessing and peace.

As I admired our decorated tree, my thoughts wandered back to the Christmas Tree Parade. Pondering the destination of each tree, I wondered what I might see if I could peek through the windows of the homes those trees adorned. Were they all happy places with pleasant families in perfect circumstances? Surely not. Had some families experienced heartache and loss in the past year? Would I have seen illness or health? Plenty or poverty? Singing or sadness? Loneliness or joy? Undoubtedly there would have been a variety of situations to observe. Perhaps some were exactly like my own—missing family.

Yet, all those people had been out in the mountains collecting Christmas trees to carry home. Why? Because Christmas represents a season of hope; hope delivered into our earthly lives because of the birth of Jesus Christ. His journey from life to death to life promised that there is Someone who cares about the day-to-day details of our lives, and wants the best for us. That kind of hope allows us to embrace life as it is and learn to be content.

*　*　*

Always on the hunt for next year's special ornament, I recently found a glass-paneled station wagon with a tree snuggled to its top. I was instantly back on that winding mountain road dodging ridiculously enthusiastic tree toters, sensing the breathtaking cold on my cheeks and relishing the fragrance of freshly cut evergreen. My heart smiled. I had to have it! Each year as I decorate our Christmas tree, for a moment I am reminded of that enchanting Christmas Tree Parade.

Two Christmas Trees

Margaret Dornan Gamber

This story of three young girls and their mother took place during the Great Depression. As always, mortgage payments on their home came due a few days before Christmas which made it difficult to spend a lot on Christmas presents.

Our mother was a very creative person, but this week before Christmas she could not find a way to buy a Christmas tree.

However, there was a row of young trees standing across the street from their home. The week before this story took place, a winter storm damaged a young tree at the end of this row. One of its middle branches, with other connecting branches, broke away from the rest of the tree. As my father was leaving early in the morning to go to work, he crossed the street, picked up the broken sections of the tree, and put them on the front porch.

After Mother and we three girls were dressed and had our breakfast, Mother opened the front door and found the tree section. She and my sister Helen carried the limbs into the small room beyond the living room. Then Mother showed us the rolls of green crepe tissue paper which were a little wider than the branches of the tree, and instructed us how to wind them around the branches.

Helen started on the top branches, and my other sister Janet worked on the middle branches, while I, Margaret, did the bottom layer. We worked, stopped for lunch, and then decorated the tree. With Mother's help we finished about 4:30 in the afternoon. Then we sat on the linoleum floor admiring our beautiful work of art, enjoying a pot of tea and my mother's Scotch Shortbread which she always made for Christmas.

About five o'clock we saw a neighbor driving home from work in his company's truck and stopping at our driveway. As he came upon our porch, Mother opened the door for him. Surprised, we all watched as he brought in a lovely fresh pine Christmas tree.

"Thank you very much, Mr. Kosmiter," Mother quickly stated. "What a lovely tree! Girls, come and thank him"—which we did. I believe Mother was smiling extra big to cover up our non-smiling faces.

When Mr. Kosmiter left, we girls burst out in tears, thinking that now we would not be able to use the pretty Christmas tree we had made.

Mr. Kosmiter and his wife had no children, Mother told us, and Mrs. Kosmiter must have mentioned to him that she knew we might not have a tree for Christmas. So as he was coming home from work, he stopped and bought us one. It even was in a tree stand! He certainly had a kind Christmas spirit. God bless him!!

After Mother explained this to us, she collected the remainder of our Christmas ornaments that she had put aside. She then told us, "When Dad gets home from work, we will have dinner first. Then all five of us will decorate our second Christmas tree!"

The Day the Kids Bought the Tree

Phyllis Ciarametaro

It was already the third week in December, and we had not yet bought our Christmas tree. The weather had been horrible for the past few days—ice storms, snow, sleet, and icy winds blowing off the ocean, not to mention that we had just moved into a house perched on the highest hill in the city. The winds up there were severe and unpredictable. Saturday started out with fog and got progressively worse. By noontime we were in the middle of an ice storm, making travel by foot or car hazardous.

My mom always purchased our Christmas tree for the bargain price of two dollars at the local Building Center (yes, that's the name). This year, however, the freezing conditions of the weather were so bad that Mom, who was plagued with asthma, decided her children were old enough to buy the tree. I was sixteen and had just got my driver's license. My brother Andy was twelve, and the youngest, Sam, would be ten in March.

Mom gave us three dollars and said not to spend more than that. In the past the trees she had brought home were in worse shape than a "Charlie Brown" tree, if that's possible. We took great care in decorating these barren trees by placing hundreds of silver tinsel strands on it to hide the absence of branches and needles. My brothers were excited about us buying a tree on our own; they whispered the word "yes" and high fived each other. I didn't know what I was in for.

After a hot lunch, I warmed the car, debating on where to go to buy this wonderful Christmas tree. Travel was going from bad to worse so I decided against driving across town to the Building Center. Instead I thought driving the two blocks to Gleason's Bait and Tackle Shop would save us a lot of time, and me the anguish of driving on slippery streets. I backed out of the driveway, and immediately lost control of the car. It skidded a quarter of a mile down the hill, and almost slid past the corner of Centennial Avenue before I could regain control. From that corner it was slow going. I finally made it over the wooden railroad bridge to Gleason's parking lot and trees.

We jumped out of the car and started for the tree lot, but were driven back by the cold pelting sleet. It turned to ice on our eyebrows, it formed icicles on our noses, and coated our clothing, making us look like aliens from another planet. Back in the comfort of our heated car, we shivered as we thawed out, deciding to look through the windshield for a tree that wasn't too far from where we parked. We had to make our decision quickly, as the car was icing up. Sam noticed a tree leaning up against the fence that looked pretty full. I told the boys to stay put, that I would brave the elements alone. I slipped and slid as I ran from the car to the shop to pay for this fabulous plant. Oops, this tree cost five dollars and included the ice. I had the three dollars Mom gave us so I dug into my pocket for my last two.

It took the three of us and Mr. Gleason to tie the tree to the roof of our Kaiser-Fraser. The trip home was scary. Ice coated the windshield making it hard to see, and the black ice made it impossible to climb the hill. I had to drive through side streets in order to make it halfway up the hill. The rest of the way to the top was slip and slide.

I said a prayer of thanks as we reached our house in one piece. We untied the rope, carefully dragged the tree off the car by the bottom, and pulled it up onto the front porch. We didn't realize how big it was until we had to open the double doors to get it into the hallway. We left it lying on the floor of the downstairs hall to thaw, and went upstairs to ready the room, shouting as we went that we had found the perfect tree. Mom had made some hot cocoa to warm us, and insisted on a thorough cleaning of the living room before bringing in the tree. We groaned, but we rushed through it.

Now we were ready to bring the tree upstairs to the living room. Andy and Sam pulled it up by the bottom and I cradled the top, being careful not to damage it. It would look great in the front window facing the street, but when we managed to push it through the door of the room and tried to stand it up, it was too tall.

Mom came into the room and screamed, "What is that? Did you bring the forest home? How much did it cost?"

I caught the brunt of this outburst as my brothers were out of sight behind the lush green branches. "We'll make it fit," I said. "Dad will be home soon, and he'll help us. You'll see it will be beautiful." I said a little prayer for help.

"In the meantime, someone clean up the pine needles in the hallway," Mom said, as she threw up her hands and hurried away.

"Boys, you'll have to hold the tree upright until I clean the hallway." I rushed to vacuum.

When Dad arrived home, he had a cup of hot coffee then came to help with the forest. "How did you get that monster in here?" He shook his head and couldn't stop laughing. "I bet your mother had nothing to do with buying this tree."

Little did he know what we had gone through to get it! "No more Charlie Brown trees for us," I said.

"Okay, hold on a little longer. Andy, come with me," Dad said as he disappeared down the stairs to the basement. They soon returned with a tarp, a white jelly bucket filled with sand, a saw, nylon fishing line, and some tools. "The tree will have to stay in the middle of the room," Dad said as he began sawing a foot off the bottom.

"Oh no," I cringed. Our beautiful, perfect tree was being butchered. Every branch cut off was carefully placed on the tarp to be used for decorating the front doors. When Dad was done with that task, he placed the trunk of the tree in the white bucket, and sent Andy to the kitchen for a large pan of water that he carefully poured over the freshly sawed tree trunk. When it stood upright, it was a foot below the ceiling.

Dad nailed hooks to the three window frames around the room and wrapped the fishing line around the tree trunk, then attached the line to the hooks to secure it. Our monster tree was finally standing by itself, but it took up the entire room. We could not get around the tree without climbing over furniture or crawling under fishing line.

When Mom came into the room to check on us, she sat down, discouraged. Luckily the sofa was in the open end of the room. "Where will we put the presents?" she asked.

Dad suggested that we stack the gifts in front of our forest instead of under it. Everyone agreed. The ornaments were brought in and each of us took a side to decorate. Dad strung the lights, and brought in a ladder to put the star on the top. We didn't have enough ornaments, and I didn't dare ask for money to buy more, so we all popped corn, made stars out of aluminum foil, and fashioned paper chains from wrapping paper to fill up the tree.

At last it was finished. We darkened the room and turned on the tree lights. It was perfect, the best tree we ever had. My brothers and I stood there in the glow, inhaling the sweet smell of pine, our eyes shining with happiness. Dad had a grin on his face and an arm around Mom's shoulder. She was crying, "It's the most beautiful tree we've ever had, and we didn't use a single strand of tinsel."

Oh Christmas Tree!

Faye Braley

Our son Brad was born in 1960, thirty-one months after the birth of his sister Beth. Also living with us at the time were two teen-aged children, Ron and Gerry Lynn, whose parents were doing translation work among the Zapotec Indians in southern Mexico.

My husband Jim was teaching at a small Christian school and our salary was barely large enough to cover our monthly expenses. To a large extent, this was made possible by one family in the school who charged a very low rent for the two-story, three-bedroom house we were living in.

Although content and enjoying our small family, we knew our Christmas would be "lean" that year. After all, meeting expenses doesn't mean you have a lot left over for extras. We were happily planning to buy a Christmas tree and decorate it together. That would be most of our Christmas spending.

For reasons that have been lost to memory over the years, we decided at the last minute that rather than stay home, we would drive 400 miles to my husband's hometown and surprise his parents for Christmas. Only Jim's "granny" was in on the surprise. We called her just before we left our home to let her know when we would arrive, and urged her not to tell anyone.

That evening Granny walked in to my in-laws' home, carrying our infant son. "Look who's here for a visit," she said. In the midst of the babble of excitement Jim, and I trailed in with the other three children.

One step into the house, and Jim spotted a two-foot high aluminum tree perched on top of the television set. "Mother!" he gasped. "You didn't!"

Never in his life had their family had anything but a real, live tree, lovingly decorated with ornaments, lights, and icicles carefully draped over the branches.

The next day Jim and his father took the children out to cut a tree. Jim's mother had not gotten any ornaments out of storage, and by the time the tree arrived she was in bed with the beginning of a two-day migraine. We spent the day helping the children make colored paper chains and string popped corn and cranberries to use as decorations.

It was a unique Christmas in many ways, and a truly memorable one. But we learned our lesson. Never again did we try to surprise anyone with a Christmas visit.

Still, over the years, as we have decorated a tree in anticipation of a visit from our own children and grandchildren, I have smiled at the memory of my husband's shocked voice: "Mother! You didn't!"

The Not-So-Perfect Tree

Betty L Arthurs

One year in the 70s, a week before Christmas, my husband, John, and our neighbor, Junior, searched the woods behind our houses along Ridge Road in western New York farm country for the perfect tree. They rode snowmobiles through the Concord grape and Catawba vineyards and snow-covered hay fields, on a holiday mission that has never changed for families over many years.

While they were gone, Junior's wife, Sue, and I and our four children drank hot chocolate in her warm kitchen, laughing and talking about our modern pioneer men.

"I sent them off with ropes, a saw, and an axe," Sue said. "Sure hope they find some pretty trees."

In an hour we heard the roar of the snowmobiles and rushed out to meet our heroes. The children jumped up and down, screaming, "The trees are here, the trees are here!"

"Junior and I climbed the pines and chopped off the top of them. We couldn't find any nice smaller trees," John told me, propping our beautiful six-foot-tall tree against the front porch railing. "Let's leave it out here so we can shake off the snow tomorrow. Otherwise it's going to get the floor wet."

Four-year-old Julie clapped her hands as she ran to the window again and again to see the tree. She told me, "Santa Closet is coming soon 'cause he loves baby Jesus." She had already been searching through our Christmas ornament box. When her brother Robbie toddled over to the box, she handed him unbreakable ornaments to play with, saying, "He's a baby an' we don't want him to get cut."

Tomorrow Rob would turn two years old. We had decided that our family tradition would be to decorate the tree on his birthday. There wasn't much money this year for presents but we had the perfect gift from the forest.

Later on in the frosty day I slipped on my wool poncho, stepped onto the porch, and touched the tree. "Fresh and fragrant beauty, that's what you are," I murmured. Tiny pinecones and melting snow glistened on the dark needles of the Douglas fir. "I'm sure the chickadees and squirrels are missing being able to pounce on your branches."

I noticed a dead vine woven through the tree from top to bottom. How quaint, but I don't want dried leaves all over my floor.

With my bare hands I pulled at the vine with dried white-colored berries that turned and twisted like brown yarn in a dark green quilt. The stubborn vine resisted my pulling and tugging so I yanked harder until it was freed.

The next morning John shook the tree free of melted snow, jammed it into its stand, and carried it into our house to the sounds of squealing delight from Julie and Robbie. Its pine fragrance enveloped the house in my favorite holiday aroma.

However, during the night I had developed a severe rash on my hands and arms. Mystified, I smeared a soothing cream over the welts. The itching intensified and in agony I tried not to scratch the burning, red rash.

"What did you do?" John asked. "What did you touch?"

Then I knew. The innocent looking dead vine still packed a punch. Poison ivy! As a child growing up in Kansas I'd had plenty of nasty encounters with poison ivy in spite of my parents showing me the three-leafed plant. "Be careful where you run when you're in the woods…don't touch."

Perhaps, thanks to the hideous vine, that's one reason why I've never forgotten our not-so-perfect tree. God knew it held a hidden danger and He helped me protect my family. That Christmas the "what-ifs" flooded my mind: What if John or Robbie or Julie had touched the plant? What if we all had a miserable red-rash-family-Christmas? What if Robbie had eaten a leaf?

The not-so-perfect tree created a humorous memory once I recovered from the nasty rash—which just goes to show that memories we cherish don't always come from perfect situations. God uses them all, good and bad—even poison ivy—to remind us of His awesome Christmas gift.

Paper Christmas on the Tree

Maria Magdalena Agullo

A little paper Dolly
hung on a tree,
with markers eyes and hair
she smiled as pretty as could be.
This was her first Christmas
of her folded paper life,
folded with care and love
by the baker and his wife.

For many days she noticed
her family in the room.
They cut and folded, tied and strung
paper flowers in full bloom.
She saw paper cones
filled with potpourri
and tiny cookies on each bough
baked from secret recipe.

"I wonder what this is about,
What could all this mean?"
she asked herself in quiet voice
beneath her swag of green.
The watching star of gold and white
smiled at Dolly far below
and with a voice so good and mild
it whispered down, "Hello.

"This is a special time," it said,
"Not about snow or things.
We celebrate the birthday
of One called King of kings.
In a place called Bethlehem
the family's Babe was born,
right beside kind animals,
right before the morn.

"There was only one like Him
sent from heaven above.
He came to bring peace to the world
and show us His pure love."
Now Dolly tells the ornaments
upon the tree each year,
the truth about the Christmas night,
and about the Babe so dear.

Christmas in Other Places

Christmas is not in a place; it's in the heart.
—Donna Clark Goodrich

Christmas in Portland

Josephine Walker

When people around me begin their journey down memory lane, recalling special Christmases, I slip back to 1957 in Portland, Oregon.

I was thirteen years old, a freshman in high school, fourth in the line-up of eight children who at this time were all living at home. Nicky, the oldest, had come home from the convent to help care for us. Mom, imprisoned in a body cast, was perched like a queen in a hospital bed in our dining room.

What a way to begin our Christmas season. Mom's back had finally given out, requiring a surgery that could not be delayed. The divorce from our stepfather came the year before. When it was final, Mom picked herself up once more. Filled with the faith that the Lord would again provide, she moved us into the rental on 51st Street. A go-getter with an amazing entrepreneurial spirit, Mom began her venture into selling Sarah Coventry jewelry, which came to a screeching halt with the operation.

There we were—ten mouths to feed (Grandma was also living with us), no job, and short on money. My two older brothers were working as box boys at the local Piggly Wiggly grocery store, I did some babysitting which helped.

I remember there'd been a few sparse Christmases, but I don't recall any of us kids moaning and groaning about it. Maybe that was because we celebrated Advent, focusing on the real reason for the season.

Somehow this year we had a tree, so I took my babysitting money to the corner hardware store, hoping I had enough to buy some lights. Not realizing it, I misread a tag on the light string thinking they were much cheaper than the real price. I was excited I had enough money to buy such a large package. This is where the Christmas spirit first showed up in the form of the owner. He must have realized my mistake by looking at the amount of money I'd put on the counter, and knowing me, I probably told him it was all I had. He said it was just enough. It wasn't until Nicky saw the actual price tag that we realized his generosity.

A couple days later, Nicky was in the kitchen making some delicate Scandinavian pastries when Mom got the call that became the beginning of Christmas abundance beyond our imagination.

Her Sarah Coventry boss, Olive, said, "Grace, I hope you don't have a tree up because the girls have bought you and the kids one, with all the decorations.

And they have presents for the entire family, especially the little ones. They're also bringing you a complete Christmas dinner, along with boxes full of food."

Can you see our dilemma? We had a fully decorated tree with silver tinsel on every branch, framing beautiful lights and ornaments, with only one room it could be moved to—Grandma's bedroom. How it fit, I don't know. Mom directed us from her hospital bed to be careful moving the tree, plus instructing us to keep our mouths shut about it.

This wonderful demonstration of the Christmas spirit was only the first of seven such expressions of love and giving. Unknown to us, someone had put our name and story on a number of organization's lists. We watched somewhat embarrassed, yet grateful, as car after car came the next two days, bringing food and presents. The four youngest of the children were ecstatic to say the least.

We, however, found ourselves faced with a serious problem. What to do with all the perishable food we had no room for. You see, each group had brought us a complete Christmas dinner. Oh, to have owned a freezer.

The answer came when my brothers shared that many of the regular customers from the store where they worked would have no Christmas dinner at all.

Our decision was easy. Back then you knew your neighbor. The boys helped with grocery deliveries so they knew where many of these folks lived. We had great fun putting together the Christmas dinners, and my brothers had no problem getting one of their friends to drive them around, delivering these boxes of food onto porches. The people never knew where the boxes came from—but we did.

What makes this the most memorable Christmas is how God again made a way for us—who were so amazingly blessed—to be a blessing to others. In this I have learned that no matter how poor one might be, they can always find a way to give.

Do I remember even one gift I received that Christmas morning? No. The most important gift received through those tough years growing up has been the truth of God's love and provision which has been the foundation of my life, proving out the legacy of faith and love left to me by my mother.

O Little Town of Bethlehem

Lucy Neeley Adams

It's delightful singing the same Christmas carols year after year. "O Little Town of Bethlehem" is one of them. This carol never ceases to be meaningful to me as I picture the many visual images in the words. I accept its beauty with joy in my heart and the simple beat of its music.

However, there was a day when I sang the carol and tears flowed. I dabbed my cheeks with a tissue, as I sang with new enthusiasm and greater joy. What had changed? It was the first time I had sung this endearing hymn in a special place—the real little town of Bethlehem.

My husband and I sat with friends who had traveled together from our home church in Tennessee. It was evident that everyone was deeply touched as we sat in the Church of the Nativity built over the spot where it is believed Jesus was born. Reading about the birth of Jesus was not the same as worshiping in His birthplace, and hearing about Bethlehem was not the same as being a part of it.

This was probably the same reaction experienced by Phillips Brooks, the composer of this famous Christmas carol. The minister of Holy Trinity Church in Philadelphia, he had visited Bethlehem in December of 1865.

Several years later, when he wanted a new Christmas song for the children to sing on Christmas Eve, he reached back in memory for inspiration from his Holy Land visit. The poem he wrote painted in words the sights and sounds of that little town of Bethlehem he had visited. What came from his pen was a Christmas carol that has lived to become a worldwide favorite:

> O little town of Bethlehem,
> How still we see thee lie!
> Above thy deep and dreamless sleep
> The silent stars go by.

When Brooks completed the verses, he asked the church organist, Lewis Redner, to compose a melody simple enough for the children to learn. Redner sat down at the piano to find just the right tune to carry the descriptive words. But nothing he wrote seemed to fit.

On the night before the Christmas Eve service Redner felt defeated, so he went to bed. During his fretful sleep it seemed that he heard music. Immediately, he got up and wrote down the melody just as we sing it today. When he joyfully presented it to Brooks, he said, "I think it was a gift from heaven." The children sounded like a choir of angels as they sang the new carol written just for them. We are blessed to continue singing it over one hundred years later.

Phillips Brooks was born in Boston in 1825 and educated at Harvard. He was a beloved and respected evangelist. After serving several Episcopal churches in Philadelphia and Boston, he was appointed bishop of that area.

This giant of a man, who stood 6 feet, 8 inches, also had a big heart that endeared him to old and young alike. He kept toys in his office for the many children who visited him, and it was a familiar sight to see the beloved bishop sitting on the floor playing games with them.

He never married but other people's children became like a family to him. When he died unexpectedly in 1893 at the age of 58, grief overwhelmed everyone. It was a child who put his death in a beautiful light. When told by her mother that Bishop Brooks had gone to heaven, she simply said, "Oh Mama, how happy the angels will be."

Christmas in a Suitcase

Debbie Burgett

Traditions don't just happen. They have to be made. How? By choosing what you want to do, how you want to do it, and then continuing to do it exactly the same way over the years. Then at some mysterious, wonderful point in time, you discover you couldn't change them if you wanted to. Your loved ones won't let you. That's a tradition. And it becomes synonymous with everything your family holds dear.

But in our transient culture where we change homes, jobs, schools, churches, and other important things almost as easily as we rearrange furniture, traditions are in danger of never being made. May we never let that happen to Christmas. In our busy, contemporary lives, often in a constant state of flux, may our timeless December traditions be the one thing our families can count on to stay the same.

And sometimes that might even mean carrying Christmas with you.

"What on earth do you have in this suitcase?" my husband inquired as he struggled to lug it downstairs to the car.

"Oh, just some things I need for the children." I tried to sound casual so he wouldn't inquire further. If I told him what was really in that suitcase, he would think I was crazy and try to talk me out of it. And that would be impossible.

"My, how long are you planning on staying?" my stepfather twinkled at me six hours later as he helped tote our pre-wheel luggage from the airport. He had unfortunately chosen to carry my suitcase and my husband hadn't objected.

"Not long enough," I answered, breathing in the ocean air of southern California.

After the flurry of hugs and kisses for Grandma when we arrived at my mother's house and as the children ran around making themselves at home, we began unloading the trunk. When Mom reached for my suitcase, my stepfather quickly assured her she didn't want to carry that one. Undeterred, she dragged it as far as the porch before surrendering.

"Um, I think you men need to get this one," she said as my husband came back out the front door. "I thought for sure I told Debbie we had our own kitchen sink."

But I wasn't worried about the kitchen sink. I knew my mother would provide all the normal everyday things we would need for our visit, and even have all the normal holiday trimmings like a tree and special food. But there were extra little touches that only I could provide for my family. Nestled snugly among my clothing was the kind of stuff that traditions and memories are made of.

So later that evening, when my young children sat washed and expectant before me on my mother's living room carpet, I opened the suitcase.

Our "homemade" advent candle centerpiece had made the trip safely. We had painted fourteen alternating red and green rings about two inches apart from top to bottom on a tall, white-tapered candle and set it on a base of holly and poinsettias. The children proudly placed it on Grandma's table along with two votives on either side. The glass votive candle holders had a small white bunny painted on one side, a red heart on the other, and holly leaves in between. The children loved those holders.

Next came our stack of Christmas books and stories (that's where the real weight came from), along with a special bag of chocolate goodies. Now we were ready to begin the tradition we did every night the last two weeks before Christmas.

We chose a story, gave everyone a treat, lit the three candles, and began to read. The fun part came when the advent candle began nearing the next red or green ring. The idea was to burn down to one new ring every night, counting down till Christmas. But what if the story wasn't finished yet? You race! I would read faster and faster and the children would giggle and squeal with excitement. Sometimes Daddy got into the act and jokingly insisted that we couldn't finish the story if we had to blow the candle out. The children would beg us to keep reading and, of course, to their relief we would grudgingly relent, blow out the candle, and finish the story anyway.

My mother watched from her recliner as our traditions, and all the love and laughter they inspired, came to life in her living room. She still talks about the year that Christmas came in a suitcase—and left even stronger in our hearts.

Christmas Down on the Farm

Carol Dee Meeks

Christmas down on the farm
finds us among bare trees
wrapped in beauty of white glimmer
falling from the sky.

Even the animals know
there's magic in the air.
They bay and watch
the activity everywhere.

Ice skaters on the pond
enjoy evening's knife cold edge.
Their laughter and their joy
warm up the barn-side ledge.

Visitors come around the bend
as friends and family appear once more
to celebrate the birth of our King.
And the animals know for sure
it is a special day.
A special Day
when it's Christmas down on the farm.

Christmas in Wartime Scotland, WWII

Margaret Dornan Gamber

Christmas during 1941 in war-torn Scotland contained hardships and even loss of life. However, a very unexpected Christmas miracle warmed my heart during those horrendous years. Christmas in Wartime Scotland tells of an unexpected Christmas blessing that filled a desperate need.

* * *

"Jingle Bells, Jingle Bells" are familiar sounds in the United States at Christmas time. Instead, however, for the past three Christmases, while sitting in our outside street shelter, our ears pick up the sounds of incendiary bombs blazing the trees around the neighborhood, whistling as they fall from the sky. It is quite a difference, believe me!

We sing Christmas carols to drown out the sounds but they are still the louder. We also play guessing games and other games to keep our spirits up. My mother and we three girls quietly pray to God that our father would be all right, as he works as a night watchman at John Brown's Shipyard in Clydebank. It is work far beneath his knowledge, but he has to work, as well as my sister Janet and I because we have to eat (when we can get some food) and we have rent to pay. We came to visit our Grandfather Dornan for a three-week vacation which turned into three-and-a-half years.

My father had a consulting meeting with the American Consulate in Glasgow Scotland, to see if there were any ships sailing to America. But there were none for taking passengers, as all the ships were commandeered by the government for war work.

* * *

My father is fortunate to be a night watchman at the shipyard. When he was having an interview with the head man, Sir Donald Skippington, he wondered why Skippington was interviewing him.

"Don't you recognize me, Peter?" he asked my father. "It's been a long time since we have seen each other. When you were a high school student and attended St. James' Presbyterian Church, I was your Sunday school teacher. I knew you as an intelligent young man. Then later as a college student at Glasgow University, I heard you had great grades. I was proud of you!"

Then he added, "It is very likely that, because of the war, you are worried about being here at this time."

"Yes, I do worry about being here at this time," my father responded. "I have my wife and three daughters here also. We only came for a three week visit!"

"Well, Peter, I know this job is well below your ability," Sir Skippington replied. "But it is outside work, and you cannot let anyone pass your building unless they show their badges.

"I will do that, sir," my father promised, "I do recognize you now. What time do I show up for work?"

"Nine p.m. will be the starting time and will end at 6 a.m. When you get here, I will have a badge for you which you must wear while working."

He shook hands with his long-ago pupil and with a great smile welcomed him aboard.

Centuries Old Scottish Christmas Delight

Margaret E. Albertson

"Mmm, the white cookies!" my ten-year-old daughter Meg said, looking at the large platter piled high with cookies.

"White cookies?" Five-year-old Don hurried into the kitchen, not far behind his sister. "These are my favorite." Don clamped his mouth down onto the still warm morsel, trying to talk as he ate.

Jonathan, thirteen, then sauntered into the kitchen wondering what all the commotion was about. Seeing the cookies, he grabbed several, popping them in his mouth. "Cool," he said as he exited the room.

In the event I just witnessed, I realized my three children joined the enthusiasm of four generations—maybe more—in devouring the delectable Christmas cookie called shortbread. Their great grandmother, who was born during 1885 in Scotland, introduced me to this wonderful delight decades after she was born. I imagine her mother and her mother before her also made this recipe because it is the "staple" of the Scottish tea during Christmas time.

What I remember most is the excitement I felt when seeing my grandmother's and my mother's round cookie tins filled with these cookies nestled safely in layers of waxed paper. For it was then I knew Christmas—the long-awaited holiday—would soon arrive.

"Granny" would make her shortbread into many wonderful shapes, but the Christmas tree was my favorite. She would even add green sprinkles to their pointed forms. While her use of shapes was untraditional, her love for shortbread was a legacy for all our families. On the other hand, in later years my mother chose the most traditional form of all, making one large cookie the size of a small pizza. In fact, she eventually used round pizza cooking sheets to accomplish this feat, imprinting the Scottish thistle into the cookie's surface by pushing the top of a silver spoon bearing the sculpted image of the Scottish symbol into the middle of the cookie. Then she pricked the middle and scored around the edges with the tines of a fork.

When this enormous cookie was pulled from the oven, we waited until it cooled, all the while being tempted by the rich smell of melted butter filling the room. Then, the fun began. Mom made some hot tea and served us from her favorite teapot. Afterwards, we all sat around the table and she placed the delectable "biscuit"—as the Scots would call any cookie—on the table. We each broke off a piece, munching it in glorious delight. Tanginess from the tea mingled with the rich taste of the shortbread forming perfection. Mom stopped us though from devouring the whole biscuit at one sitting. Oh, it was so difficult to quit munching it!

While shortbread found its beginnings in the twelfth century, it wasn't the same cookie we have today. The "modern" recipe was perfected by Mary, Queen of Scots in the 1500s. Shortbread was expensive to make, so it was usually reserved for Christmas and New Year's Eve. No matter the century, shortbread is a delight for any Christmas.

Shortbread

½ cup sugar
1 cup butter (it must be real butter)
2 cups all-purpose flour (centuries ago oat flour was used)
Cream room temperature butter with sugar. When it is "creamy," add flour slowly, mixing it continuously. You'll know it is time to stop mixing when the dough is in small balls resembling peas. Knead the flour; then form two large balls.

Traditional Cookie
If you make the traditional large cookie, roll out one ball to about ½ inch thick on a floured board. Form a large ½ inch circular pizzalike dough. Place dough on a large ungreased cookie sheet or pizza pan. Prick the center of the cookie with a fork multiple times. Then push down on the edge of the cookie with the tines of a fork which are parallel (flat) to the dough. Bake at 250 degrees for at least ½ hour. Note: It could take longer or shorter depending on your oven and the thickness of the dough. The cookie should be golden brown on the edges and not dark underneath. Remove the cookie from the oven and cool in the pan. When the cookie is cool, transfer it to a large plate or platter using two spatulas.

Cookies of Today
When the dough resembles peas, do not make large balls. Instead, scoop dough with a teaspoon and roll dough into small balls using your hands. Then flatten cookie while still between your hands. Place on cookie sheet and prick and score the cookie using the tines of a fork (see directions above). Bake at 350 degrees for about 10 minutes. Cookies are done when golden brown around the edges and not dark underneath. Cool slightly on baking sheet. Then transfer cookies to waxed paper to cool the rest of the way.

A Christmas to Remember

Anita Mellott

"Anita, your ride's here," Vivian, my host parent, called.

"Coming." Trying to hold back my tears, I grabbed my backpack and headed upstairs from my room in the basement.

Christmas, my favorite time of the year was approaching, and memories filled my mind...the Christmas tree glittering in the muted light of my parents' living room, the squeals as we opened our gifts, carol singers whose voices filled our home, the laughter and hugs from neighbors and friends, the aroma of Christmas delicacies floating through the condo hallways...

I sighed. What would Christmas be like thousands of miles away from my family in India? Though Vivian and Kevin Bennett had opened their home to me, an international student, I yearned for the familiar comfort of home and family.

As I stepped outside, the cold Canadian wind whipped through my layers of clothing, accentuating the lonely ache in my heart. Shivering, I climbed into the warm car, and tried to smile at my friend as we headed to the University of Windsor.

Despite the candy canes and the lighted tree, the graduate lounge was depressing. International students from my class sat around moping, everyone dreading being alone for the holidays.

"You're lucky, Anita," one of my Chinese friends commented. "At least you don't live in an apartment by yourself. There's family around you."

But not my family. It's not the same. I shrugged.

Several hours later, I shook the snow off my boots and entered the Bennett's house. The smell of spaghetti sauce greeted me, while the kids chased each other in between setting the table.

"Hey, Anita," Vivian called.

I walked in and stood near the stove. "What can I do to help?"

She gestured to the salad fixings on the counter. I washed my hands and began to chop the tomatoes.

"What are your classmates—the international ones—doing for Christmas?" Vivian asked.

"Nothing."

"Kevin and I decided to have them over on Christmas Eve," she continued.

I stared at her. "But…but…what about the Bennett family get-together?"

"Oh, that's Christmas evening. We talked to Kevin's mother about having the international students over, so she changed the time." Vivian glanced at me. "You're invited for the family dinner. She was clear about that."

I froze.

"You're part of the family, for better or worse, you know. The kids call you their 'big sister.'" She grinned.

I bent my head and concentrated on the salad. My cheeks felt like they were on fire. I was part of the family! Lord, I'm sorry for not seeing Your blessings.

The next few weeks passed in a blur of preparations: settling on a time, inviting the international students in my graduate class, and making arrangements to pick them up from the university, a good half-hour's drive away. And the best part of all—baking dozens of cookies and goodies, and helping Vivian and the kids choose gifts for the students.

Christmas Eve arrived.

"They're here, they're here," screamed six-year-old Nathan, jumping up and down as the lights of the van flooded the snow-filled driveway. Eight-year-old Melissa threw open the door, oblivious to the wind and snow blowing in. "Come in, come in," she cried even before the van doors opened. Soon we were hanging up jackets and putting away scarves and mittens. I could hardly hear myself introduce my classmates.

We played board games, drank hot chocolate, and even braved the frigid outdoors for a snowball fight. Later we gathered in the living room, the fire crackling and drawing us in with its warmth. The candles flickered, throwing a golden hue around the tree, which glittered as its garland of lights blinked on and off.

The students were fascinated with the tree. "What do the decorations mean? Why are there gifts under the tree?" they asked.

"The star on top of the tree is for the star that led the Wise Men to where Jesus was born," Melissa explained. Nathan chimed in, "Do you know Jesus? He really loves you. That's why He came to earth." Vivian and I shot each other a look. I held my breath. Would my classmates be offended?

But the questions kept coming, and the kids related the Christmas story in their simple, childlike way.

We ate cookies and sang some carols, off-key at times. Again questions flowed about their meaning. My classmates giggled as the kids tried to explain the meaning of the songs. Other students helped with translations into Mandarin. My heart overflowed at Melissa's and Nathan's excitement as they innocently shared Jesus' love.

All too soon the evening was over. My classmates beamed and their eyes sparkled as the kids began handing out gifts—boxes of homemade Christmas goodies, and tapes of the Gospel of John in Mandarin.

"I never knew what Christmas was about," whispered one of the students on the way out. "Thank you for sharing your special day with us." Her eyes shone with unshed tears.

The kids and I stood at the bay window watching the red taillights of the van as it sped down the driveway. I lingered there long after the van disappeared from view, the joy and gratitude on my classmates' faces etched in my memory. My dull ache of loneliness had been replaced by a deep peace and sense of fulfillment. I had experienced what Christmas was all about—selflessly giving, reaching out in love regardless of race and faith, and bringing hope and joy to others.

A Colorado Christmas

Peggy Halter Morris

Beth, wife of Jeffery and mother of their three spirited children, called the excursion: building new family memories in a foreign land. Jeffrey had managed to squeeze in a brief lunch break, away from the frenzied shoppers at Carlson Drugstore, for this Christmas tree hunt. The family trudged from lot to lot trying to agree on the perfect tree, each child selecting a different one.

"Do you think our kids will ever cooperate on anything?" Beth jokingly asked Jeffrey. She knew Colorado wasn't really a foreign land but it seemed so far from home and friends where they fit in and had deep roots. They hadn't had enough time to find where they fit in this new place. Carlson Drugstore never gave much advance notice when they offered an employee a promotion to another location, but Jeffrey had taken it anyway.

Beth felt lonely away from her friends. Did the kids too? But they had said they were dreaming of a white Christmas, like the song says. That was one thing—snow never fell back home in Phoenix. But have Jeffrey and I taught the kids enough about being resilient? About blooming where they are planted? About making lemonade when life serves them a lemon? About all those clichés?

Beth worried at how secretive the kids were being. She knew they were disappointed that they arrived in town too late to audition for parts in the Christmas pageant at their new church. The pageant had been a highlight of their holiday season in previous years. Well, maybe next year. This first Christmas in Colorado, they'd just have to sit this one out.

Later that night, Beth moved wrapped presents from the bed. At least that was done. But so much to do tomorrow, Christmas Eve Day. Why can't I get things done ahead of time? Beth longed for a Christmas with its true meaning, but she and Jeffrey both fell into the holiday season's pace of rush, hustle, and hurry.

The bedroom light didn't disturb Jeffrey's sleep. He deserved a restful night. Retail in December was brutal. Sixteen-hour days were common for him in his new position as assistant manager. He was up to his eyeballs in retail "good cheer" at the store. Managing employees, stocking shelves, ordering merchandise all landed on his shoulders, along with dealing with the pushing crowds and cranky customers. No wonder he echoed Scrooge's sentiments about Christmas: Bah! Humbug!

Beth reviewed her to-do list: vacuum, dust, clean bathrooms, bake pies, tackle mounds of dirty dishes scattered on the kitchen counters, help the kids decorate the tree, then attend Christmas Eve services at the church. She could worry about all that tomorrow. She laid her list on the nightstand and crawled into bed, welcoming sleep the moment her head touched the pillow.

Brring. Brring. The annoying middle-of-the-night telephone call. Any time the store alarm went off, the alarm company called Jeffrey, the go-to guy. Usually it meant nothing, just a false warning.

On the second ring tonight, Jeffrey picked up the bedside phone.

"Jeffrey Andrews here." He listened longer than usual. "All right. I'm on my way." He hung up the telephone and scrambled out of bed. "Front window smashed in." He grabbed his clothes. "They've called the police. I've got to get there. Want to come with me?"

"Sure. Let me tell the kids." Beth changed, then tiptoed to the girls' bedroom. She gently shook Annie, trying not to wake Megan. "There's been a break-in at the store. Your dad has to check it out. I'm going with him."

Megan lifted her head from her upper bunk. In a sleepy voice she said, "Remember, Mom, we have a surprise for you."

Within minutes, Jeffrey and Beth's van sped toward the store. As they pulled up, they spotted two police cars parked in front, lights still flashing.

"Look. The whole plate glass window's shattered." Jeff groaned. Beth shivered as a blast of icy Colorado night air swept through the parking lot. She prayed as the officers searched the store for hidden suspects.

"Looks like someone tried to get into the pharmacy. Took a crowbar to the door," the first policeman said. "Probably hoping to get some drugs."

"Check to see if anything else has been disturbed," the second officer said.

Nope. Nothing else was amiss. Nothing more the officers could do, just write up their report and leave.

Beth stood by Jeffrey as he surveyed the damage. "Security system's gone. Right?"

"Yep. I guess we're security for the night," Jeffrey replied. "I'll turn on all the store lights. That way no other crazy can take advantage of that broken window. You want to stay?"

Beth hesitated. Exhaustion consumed her after weeks of packing and unpacking with the recent move and of trying to fit into their new community. Could she stay up all night and still have energy to make Christmas Eve memories with her children? Thinking of her undone list made Beth's stomach twist in knots. But *Jeffrey needs me too.*

"Yes. I'd like to keep you company. I'll chase the boogie man away," she joked. "Two are better than one."

What a long night.

1 a.m. Beth helped clean up the broken glass. Jeffrey pulled down and built new displays.

2 a.m. They stocked and straightened shelves ransacked by frantic last-minute Christmas shoppers.

4 a.m. Beth dusted Jeffrey's office and even scrubbed the table and chairs in the employee break room.

7 a.m. "When are we going home to get some sleep?" Beth asked.

"As soon as Ron gets here."

8 a.m. Beth let the check stand hold her up while Jeffrey and Ron, the general manager, discussed break-in details and getting the window fixed.

8:30 a.m. Ron said, "Stay home the rest of the day. Get some sleep."

Stay home? On one of the busiest retail days of the year? Incredible! That was unprecedented in the history of Carlson Drugstore.

Beth felt herself smiling. Family celebrations could begin early. If only she didn't have so much work lined up...

9 a.m. As they headed out with the wrapped presents Jeff had kept hidden from the children in his office, Beth's thoughts turned to the kids. They would love the surprise of having their dad home for the day. That would make up for some of the uprooted feeling.

At home, the smell of Scotch pine greeted them. The kids followed as Beth and Jeffrey "hid" the newest presents in their bedroom, peppering them with questions about the break-in—and the presents.

Beth flopped on the bed. "I need sleep before I attack the day."

"Me too," Jeffrey said.

Annie, Megan, and Scott backed out of the bedroom, eyes lingering on the presents. Annie pulled the door shut behind them.

"Tada!" All too soon three voices rang into the bedroom in perfect three-part harmony. Jeffrey leaned up on one elbow at the sound. Beth stretched while trying to focus her sleepy eyes. She grabbed the clock at her bedside. Three o'clock! How could they have slept that long?

Annie carried a pumpkin pie. Megan balanced a cherry cream pie in one hand. Scott followed with freshly baked chocolate chip cookies. Unbelievable!

"Mom, Dad, come see what we've done," Scott said as he led Beth, Jeffrey, and the girls down the hall to the living room

"You've vacuumed!" Jeffrey said.

"You've dusted!" Beth added.

"And look," Megan said as they moved to the family room. The Christmas tree glittered; blue lights twinkled. "Annie strung the lights and we all added the decorations."

"It's a little crooked, but I built the stand," Scott said proudly.

Annie added, "Scott did the tinsel and didn't even throw it!"

All the family laughed, including Scott.

"You are all amazing!" Beth said as she plopped on the sofa. How could she have slept through it all—the fragrance of baking pies and cookies and droning of the vacuum sweeper?

"That's not all," Annie said as she reached for Beth's hand, pulling her up and leading her to the kitchen. "Come on, Dad."

The pile of dirty dishes—gone. The counters shined. Beth gathered Annie and Megan in her arms while Jeffrey tousled Scott's unruly hair. "Such a welcome surprise," he said.

"But that isn't *the* surprise," Annie said.

The family spent the rest of the afternoon enjoying cider and chocolate chip cookies while playing board games beside the glimmering tree. Then at seven that evening, they all piled into the van to head for the church.

"Let us out at the door, Dad," Megan said.

"Please," added Scott.

"Now what do you suppose they're up to?" Beth asked as Jeffrey pulled into a parking spot.

"No telling."

Beth and Jeffrey slid into the pew just as the service started. The preschoolers sang "Jesus Loves Me," and other children followed with "Away in a Manger."

Beth was touched as the youth group acted out the Christmas pageant, telling of the birth of a Savior. Then, puzzled, she reached for Jeffrey's hand as her three children stepped forward. What are they doing? Looking at her bulletin she read: "Fitting Our Hearts into Christmas, written by the Andrews: Annie, Megan, and Scott."

Tears traced Beth's cheek as the three acted out a vignette describing the timeless message: fitting Christmas into the heart—regardless of where you are.

So that was the surprise. A Christmas play written by her children, expressing their understanding of fitting in.

The service closed with a solo of "Oh Holy Night."

After hugs and tears, the family stepped outside to lacy snowflakes falling through the air. Snow blanketed the ground.

Beth drew in the nippy Colorado air and lifted her heart to God. Be pleased to fit into our hearts this Christmas—our first Colorado Christmas.

"Yah Sure, Swedish Pancakes"

Sharen Pearson

I'm the mutt in my husband's family genealogy. I was scandalously of English, Irish, and German heritage. Everyone else was of Scandinavian descent. Having moved from "the old country" to settle in Minnesota, they brought along their charming holiday food traditions.

Trying my best to fit in, I bravely smiled while enduring my first helping of the revered lutefisk. I took a turn at gently dipping and frying delicate rosette cookies, sprinkling them with powdered sugar, and lit the angel candles in the center of the table.

Of all the cherished Christmas foods the one that became part of our family tradition for good was the rich, crepe-like Swedish pancake, served with powdered sugar and melted butter. (Heaven forbid that you pour maple syrup on them, although I do sometimes.) True Swedes enjoy them with lingonberries, but they are illusive in the U.S. and I find them rather bitter.

Through the years, the making of Swedish pancakes on Christmas morning has passed from my hands to my husband's. Yah, sure, you betcha, but don't tell the Scandinavians, please. He enjoys making them, is better at it, and gets up earlier. I happily concede. As each of our three sons have grown and married, they have carried the pancake torch. Our two daughters have now taught their husbands. Too yummy for just Christmas, Swedish pancakes can be consumed any Saturday morning in any of their homes with seven new little "mutts" helping pour and measure. And so the tradition continues.

Grandma Signe's Swedish Pancakes

6 eggs
2½ cups milk
2 cups flour
2 Tbsp. sugar
1 tsp. salt

Beat eggs by hand or with mixer until lemon-colored. Slowly stir in flour, sugar, and salt. Do not overmix as too much air in the batter will change the texture of the pancake. Strain batter if there are remaining lumps.

Drop by tablespoons into moderately hot, buttered Swedish pancake pan or make single, large pancakes in a nonstick pan. Spread batter evenly. Pancakes are quite thin. Turn when light brown on the bottom.

To serve: Spread pancakes with melted butter and sprinkle with powdered sugar. Serve with lingonberry sauce (optional).

The Posada—A Southwestern Tradition

Carol Mottinger Ramirez

One Christmas I received a beautiful nativity and crèche. As I joyfully arranged Joseph, Mary, and Baby Jesus—along with shepherds, stable animals, the three wise men, and angels—I remembered the posada celebrations that take place each year in my Southwestern hometown.

I was privileged to participate in a posada one year when several of my students invited me to join their families and be a part of this ancient Christmas "traveling play."

It was December 16, the traditional time of the posada. The sun had set, and darkness settled in quickly. A brisk wind blew down from the mountains in the desert Southwest making coats, gloves, and hats essential. Families and groups of friends assembled at the end of the street. Each individual who gathered this night received a lighted candle.

Slowly, the entourage trekked down the street. Two individuals led the procession, carrying images of Joseph and Mary.

The party marched to the first house, knocked on the door, and pleaded, "In the name of heaven, I ask you to let us in. We need shelter for the night because we've traveled a great distance. Have charity toward us and God will reward you."

"Be on your way! Go somewhere else. You might be evil and not who you say you are."

The entire party walked to the next abode and cried out, "We are exhausted and come from Nazareth. I am Joseph, the carpenter. My wife is Mary. Please provide us a room."

"I don't know you. Let me sleep, for I'm tired and you are waking my family. I will not open my door. How is it that you're out so late? Leave my property!"

The travelers tried several other houses. Finally, at the last house everyone was allowed in. "God will repay you for your charity. Heaven grant you joy forever and forever."

Soon the song "Enter, Holy Pilgrims" filled the air.

The posada (Spanish for "resting place" or "lodging") is the characteristic Christmas ceremony of Mexico commemorating the journey of Joseph and Mary. Often family groups in an entire neighborhood participate together. A party follows to honor Mary and Joseph and to conclude the ceremony. Even though the spoken parts are somewhat scripted and the songs memorized, and even though folks knew which houses to visit, my students assured me that each year's posada affords them a meaningful experience. I know it was meaningful to me.

Shiny, Happy Cards

Coleene VanTilburg

Walking into the beautiful flower shop at Christmas, the wintry foliage and greenery sparkled with wonderment, displaying its unique arrangements and Asian influence. Scanning the counter, I spotted several extra copies of a regional magazine delivered to businesses, in which my essay had been printed. I asked the owner if I could have the extra ones. Agreeing, she wanted to read my story first.

Jennifer was a beautiful Asian, probably in her late twenties. I complimented her on the gorgeous displays of Christmas arrangements and wreaths decorating her flower shop. More interested in finishing my article, she looked up at me. Eyes glistening a little, she smiled and nodded her head as to give me that conveyance of sympathy as she read my story about a special Christmas decoration that had survived a fire and now reminded me of my deceased son. She then began to share with me her own Christmas story.

She touched her head and then her chest saying, "I have memory right now, I do not think of for long time. In my country when I was little girl, we get old Christmas card." She proceeded to be very animated with her hands, describing the cards. "You know...the card come already used...somebody already read them and they have writing in them for someone else... then we get card in Taiwan. We get from relative in America...many shiny Christmas card. We don't look at writing, just picture on front; picture so shiny and happy. As children, we love the shiny cards of America. It was a favorite thing. We look at picture for long time thinking about America and hoping someday..."

Holding her hand out, with the imaginary card in place, the other hand passed over as if she physically felt what gave these cards their special iridescence. She touched her head again, her smile never leaving her face, and thanked me for sharing my story that brought back her childhood memory. Realizing she is now living the "shiny, happy Christmas card" dream in America, I am suddenly humbled and thankful.

That brief conversation stuck with me. Arriving home, my eyes scanned the Christmas cards secured to my staircase, each one representing a loved one, family, or friend. Blessed to be an American and to have many shiny, happy cards arriving in my mailbox, I reached across my coffee table, seeing today's unopened stack of Christmas mail.

Media bombards us with all we should buy at this time of the year, but what better gift to receive than a card with a picture of a growing family or holiday greeting from a cousin across the country. Whether it is a cartoony snowman or a reproduction of a Courier and Ives winter scene, a significant star over a stable or angels singing "glory hallelujah," each card represents a moment someone took to show thoughtfulness in a busy season. These are the true blessings of this time, a reminder of the simple joys that bring smiles.

Jennifer lives today in her "Christmas card" dream of America. Touching my heart with gratefulness that I have a life as well in this country, although not perfect, it still allows me to shine at my best effort. Realize your dreams. Surround yourself with what is shiny and happy, even if that is within your own spirit. Send someone a card; you never know what that little act can do for someone's Christmas dream.

An Arkansas Christmas

Anna Roberts Wells

The source of this story is the son, Bill, who told my sister and me of this family custom. Strangely, none of the children, now grown, of the landed people seemed to know that this ritual took place in this midst. A true act of charity.

A stranger passing through Scott, Arkansas, would not likely notice that Christmas touched this tiny farming community in any way out of the ordinary. Life in the flat Arkansas River delta southeast of Little Rock was standard and predictable. In the post-World War II years when I was growing up, the homes of the community were scattered. Landowners lived on their plantations or farms in comparative luxury to the sharecroppers who lived near the fields they worked.

We were landowners. At least, my grandmother was, and that is where I lived—in her large white house with its big rooms with twelve-foot ceilings and four fireplaces. We were not wealthy by the standards of many of those who lived around us. In fact, my father laughingly called us the gentile poor—long on lineage, short on cash. However, compared to the people who hoed and picked our cotton, we were rich indeed.

Most of the people of the community fell into one of these two categories, but there were three storeowners and the postman. During the Christmas season, the landowners and shopkeepers decorated their homes with garlands of fresh cut greens held in place with red bows—except for Miss Virginia, who was still living and driving a car at 103. She always had rich greenery wound with gold roping and large gold bows ending in drapery tassels. It was as close as anyone dared come to being ostentatious.

I never knew anyone who lined their homes with electric lights until I was in my late teens. However, we (and most of our friends) had electric candlesticks to set in the windows, and we had real lights for our trees. We purchased a tree from one of the charity lots except for the year I begged Daddy to cut one of the ubiquitous eastern cedars that grew in our area.

The homes of the sharecroppers were usually unpainted, three-room shotgun structures, so-called because the rooms were lined up so that a person could stand at the front door, fire a shotgun straight through the house, and not hit a thing. We had one family so large that two of these structures were joined like a duplex but with a door or two cut through to join rooms. In the winter, these gray-brown structures sat on the edge of tan stubble-dotted fields. There were few trees or bushes in the yards. Most of the bits of land around their houses were for vegetable gardens. Some sharecroppers planted annuals out front in the summer but they were long dead by Christmas.

The homes of the sharecroppers had Christmas trees, but they were the prickly cedars cut in the woods and decorated with paper chains and handmade ornaments. A few had lights but most did not. One family on my grandmother's farm saved tinfoil all year to cover a growing collection of ornamental shapes cut from cardboard. They tied these to their tree with red yarn, along with garlands of popcorn. I thought they had the best tree I ever saw—all green and silver and red, shining in the light of their polished kerosene lamps. The father had even made an eight-sided star for the top of the tree which was carefully kept in a small box of its own and taken out year after year. This tree sparkled and shone as much as our electrically lighted one. This imaginative, creative approach brought much color to those brown delta winters.

Two of the most colorful characters in our community were "Mr. Bill" and "Miss Elizabeth" Cotham. Mr. Bill ran a general store that still sits on the edge of the main highway that runs through Scott. He carried a wide array of items in his store—from penny candy and nickel Cokes to groceries, farm tools, overalls, shoes, and inexpensive cotton housedresses. One of the oddest things about the store was that the back half was built on stilts so that part of the store was suspended over a bayou. Years later Mr. Bill's son, also a Bill, would turn half of the store into a country restaurant that became a favorite haunt of Bill Clinton who loved the famous house specialty—hubcap hamburgers with chunky country fries.

The other oddity of that building was that it had a front porch with a steeply pitched tin roof. It was that roof that gave Mr. Bill and Miss Elizabeth their Christmas idea. Those who knew this couple knew that Miss Elizabeth, though quietly reserved, was a generous and compassionate soul. She was particularly concerned for the children of the poorer sharecroppers. Each Christmas Eve, the Cothams would close their store to the public at 5:00 p.m. and then reopen it at 6:00 p.m. to families who had received invitations. The parents could pick out clothing for their children and themselves and a nice toy for each child. They could also pick up a box packed with all the makings of a good Christmas dinner. If the family was able to pay anything, they did. If there was no money, it didn't matter. They were all treated as valuable customers.

The real treat for the children began at 9:00 p.m. at which time Mr. Bill built a big bonfire on the front corner of his parking lot where everyone gathered and drank hot chocolate and ate cookies. They roasted marshmallows and sang Christmas carols until Mr. Bill brought out his big gallon pickle crock. At the very sight of it, the children would begin to dance about and fairly tingle with excitement.

You see, Mr. Bill saved all his pennies for the whole year, keeping just enough in his cash drawer to make change in the store. All the rest went into that crock, along with a smattering of nickels, dimes, and quarters. By the end of the year, it was usually full. In the light of that glowing fire, he would reach into that crock, grab as many pennies as he could, and fling those pennies onto the roof of the store porch. Because of its steep pitch, nothing would rest on it so that the pennies he threw began to slide down and fall on the parking area where eager children dove to catch as many as they could. Over and over, he dug deep and over and over, the children reached and squealed and danced and laughed with sheer delight.

Miss Elizabeth, whose idea this was, stood back and smiled her quiet smile. The night was full of laughter and copper coins flashing in the light of the fire. The precious nickels, dimes, and quarters were turned over to parents; but the children filled their pockets with the pennies that seemed in the firelight to be made of gold.

No one cared that Mr. Bill and Miss Elizabeth would probably see all of those pennies again when they were exchanged for B-B Bats, bubble gum, or Tootsie Rolls. All they knew was that while other children in our community were trying to get to sleep so Santa would come, they were being showered with Christmas love in the form of pennies rolling off a tin roof.

Poppy Seed Cake

Suzanne Gene Courtney

1 box yellow cake mix
1 box instant vanilla pudding
½ cup Wesson oil
1 tsp. almond extract

Mix above ingredients on medium speed. Add 4 eggs, one at a time. Beat well. Add: 1 cup hot water and 2 tablespoons poppy seeds. Mix well. Pour into well-buttered Bundt pan. Bake at 325 degrees for 45-50 minutes. Sift confectioner's sugar over the top.

When we lived in Hawaii years ago, our Japanese-American neighbor would occasionally bring us some delicious local fare. One of her delights was Poppy Seed Cake which was to be served on New Year's Day, a symbol of good luck for the coming year. That started a tradition in our own family for years to come.

Two Memorable Recipes from Historic Malta

Raymond Fenech

Christmas was around the corner and I hardly thought I would actually be writing about youthful memories and food at the same time. But there were instances in my life that have made me go back in time inspired by sensations of taste, sound, or even sheer smells.

Lately I had one of these special moments when walking through the main gate of our capital city, Valletta. Described by Sir Walter Scott as "a splendid town, quite like a dream," Valletta bears the name of Malta's national hero of the great siege of 1565, Grand Master Jean Parisiot de La Valette. When talking about the Maltese capital, perhaps it would be interesting for the reader to know something about it and how it has become one of the most important landmarks in Maltese and European history. Valletta was the first planned city of Europe.

The Great Siege of Malta came about when Suleiman, known as "The Magnificent," sent his great armada consisting of about 40,000 Turkish troops aimed at annihilating the Knights of St. John once and for all. But the bravery and heroism in the defence of Malta during the four months that followed earned the Maltese and the Knights a historic victory. It is important to note that Grand Master La Valette had only 600 knights and about 7,000 men under his command in the battle of the Great Siege of 1565.

Soon after the Turkish armada's devastating defeat, the Knights of Malta gave priority to the rebuilding of Valletta's new fortifications. The high ground of Mount Sciberras, which overlooks the Grand Harbour and Marsamxett Harbour, was chosen as the foundation of this great city, so rich in culture and history. Valletta was designed by Francesco Laparelli, assisted by Gerolamo Cassar. Grand Master La Valette supervised the construction work personally. After the Grand Master's death, Laparelli left the island, but the project was continued by Pietro Del Monte and Gerolamo Cassar and completed in 1571.

But now, let me go back to my inspiring walk through Valletta. It was late evening when I strolled through Republic Street, the main street of this wonderful city. I distinctly remember flinching my nose at the wonderful aromatic smell of Imqaret (Date Slices), a traditional Maltese sweet that automatically sent my senses reeling into the past. Before I get down to giving you this most unusual and delicious recipe, I will proceed to recount something about the memories, which this sweet arouses in me every time I get a whiff of its cooking.

My late father, Vincent, used to love Christmas, especially the preparatory phase when every member of our family—four in all—were busy cleaning, decorating, and cooking. My dad loved the cooking assignments and directed these in a wonderful, harmonised manner together with my mother, Maria Aurora. One of these many special tasks was the cooking of this marvellous sweet, which oftentimes was served either during tea time or as a special Christmas or New Year dessert, sometimes washed down with sweet liquors, champagne, or fizzy wines. Even our next-door neighbours benefited from this annual family tradition as my parents always presented them with a bowlful of these mouthwatering Imqaret.

What really smells so wonderful when cooking this recipe is the considerable amount of anisette that goes with it and that makes one's senses reel and look forward to this tasteful dessert.

Speaking about odours, I also remember the smell of fresh pine tree branches and heather, with which my dad and I embellished the hall and the dining room during Christmas. By now, I am quite sure you are simply craving to know the ingredients and cooking method of this recipe.

Ingredients Imqaret (Date Slices)

1.2 kg dates
a pinch of ground cloves
½ orange peel grated
½ tangerine peel grated
½ lemon peel grated
½ bar of cooking dark chocolate (100 grams)
1 Tbsp. orange flower water (ilma zahar)
1 Tbsp. anisette
1 Tbsp. black rum

Method: Stone the dates and soak in water for 30 minutes. If you can find dates that have already been pitted, it will make the job easier. Mash well and mix with the rest of the ingredients.

Dough Ingredients

400 grams flour
1 Tbsp. lard
Orange flower water
1 Tbsp. margarine
1 Tbsp. sugar

Method: Rub the fat into the flour, add sugar, and mix thoroughly. Then moisten with orange water and make into soft dough. The dough can be rolled out into a long strip. Spread and apply filling along dough to within ¼ inch. Cover filling and wet edge of pastry so it can be folded. Make sure pastry is stuck well at the edges, as the next step will be to cut into diamond shapes. Fry in boiling oil in deep frying pan until golden. After frying, it is recommended that date slices be placed on kitchen roll paper so as to absorb the unwanted oil. Date slices are best served hot, but are still delicious even at room temperature. Store in a metal biscuit box. The above ingredients are enough to produce about 24 slices.

From childhood, I remember another dish, often presented at dinner or lunch on special occasions, usually on Sundays—Ross il-Forn (Oven Baked Rice). This dish was my favourite, and my aunt—with whom I spent most of my childhood days—cooked it in a marvellously delicious way. Usually she prepared this dish on the occasion of the village feast day, which marked Our Lady of Mount Carmel.

Those were indeed happy days for all my cousins and myself. The festivities used to start on Thursday, with traditional band marches (village bands) passing through the main village streets, including The Strand Road, Gzira, where my grandparents' house was situated. All the cousins—about six of us—gathered on the roof preparing confetti paper and fireworks. The climax of the festivities was highlighted by the procession with the statue of Our Lady of Mount Carmel that passed right in front of the house.

Speaking about "festas," religious feasts in Malta are usually celebrated during the long hot summer months when temperatures soar up to an average of 34 degrees centigrade. Every weekend a village marks the feast of its patron saint. These feasts are one of the greatest tourist attractions, not only because of the folklore and tradition but also because of the firework displays, which are quite unique in the world. Every village celebrates the feast of its patron saint once a year.

Among the most popular feasts, with both tourists and locals alike, are the feasts of L-Imnarja (the feast of St. Peter and St. Paul) on June 29, and Santa Marija (the Assumption), on August 15. Another one, Il-Vittoria (Our Lady of Victories) on September 8, marks the defeat of the Turkish Armada during the Great Siege of 1565.

But now back to the recipe, which is often used by many a Maltese family on feast days, including those during which the village festa is celebrated.

Ingredients for Ross il-Forn (Oven Baked Rice)

1 packet or two of 500 grams rice
500 grams beef minced meat
1 lg. tin (500 grams) corned beef
4 tins of tomato pulp
1 chicken cube
2 Tbsp. tomato paste
5 Tbsp. sugar (make sure to taste the sauce until it is sweet)
½ sm. packet Parmesan grated cheese
2 eggs
Pepper and salt

Ingredients for White Sauce (Béchamel)

½ packet butter cut into knobs (round pieces)
1 tin Nestle cream
Milk
Flour

Method:

Boil rice for five minutes, drain, and put aside. In large saucepan, fry minced beef and mix in the corned beef. When brown, add the two tins of tomato, tomato paste, half chicken cube, and the sugar. Boil for 20 minutes on moderate heat. Add rice, eggs, and cheese to mixture, mixing well. Take an ovenproof dish and grease well with butter. Add the mixture.

Melt the half packet of butter in a small pan. Add flour with tablespoon until butter becomes pasty, then add tin of Nestle cream and mix well. Add milk until mixture becomes creamy. The whole procedure should be performed on an extremely low flame. Take the béchamel and spread it evenly on top of the rice.

Sprinkle with grated cheese and salt and pepper. This dish should be served hot. For best results allow the oven-baked rice to cool down completely and serve a day after it is cooked in order to allow to settle.

The Strufolli Tradition

B.H. Haropolous

Strufolli has always been a Christmas tradition in my family. My mother's family is Italian-American, raised in New Jersey (naturally). My mom and I would spend several days at her sister's home and we'd gather around the table to make the strufolli. Those small, fried balls of delectability were quickly consumed. It seemed we could never make enough.

Christmas does not "officially" arrive until Mom (now me) is breaking out the fryer and the honey. Now, in this technologically advanced age, my cousin and I send our strufolli pictures to each other via text messages. It's a contest to see who makes them the earliest in the month of December. We always laugh on the phone after the first picture is received.

Strufolli (Italian Honey Balls)

2 lbs. flour (8 cups)
6 eggs
½ lb. butter
¾ tsp. baking powder
1 tsp. vanilla
½ pt. sour cream
1 cup sugar
1 bottle honey
vegetable oil
spritz

Put all ingredients in a mixing bowl except the flour and mix well. Add flour slowly until well blended (dough is thick). Roll out dough on a well-floured surface into ropes about ½ inch to ¾ inch thick, and 18 inches long. Cut into ½ inch to ¾ inch balls. Heat a large pot of oil/Crisco and fry balls until lightly browned. Drain on paper towel, then place in a bowl. Add some warmed honey to each batch and mix well. Sprinkle with spritz.

*Tip: Do ALL rolling and cutting first!

Three Wise Decisions

Reba Cross Seals

The camels' hooves made no sound as they plodded through the sand with their hooded eyes, bearing burdens of luxurious robes, goatskin water bags, and unusual gifts for an unusual purpose. Equally silent were the three travelers on their backs, fatigue showing in strained faces. Of the three, Gaspar—the Asian philosopher and astronomer—seemed the most impervious to the howling winds and blowing sand. He patiently followed Balthazar, the black-bearded African who had traveled the farthest to meet his learned companions, and both men followed behind Melchior, the European who looked like the king he was with a flowing white beard.

Their journey together began in Babylon of Mesopotamia, where the strangers met after months of peering through telescopes in their own countries, studying ancient scrolls, and consulting other learned men. Each separately came to the conclusion that great portent was meant by the never-before-seen lining up of Jupiter and Saturn in the eastern sky creating a star that was more brilliant, more piercing than any ever seen. After years of studying the great manuscripts of Isaiah and Daniel, they each came to the conclusion that they were in a moment of history that had been foretold centuries before in ancient Jewish manuscripts, a time when a king would be born who would save the world, and each felt compelled to go verify the event.

"Stop, Melchior, I beg you!" pleaded Balthazar with sweat dripping from his forehead. "We need to rest, as we are rapidly chasing daybreak." He didn't mention the pain in his withered arm. He was so used to living with pain, that it was almost as familiar to him as his black beard.

Melchior nodded, yet kept steadily moving. "Yes, Balthazar, we are approaching daybreak where we will not be able to follow our star, but my maps tell me that soon we shall approach a large oasis. There we shall spend the day and rest us and our animals. The hardest thing as usual will be explaining to nomadic herdsmen why we wish to travel at night instead of carousing with them around the campfires."

The added possibility of theft from bandits who frequented desert oases was not mentioned, although that fear drove Melchior past many watering holes where they could have rested. Indeed, Melchior shuddered as he thought of losing the rich gifts they were carrying. Even though he was a wealthy man in the provinces of Europe, he was burdened by the treasures he and his small caravan carried as they followed the brilliant star.

As they crossed the dunes and began to see small twinkling lights from village oasis campfires, Gaspar reflected upon what he was doing with this unusual pair of men. True, they were scholars like himself, revered and thought kingly in their own countries, but he knew them not and he despised them for their strange looks and different cultures which did not have the wisdom, history, and beauty of his Asian heritage. Gaspar didn't know why he chose myrrh—a rare, expensive spice used in embalming—to bring to a baby, but it seemed to match his mood. While a valuable gift, it reflected the despair in Gaspar's heart, which was hard and full of churning hate. He did not know if he could bring himself to complete the journey with these strangers.

After greeting the village elder who welcomed them by warning of increased bandit activity in the oasis ahead, the three travelers erected their tent and built their own small campfire. Sitting around it with their backs to the rising sun, drinking tea brought by Gaspar from China, they were almost too weary to speak. Eventually the African Balthazar nerved himself to voice his thoughts. "Friends, over many dunes and through many nights I have considered. We embarked on a journey to find a king who was promised to the Jews many years ago, who will right the world and save mankind. But I must tell you of physical pain I carry with me constantly, and feel it increasing each day, and I feel that I must turn back. Besides," Balthazar added nervously, "my family in Africa is large, and the youth need guidance, and my wife needs my companionship. I must turn back."

The other two considered, each apprehensive about revealing his own heart. Finally bitter, unreadable Gaspar spoke up. "I might have known that you would fall out. You and your people do not have the wisdom of the ancients that my people do, and your ways are not dependable. In fact, Melchior, I expect you also to go back on your word on our journey to see the king in the east!" Venom was in his voice as he stared at his companions, concealing that he too was considering the idea of retreat.

Melchior looked startled for, indeed, his fear of traveling into dangerous territory was increasing. Not only was he worried about the wealth in precious gifts that the three carried, but he feared for the safety of his worldly goods at home. Perhaps he needed to be back there to defend his possessions and family compound. Melchior thought of the gold bars he had brought for the new king of the Jews. They represented little of his accumulated wealth, but they would be valuable indeed to an infant Jewish king. Still, he didn't want to waste them if they would just get stolen somewhere along the journey. Perhaps he too should reconsider traveling on with his two companions.

Silence fell complete around the campfire as sleep overtook them, and without more comment, they each rolled up a robe into a pillow and retired into their tent. Eventually all three fell into deep slumber.

Suddenly near dawn the flap to their tent was thrown back, even though Melchior had secured it firmly with sturdy rope. The three men awoke, each groping for something nearby to use as a weapon, when they heard a voice say, "Nay, do not fear, my good men. I mean you no harm. I came to remind you that 'For unto us a child is born, unto us a son is given; and the government shall be upon his shoulder; and his name shall be called Wonderful, Counselor, the Mighty God, the Everlasting Father, the Prince of Peace.'"

Standing before them at the tent entrance was a man who looked like Father Moses with a flowing white beard that put Melchior's to shame. The men glanced at each other, then back again to the elder. "Sire," said Balthazar, "we know that verse from the ninth chapter of Isaiah. It is one of the reasons we are here in this desert oasis. We were on our way to see this newborn king."

"Ah," said the one who looked like Father Moses, "you said 'were,' did you not? Are you not still going on the journey to see the savior of the world?"

The three men were seated cross-legged on their robes by now, trying to explain their various reasons for turning back to the imposing elder. "You see, sire," said Melchior, "I fear that with our load of valuables, we are a target for every bandit who ever brandished a sword between here and the Red Sea. We don't want to lose all that we have, even our lives!"

Balthazar then spoke. "Sire, I'm afraid that this new king may not be worth what I am going through either. He is a mere baby who will one day grow up, but I am in great physical pain today, and what good can he do me? I know that baby will shoulder the government and make life better for me and my people, but my family needs me. But if you are going that way, you can take this frankincense with which to worship him!"

Finally the silent Gaspar was moved to speak. "I hate the difficulties of this journey and would like to be back on my mountaintop alone with my telescope. I do not like the desert, the sand, or the wind, and I am having second thoughts about a baby ever being able to bring peace. War is all my country has ever known, and indeed, the whole world has known little more. Peace!" he spat. "There will never be peace!" While Gaspar's face remained passive, his eyes revealed his hate.

The man who looked like Father Moses was silent for a while, leaning upon his staff. "Ah, let me see," he finally said. "You all are giving up the journey for these reasons, and you do not think the newborn babe will ever be able to make a difference. I hear greed and fear, family duties and physical problems, and finally, hate and despair. Am I correct? Are these not the real reasons you are giving up following the brilliant star to find the one who will someday be a counselor, a prince of peace, and a wonderful healer?"

Silence greeted these questions, and they contemplated them in stillness. Each man knew in his own heart that the man who looked like Father Moses had accurately targeted his basic reason for not fulfilling his mission. While their reasons to turn back were real, while all their reasons were true and valid; nevertheless, they knew in their hearts that the purpose of their journey was noble, their quest was important, and that the world needed to hear what they discovered.

So, as the sun was sinking in the west, and the first star that could be seen was already shining brilliantly behind the head of the man who looked like Father Moses, the three travelers rolled up their robes and tent, loaded their camels, and prepared to journey on.

Wise men still seek Him.

A Sweet Treat for my Sweetheart

Alice King Greenwood

My husband has been a diabetic since childhood. When we married, I began preparing healthy meals as he was very self-disciplined, eating only the foods allowed in his diet. When holidays rolled around, he watched as others in the family indulged in rich desserts. I felt sorry that he was not able to enjoy something special too.

Then one day I chanced to see a recipe for a cake that contained no refined sugar and immediately knew it was one I needed to save. Since that time I have made this cake every Christmas, and sometimes for birthdays. It was good to see my husband enjoy Christmas goodies along with the rest of the family. This is the recipe below.

Diabetic Date Nut Cake

1 stick margarine, creamed

Mix together and add to margarine:

1 egg
1 tsp. vanilla
½ cup sugar substitute that measures like sugar
(or 1 Tbsp. liquid artificial sweetener)
1½ cup (or 14 oz. jar) diet applesauce

Sift together and add to first mixture:

2 cups flour
2 tsp. baking soda
½ tsp. cinnamon
¼ tsp. cloves

Beat with electric mixer until well blended.

Add: 1 cup chopped pecans
1 cup chopped dates

Turn into greased loaf pan and bake 1 hour at 350 degrees.

Unexpected Surprises

"And now you know the rest of the story."
—*Paul Harvey*

Megan and Zoe

Rebecca D. Bruner

The last day of school before Christmas vacation, I was so excited I could hardly stand it. I skipped all the way home from the bus stop singing "Jingle Bells." Christmas was just around the corner!

I rushed into the house, flung my arms around my mom (who was on the phone) and gave her a big hug. "Only five more days 'til Christmas!" I said.

"Shh," Mom said with a frown. She scrunched the receiver to her ear with her shoulder, while writing furiously on a notepad.

Even her grouchiness couldn't spoil my good mood. I kept humming as I pulled a packet of popcorn out of the pantry and put it in the microwave.

"No, don't worry about it," Mom told the person on the phone. "We'll go pick her up....All right. See you later." She hung up.

I grabbed the popcorn out of the microwave.

"Here," said Mom, taking it out of my hands.

"I can do it myself," I protested. I hate being treated like a baby. After all, I am in third grade.

"Well, you're going to have to bring it with you in the van. We have to go to the airport to pick up Megan."

Oh no, not Megan! I had forgotten she was coming today. No wonder Mom had seemed so grouchy.

Megan is my sister, but she never lived with us. She's eight years older than me, so when I was born, she was already as old as I am now. She lives in Minnesota. I live in Arizona. We really don't have anything in common—except our dad. That's why she had to come and stay with us for Christmas vacation but I wished she could have just stayed home. Megan never wants to play with me or do anything fun because all she thinks about is acting cool. If she tried any harder to be cool, she'd probably be frozen solid.

Before we moved from Minnesota to Arizona, Megan used to stay with us on weekends for "visitation" (which means that the judge said she had to come, even if she didn't want to). She spent most of her time in her bedroom. The only time she ever played with me was when Dad made her, and then all she wanted to do was play hospital.

"You be the doctor, I'll be the patient," she'd say, lying down on the sofa and closing her eyes. "And I'm in a coma."

I was almost six when we moved to Arizona, and Megan was thirteen.

Because we lived so far away, she couldn't come on the weekends anymore, but I sure didn't miss having her around. Then Christmas break came and we got her for the whole two weeks! She didn't want to do anything. She didn't want to drive around and look at Christmas lights, or see Santa Claus at the mall. She didn't want to sing Christmas carols, or decorate sugar cookies, or make gingerbread houses. She didn't even want to watch "How the Grinch Stole Christmas."

I was dreading the coming week as I sat in the backseat munching my popcorn.

"Mom," I said, "why does Megan have to come?"

"We've been over this, Zoe. She gets to spend every other Christmas with Dad."

"But she'll ruin everything."

Mom sighed. She knew I was right but wouldn't admit it. "The fact is that Megan is your sister, and if there's one thing you have to learn during the holidays, it's how to tolerate difficult relatives."

"I wish we could have Christmas like last year, with just us."

"Well, honey, that's not the situation. Megan is coming, and we have to make the best of it."

Making the best of it didn't sound like much fun to me.

When we got to the airport, Mom parked the van and we hurried to baggage claim. We found the carousel where Megan's luggage was supposed to show up and stood around waiting. Finally, I caught sight of her. Her black hair matched her black, oversized coat and the black makeup around her eyes. A pair of earbuds dangled around her neck. She walked up to us and hiked her army-green canvas backpack higher on her shoulder. She looked from my mom's face to mine and then scanned the crowd of people behind us.

"Where's Dad?" she asked.

"He was planning to be here, but he got tied up at the office," Mom said with a stiff smile.

"Figures," said Megan. Without another word, she walked past us toward the baggage carousel.

"Merry Christmas to you too," I muttered.

"Zoe," Mom frowned, "don't start. We're all trying to make the best of this, remember?"

I remembered all right, but it wasn't going to be easy.

Two days before Christmas, Mom had to go in to work. Dad was home but he was "telecommuting," which means he was chained to his computer.

"I tell you what, girls, if you can occupy yourselves and not disturb me, I'll take you out for lunch," he promised. "What do you say?"

"I won't hold my breath," Megan muttered. I don't think Dad heard her.

He shut the door to the office and Megan went into the guest room. Pretty soon, I heard the sliding glass door open. I turned around to see Megan disappearing out back in her bathing suit! She couldn't be crazy enough to go swimming in December, could she? I hurried outside to see what she was up to.

She was lying on a lounge chair wearing sunglasses and a two-piece bathing suit. I shivered. I was cold even wearing my sweater and jeans.

"Aren't you freezing?" I asked.

Megan snorted. "Are you kidding? Back home, the lakes are frozen and the snow's as deep as your armpits. Living in Arizona is turning you into a wimp."

"I am not!" I said. "You know, if you love Minnesota so much, why don't you just stay there?"

"You think I want to come here? I'd rather spend Christmas break hanging out with my friends, instead of a snot-nosed little brat who won't leave me alone!"

I never knew before that Megan hated being here as much I hated having her around.

"But since I'm stuck in this God-forsaken desert," she went on, "I might as well come home with a tan."

She turned over on her stomach and pretended to ignore me. I started walking along the edge of the pool like a tightrope walker in the circus. Looking down, I could see the sunlight dancing on the bright blue water.

"You know what I think?" I said. "I think you're the wimp."

I dipped my hand in the water and splashed her.

She shrieked and sat up. "Cut that out!"

"I dare you to jump in!"

"No!"

"You said it wasn't even cold," I said, stepping onto the diving board.

"It's not."

I started tightrope walking out toward the end of the board.

"Megan's a chicken, Megan's a chicken." I flapped my arms like wings and bounced up and down.

"Get off of there or you're gonna fall in, you little freak, and don't expect me to rescue you."

"Don't worry about me," I said. "I know how to swim." I stood tiptoe on one foot and lifted the other leg out behind me, spreading my arms like a ballerina.

"I mean it, Zoe. Get off!" she shouted.

"Make me," I started to say, when suddenly I lost my balance. I wobbled for a moment, and then splashed into the pool.

It was so cold, it took my breath away. My sweater and jeans felt like they weighed a thousand pounds and my soggy tennis shoes made it really hard to kick. I held my breath as my head bobbed under the icy water.

The next thing I knew, there was a huge splash and Megan was dragging me to the side.

"Let me go," I tried to say. "I can swim," but my mouth was full of water. Finally, she hauled me out of the pool.

Dad stuck his head out the sliding glass door, looking worried. "What's going on?"

Megan and I lay panting on the cool deck.

"Are you two okay?" he asked.

"We're fine, Dad," Megan answered. "Zoe just thought it would be fun to go swimming."

"Are you crazy? It's the middle of December."

Megan looked at me and rolled her eyes. My teeth were chattering, but I started to giggle. Then Megan started giggling too. Pretty soon we were both laughing so hard, we couldn't stop.

"Come in the house before you catch pneumonia!" Dad ordered.

In no time, we were bundled up in bathrobes and blankets in front of the fireplace. Dad switched on the gas log and went to make us hot chocolate.

"Your lips are blue," I said.

"So are yours."

"Here we are," Dad said, holding out a tray with two mugs of steaming chocolate.

I grabbed one and Megan grabbed the other.

"So, what do you girls want to do this afternoon?" Dad asked.

"I'm up for anything…except swimming," Megan said.

"Wimp!" I said.

Megan stuck out her tongue at me, and then we both started giggling again.

"You know," said Megan, "for a snot-nosed little brat, you're a lot of fun."

"So are you," I said with a grin, "for a cranky teenager who's too cool to move."

"I moved pretty quick when it came time to pull you out of the pool!"

"I really didn't need help," I said.

"Sure you didn't," she said with a nod.

I snuggled up close beside her and watched the fire, counting the stockings that hung on the mantle (one for Dad, one for Mom, one for Megan, and one for me). I slurped some more cocoa and thought how Christmas really is the best time of the year.

Behind the Mask

John Brewer

He appeared to be a jovial man. A smile was etched permanently into his face and laughter seemed to dance in his eyes. A great flowing white beard hid his chin from view. He wore a bright red suit trimmed in white fur and set off with glossy black leather belt and boots. The public character of Santa Claus had not changed a bit from childhood memories. He was still the epitome of love and joy. The line of people, formed in front of this legendary fulfiller of dreams, waited patiently, each for a chance to touch destiny; not one seeing beyond the mask; not one seeing the man hidden within.

A little boy waited expectantly in line for his turn to be with Santa. The boy's mother walked ahead and spoke to the jolly little man who was sitting patiently on his throne in the middle of the shopping mall. She whispered briefly in the white-haired man's ear. He nodded compassionately and shortly the little boy's turn came. Searching Santa's face, the lad saw eyes aglow with love. The red-suited man opened his arms wide and scooped the young fellow up to give him a warm gentle hug. Then setting him back down, Santa Claus formed the deaf-mute sign with his right hand that says, "I love you." Happy tears formed in the little boy's eyes as he waved good-bye.

Day after day children lined up to have their pictures taken with Santa Claus and to whisper their secret desires to the fabled toy king. Often, older children would line up too—some in their teens, twenties, and thirties; others in their sixties and seventies. Each one was still a child when they sat in Santa's lap. He gave each person a plastic Christmas ring as a personal gift.

One day a line of "special" school children were ushered into place by several teachers. They were the unloved, unwanted, slow learners, and handicapped. Today, however, they were truly special. Every hug the big-hearted Santa gave had a genuine tender love behind it. The children knew, as only children can, that this gentle giant truly cared about them. Time seemed to waver a moment as each child lingered in that warm embrace. Then, all too quickly, it was over and they were gone. The only sign of the children having been there were the tears left in Santa's eyes.

After the lines of children were taken care of, their secrets heard, their pictures taken, Santa would often get up from his throne and sing and dance. Standing on the dais by his throne with a leather band of jingle bells in his hand, his big belly would shake as he began to sing. A small crowd of shoppers would pause and momentarily shaking off "retail madness," they would gather 'round the throne and join in for a chorus of "White Christmas," "Jingle Bell Rock," or "Silent Night."

At other times Santa would step down from his throne and talk to little old men, recalling when ten cents would buy a big bag of assorted candies. Or, he would take old ladies by the arm and dance a little jig with them. For a moment the frail bent backs of these men and women would straighten and, with renewed vigor in their eyes, they would be like little children again, full of life.

On Christmas Eve, Santa was interviewed live on the local television news show. He told of all the toys the children were looking forward to, and recalled when the anchorman was just a young boy himself, sitting on his Santa's lap. Now, here he was all grown up and still coming to Santa with his questions. The anchorman admitted that he was still a child at heart. Santa wished everyone a merry Christmas and admonished all children watching to obey their parents and be good.

Then the television crew left, and the mall emptied of shoppers. A few storekeepers were cleaning up or holding little get-togethers for their employees. Unnoticed, a young man wearing a cowboy hat and dressed in blue jeans and a blue plaid shirt walked out the mall exit, tucking a small red bundle under one arm. Clutched in his other hand was a small bag of plastic rings. He spent Christmas Eve in the back of a small quiet bar; however, the beer he drank that night couldn't fill the emptiness he felt. When the bar closed, an acquaintance drove him home.

Christmas morning came all too quickly for the young man. He dressed and walked into the empty living room of the cold trailer. The lights in his tree had lost their twinkle a month earlier when the electricity had been cut off. There were no presents under the tree. Lifting his head the young man heard the joyful sound of children playing with their new toys and treasures in the courtyard outside. Glancing toward the front door, he saw an empty red suit lying crumpled on the floor. No one could see the tears in his lonely eyes, but he walked quickly to the kitchen sink to rinse his face anyway. It was time to put on the "everything is all right" mask and face the new day.

The Christmas Visitors

Michael M. Alvarez

A cold chill trickles down my spine as I see Old Man Valentine's house. Its dark windows peer out like angry eyes. The front porch sags as if tired from all the years of standing in place. I pull up my car and stop near the chained gate and the sign that announces:

KEEP OUT PRIVATE PROPERTY

In the winter of 1964, my friends and I were fearless as we stood in front of Old Man Valentine's house and dared each other to knock on the door. We had no way of knowing that what lay behind the door would change our lives forever.

* * *

"I dare you!" Tony said to me. "I double dare you."

"They say he's crazy, went nuts when his wife died," Larry added.

I stood between the two best friends any eleven-year-old could have and swallowed the huge lump in my dry throat.

It was two days before Christmas, and everyone was getting ready for the holidays. My mother and grandmother were busy making tamales and enchiladas and a turkey to serve all my uncles, aunts, cousins, and other friends who were coming to our house on Christmas Eve. That morning I had helped my dad put up the six-foot aluminum tree and set up the revolving color wheel on the floor next to it.

The fierce coldness of the day seemed to penetrate into our bones. We wrapped our arms across our chests and stamped our feet to keep warm. My teeth chattered so badly I thought they might jump right out of my mouth.

"C'mon, Mikey, you gonna stand there all day, or you gonna go up and knock on the door?" Tony challenged me.

"Don't rush me," I said.

Just then we heard an eerie sound that rooted us to the ground. We stood like marble statues. The wailing sound was sad and terrifying, all at once. *Maybe it was just the wind inside the old house?*

"I'll go if you guys come with me," I said. "We have to go together and knock on the door."

"Okay," they said, almost in unison.

Slowly, one cautious step at a time, we moved toward the house that most people in town swore was haunted. The story was that when Old Man Valentine's wife was alive, they were both happy and friendly with everyone in town. But then Mrs. Valentine got sick. No one really knew what was wrong with her, but after a while neither of them seldom left the house. Some days Old Man Valentine went into town to buy groceries and pay bills, but the rest of the time he and his wife stayed inside their big, rambling house.

A few years later, someone in town said they'd heard from Doc Johnson that Mrs. Valentine had died. The story goes that Old Man Valentine went crazy and kept his wife's body somewhere inside the scary old house. Perhaps, they say, he might have buried her in the backyard so he could visit her whenever he wanted.

Standing in front of the splintered wooden front door, we looked at each other. This was our last chance to run for our lives. I gave Tony and Larry a thumbs-up sign, and we all knocked on the door at the same time.

A few seconds ticked by; I could hear my heart pounding inside my chest. It was so loud, I was almost sure that Larry and Tony could hear it too. We stood our ground. I realized I was holding my breath.

"Who's there?" came a voice from behind the door. We were ready to turn and run when in the next heartbeat the front door screeched and began to open slowly. Finally, the front door was slightly ajar. Beyond, there was only darkness.

"Well, might as well come in, boys, and close that door! It's freezing outside." The voice didn't sound mean or harsh. It seemed almost friendly.

Once inside, the front door swung shut. Trapped! My mind was racing. *What would the Lone Ranger do?*

"I'm in the kitchen, boys. Just follow the light," the voice said.

I looked at Tony and Larry. They both just shrugged, so we all followed the shaft of lonely light coming from the kitchen.

Old Man Valentine didn't look like a monster. He was old, but he didn't look like any of us had imagined. He was a little hunched over, with white hair, and he used a walking cane carved out of mesquite. He seemed almost happy to see us.

"Just in time, my friends," he said, as he pulled a tray of cookies from his old oven. "I'd like your opinion on my pumpkin cookies. I tried to follow Millie's recipe, but I'm afraid I'm not as good a cook as she was."

We didn't know what to say. Finally, we slowly pulled out some chairs and joined the old man at the small table.

"You don't look crazy," Tony said in a tiny voice.

The room was dead silent. I thought we were goners, but then the strangest thing happened. The old man threw back his head and belted out the biggest laugh I'd ever heard.

"I'm not crazy, boys. Guess just a bit lonely most of the time. When I think of Millie being gone, I get a bit sad, but I ain't crazy." His face grew dark.

"This is good!" Larry said, munching a cookie.

He was right. They were good. Tony and I slowly chewed one, swallowed carefully, and then tried another.

"Sorry, I don't have any milk," said Mr. Valentine.

"So where's your wife?" Tony blurted out.

The old man leaned on his cane and gently shook his head. "Suppose in the same cemetery where she was buried twenty years ago. Got cancer, Millie did. 'Course the docs didn't know what to do in those days. All they could do was watch her fade away."

"I'm sorry about your wife," I said.

A sad smile appeared on his face. "I miss her the most around the holidays. Millie loved cooking during the holidays..." His voice trailed off.

That day in 1964 we discovered the truth about Old Man Valentine. He wasn't a mean, crazy old man who lived in a large, spooky house, only a gentle, quiet man, who loved his wife very much and cherished her memory. He wasn't a man to be frightened of—he was a man who needed friends, especially around the holidays.

Tony, Larry, and I made a promise that day: The three of us would always get together for the holidays and visit Mr. Valentine.

* * *

Now, Christmas Eve many years later, I wait patiently in my car. I smile as I see two cars drive up. It will be good to see Tony and Larry again.

I'm sure Mr. Valentine will be happy to see us too.

I'll Be Home for Christmas

Sandra Fischer

Kevin sat waiting for Marcy by the mall fountain, watching the moving mosaic of shoppers, listening to strains of Christmas songs on the loudspeakers. The dancing waters mesmerized him. *I never knew shopping could be so exhausting. But then, Annie had always done it.*

"Daddy, Daddy, look!" Kevin's heart skipped a beat as he turned toward the familiar-sounding voice of a child. *Missy?* Instead of seeing corn-silk curls coiling around the rosy cheeks he had touched so many times, he beheld a pint-sized brunette tugging on her father's sleeve. A twinge of envy struck him. *Oh, how I wish it were you, Missy! If only. . .*

"Kev, babe, you doin' okay?" Not waiting for an answer, Marcy handed him three shopping bags, then leaned over and kissed him. "You're my best Christmas gift this year." She winked. "Just have a couple more to get. . .be back in a jif."

Strains of Perry Como crooning the Christmas classic "I'll Be Home For Christmas" wafted over the loudspeaker to the oblivious shoppers, but the lyrics penetrated Kevin's thoughts. *Home. Where is home this year?*

He closed his eyes and a memory thrust itself forth—Annie and Missy in the kitchen making Christmas cutouts. Missy, cheeks aglow with excitement and smears of red icing, standing on a stool waving a spatula, "Look, Daddy, we're making cookies for Santa. . ."

What had he said? Something like, "That's nice," or "I don't have time for Santa or Christmas cookies." Last Christmas was a fog; so much had happened since then. The ugly arguments were either stilled by a wall of silence on Annie's part or by his spending less and less time at home.

He noticed the fountain again. The water droplets exploded into tall designs of individual beads, then cascaded to the sea of water below. *That's how it was with Annie and me – each of us seeking our own selfish desires, our actions and words erupting until we gave up, consumed by the prevailing waters of the culture.* He had succumbed to the echoing voices, *"If you're not happy, get a divorce. There are plenty of women out there eager to please."*

It was true. Shortly after Kevin moved out, Marcy appeared—young, bubbly, and vivacious, smothering him with attention. She was all too eager to keep him from thinking he had failed, particularly as a father to Missy.

"She'll be fine," soothed Marcy. "Kids adjust. Besides, now you're free to spend time with little ol' me."

At first, he had felt free. He needn't hurry home after work, he could sleep in if he wanted on weekends, and he could follow all his sports fantasy teams without reproach. As Christmas approached, however, something kept gnawing at him, a restlessness he couldn't seem to suppress.

The words of another familiar song broke the reverie: Bing Crosby was dreaming of a "white Christmas" as he had done for decades before Kevin was born. *Was every song about dreams? Was life filled only with disappearing visions like the mist in the fountain? He had dreamed of having a family of his own, a place to call home, and now. . .*

A gritty, unshaven man in a stocking cap, wearing layered, mismatched clothing and tattered tennis shoes caught Kevin's attention. He stooped under a bulging, threadbare backpack as he shuffled from one trash can to another, rummaging for discarded aluminum cans to add to the plastic shopping bag he dragged along.

Poor homeless soul. The lightning thought pierced Kevin's consciousness and his eyes stung with reality. That's me! He tried to swallow, but the yearning would not yield this time. *Oh, God, what have I done? Was it too late?*

"Here I am, sugar. Sorry about the wait," Marcy bubbled. "Hey, Kev, you catchin' a cold or somethin'?"

"Marcy, we need to talk, Marcy. . ."

* * *

Kevin punched the speed-dial number on his cell, then waited and prayed. *Please, Lord, give me another chance.*

"Wilson's residence." Annie's greeting warmed and surprised him at the same time. "Hello? Anyone there?"

"Annie. It's me. I was wondering. . .uh. . . how you and Missy are doing."

He waited. He knew Annie would be weighing her response.

"We're doing okay. How about you?"

"I'm doing okay too."

"That's good. Would you like to speak to Missy?"

"Yes—no, I mean—not yet. I want to talk to you. Annie, I lied. I'm not okay. I'm miserable. I was wondering. . . Annie, I'm so sorry about everything." He waited for a response. "Annie? Are you there?"

"Yes, I'm here." Three simple words, spoken slowly, deliberately, and tenderly gave a glimmer of hope.

"You were wondering?" Her voice was soft, open.

"I was wondering if you could forgive me—if we could try to. . .if I. . ." he choked. "I want to come home." There it was—all the longing of his heart spilled out in a mixture of hope and fear.

"Is that Daddy?" Kevin heard Missy's voice in the background.

"Yes," Annie answered her. "He wants to come home!"

"Annie? Did you hear me?" Kevin awaited her response. Before she could reply, Missy's excited squeal in the background gave him the answer. "Daddy's coming home, Daddy's coming home!"

"Can you be home for Christmas?"

"Yes, Annie, I'll be home for Christmas. You can count on me."

Mistletoe and the Bell

Nikole Hahn

Tinkle. Tinkle. Tinkle.

"Day in. Day out." Lena shoved more scented candles onto the shelf. "Red. Green. Peppermint. Gingerbread sold out yesterday. Not sure if I am going to get that candle in before Christmas—being that Christmas is two days away."

Cold air brushed against her cheek. A customer walked in on the wake of "Merry Christmas! Thank you, Ma'am," and the clink of coins hitting the kettle.

Tinkle. Tinkle. Tinkle.

"I'm going to chuck that bell any day now." Lena finished stocking the scented candles and noticed the curious expression on the customer's face. "Sorry."

She paused in front of a mirror, and with a quick glance over her shoulder, combed her fingers through her long dark hair. She wet her finger and rubbed at the mascara smudges beneath her gray eyes. Her small shop did well at Christmas as she stocked all the popular candles and potpourri for the season. A few gift items and incense sticks adorned the shelves too. The owner of the mall raised the rent for the second time this year, and Visa and MasterCard doubled their fees. More money went to bills than into her bank account. Last month she had to lay off her only employee. This doubled her hours.

"This is why I am single and divorced. This is why I don't have time to date." Lena whispered into the mirror.

The economy weighed heavily on Lena. Thankfully, she and her ex-husband never had any children. Like every Christmas, she would warm up a microwave meal and watch "It's a Wonderful Life."

"Having a hard Christmas?" The customer appeared nearby. She wore a nice beige overcoat and her expensive scarf fell around her shoulders.

"Sorry...again." Lena gave the older woman a half-smile.

"You've been mumbling for the last ten minutes, first picking on the Salvation Army bell ringer and then going on and on about your business."

"Sorry. It's just that you aren't here from 9 a.m. to 6 p.m. hearing that bell ring over and over again. It loses its meaning after a while."

The woman mumbled under her breath something about poor Christmas spirit and walked out of the shop.

Lena looked out the display window. Piles of snow capped the grass from last night's light snowfall. Then she noticed the girl smiling and ringing the bell. She had purple highlights in her blonde hair, and a nose ring glinted in the morning sunlight. Lena put her hands over her ears.

"Merry Christmas!" She stabbed a pad of paper with a Bic pen, and watched the blue ink bleed out.

"Merry Christmas…Oh! Are you okay?"

Lena noticed the bell ringer standing there. "Yeah. Sure. What can I do for you?"

"I don't suppose you have a cup of coffee you could share?" The girl's eyes roamed the shop. "It smells so nice in here."

"Some." Lena stood and walked behind the partition that separated the main shop from her back room. Her cold mug of coffee sat next to a pile of mail. The only other cup had a chip in it. She grabbed that one and poured the last of the lukewarm coffee into it.

"Thanks!" The girl inhaled the fragrant coffee. "It gets so cold out there. My name is Mistletoe."

Lena blinked. "Mistletoe?"

"My parents were Christmas-a-holics. They named my twin sisters Holly and Ivy. The story goes that my parents conceived me on Christmas under the mistletoe." Mistletoe blushed. "I used to get teased."

"You must be very lucky."

"I was."

"Was?"

"They were too generous. Dad lost his job. Mom became an alcoholic. I ran away more than once. Holly and Ivy were taken away by CPS. But I have a feeling this year will be different somehow." Mistletoe sipped her coffee and looked over the shop.

The bell sat on the counter. Lena considered grabbing it, but instead asked, "Why do you think it will be different?"

"Made some new friends. Got my first apartment. Mom is in rehab again. Dad and I are hoping this time it sticks. I even bought a real tree. It was hard. Couldn't really afford it and it doesn't have really much on decoration, but it smells like Christmas every time I come home. That, and I started attending church."

"Church?" Right. Lena rolled her eyes. It's the cure-all. Go to church, get "born again," and all of a sudden your whole world was right again.

"Yeah. I never really got that baby Jesus thing. Not here." Mistletoe thumped her chest. "It just suddenly made sense. Suddenly, I got the whole relationship thing. I never thought of Christ that way…like a friend."

Mistletoe walked over to a display of medium-sized candles. She touched a yellowish-beige candle and brought it close to her nose. "Vanilla? Cinnamon? Reminds me of home. How much?"

Lena stared at the bell. A friend? She used to sing "Away in the Manger" in the car. So many Christmas carols talked of Christ's birth. She loved Handel's "Messiah."

"What's wrong?"

"Mmmm?" Lena stopped staring at the bell.

"How much for the candle?"

"It's my gift to you." Lena smiled weakly.

"I don't need charity." Mistletoe walked over and retrieved her bell.

"It reminds you of home." And you reminded me of Christmas.

Mistletoe walked out of the shop smelling her new candle.

Tinkle. Tinkle. Tinkle.

The bell didn't bother Lena anymore. She retrieved the religion section out of the trash can and with a highlighter picked out churches that were having Christmas Eve services.

Christmas Riches

Londa Hayden

'Twas the night before Christmas and all was not well. Cutbacks with my father's work made money even tighter than usual. My mother told us not to expect much, if anything at all, under the tree.

My family rarely spent holidays with either of my grandparents. Therefore, my mother depended on my great aunt, who basically took the place of my grandmother. On Christmas Eve, we always arrived in time for dessert, which included my aunt's famous pecan pie. That fresh baked aroma welcomed us at the door as a sweet prelude to help ease into the agony of what followed.

Moments later, my brother, sister, and I sat together in the living room and faced the grand Christmas tree surrounded with presents. Our two cousins, Casey and Roxanne, opened one present after another.

"Designer jeans, just what I wanted. Thanks Grandma," Casey said, while tossing the box aside and grabbing another present.

"Whoa, cool!" Roxanne held up a Walkman, something I was hoping to get.

We watched with envy as our cousins opened one present after the other. The colorfully decorated paper flew overhead with screams of joyous anticipation that made my skin crawl. They paraded each gift as if to rub in the fact that we had nothing. At first, thoughts of jealousy and evil plots of revenge whispered in my ear. *Hide the designer jeans under the sofa. Break the headphones to the Walkman.*

Anger rose up towards my mother for putting us through such cruel and unjust treatment year after year. There we sat with no gifts at all. I watched and wondered if there might be at least one for me. Surely one, of what seemed like hundreds of presents beneath that tree, had my name on it. Self-pity welled up in my eyes, but I did my best to hold back the tears.

While we lived in a more humble part of town with modest means, my aunt and cousins enjoyed a wealthy lifestyle further away. It seemed as though they had everything and we had nothing. My final breaking point came when I leaned over and begged my mother, "Can we please go home now?" But she refused.

Finally, my aunt presented one small package to each of us. The feelings of unworthiness subsided for the moment. My eyes sparkled with anticipation as I reached for my gift and opened it.

"A watch!" I said, and slipped it onto my wrist. "Oh, thank you so much." It wasn't a cool watch with a glittery band and interchangeable faces like the one Casey got earlier. No, this looked more like something for my mother. Who knows? Maybe it was a misplaced name tag. Either way, it was difficult to understand why my cousins got so many gifts and I only one. I glanced at the two dogs sitting nearby and understood what it must feel like to beg for a handout. Why did Mother put us through this every year? Father never came and now I knew why. I tried to understand how my aunt could be so generous with her husband's family, but treated her own like second-class citizens.

Before the next year's holidays rolled around, something happened that changed everything. One fateful day, Casey arrived home from school and called out for her mother. Checking the bedroom, she found her mother lying in a pool of blood on the bed. The police called it a suicide. Casey and Roxanne had everything given to them all their lives, but nothing prepared them for this. Suddenly, their mother's tragic desperate cry for help turned their lives into a nightmare.

When I heard the news, all my self-pity collapsed into shame. The shock, the confusion, and the pain of what happened affected the entire family. I began to understand how the misery of their mother made it incredibly difficult to live with at times. A sudden realization came to me that perhaps that's why my aunt and uncle lavished so many gifts upon them, and not just at Christmas. Perhaps, unbeknownst to the rest of the family, the gifts served to make up for the raging alcoholic my cousins suffered in secret with at home.

The next Christmas Eve brought an unexpected change to the usual gift giving spree. In fact, I don't even remember opening gifts. My cousins only talked the entire evening about how much they missed their mother. All the gifts in the world and tons of money never made up for their loss.

Although my family didn't have a big fancy house and lots of presents to give, I suddenly understood wealth in a different way. My family and the people I love gave me all the Christmas riches I needed.

The Gift She'd Always Wanted!

Leola Ogle

Talk about being confused, forty-five-year old Bill was in a total state of bewildered panic. For weeks, he had been looking forward to attending this NBA basketball game of the Phoenix Suns vs. the Los Angeles Lakers, but here he sat unable to even enjoy himself. His mind kept replaying the last few months while he tried to figure out how this horrible misunderstanding and predicament he was in had happened.

It all started a number of years ago. Bill and his wife, Connie, had been neighbors of Diane and her widowed mother, Martha, for twenty years. Both Diane and Martha were sweet, church-going ladies, and they all had a friendly, neighborly relationship with each other. Bill often lent a hand, helping Diane and Martha with anything around the house or minor car repairs that needed a man's touch.

Diane was an attractive, thirty-seven-year old year old woman who was still single. She certainly never kept it a secret from anyone that all she had ever wanted was to get married and have children. She talked about it all the time. All the time!

Unfortunately, for whatever reason that no one could figure out, marriage just hadn't happened for her. Bill couldn't count the number of times Connie had said to him, "Diane is really very pretty. I bet if she lost some weight, she could have any man she wanted."

It was true that Diane was a bit on the heavy side. Well, maybe more than just a bit, perhaps quite a bit, but from Bill's purely masculine point of view, he thought that some man would be lucky to have Diane. By golly, if a man was a real man, a woman's weight shouldn't matter. It was the character and beauty inside that was important.

It was a grim, dismal time in Bill's life when two years prior to him being at this basketball game, Connie had left him for another man, taking their daughter with her. He was completely blindsided, and such an emotional wreck that he lost his job because of it. Most days, he just couldn't even get out of bed. Diane and Martha had been such a blessing, reaching out to him, inviting him to dinner, encouraging him, even sending their pastor to pray with him. Their kindness really helped pull him through that dark time. He bounced back, got another good job, saw his daughter on the weekends….and continued to hang out at

Diane and Martha's, enjoying their home cooked meals. Those women sure knew how to cook, and they seemed to enjoy having an appreciative man to cook for. The way Bill saw it, it was a two-way street. Martha and Diane were happy to cook for him and he was more than happy to partake of the food they cooked.

Both Bill and Diane, being avid Phoenix Suns' fans, would watch the basketball games together on television. Looking back on it, he wasn't exactly sure how it began or whose idea it was, but the two of them starting going out to eat and to the movies together about once or twice a week. In all fairness though, at first Martha would go with them. Bill couldn't even remember when she started making excuses about why she couldn't go. He certainly never considered that going out alone with Diane could be construed as dating because they each paid their own way. Doesn't a man usually pay if it's a date? At least that was his understanding about dating, but who knew nowadays with all this equal rights stuff?

He hardly noticed how frequently Diane mentioned that she wanted to get married. Shucks, he knew that already. She's always talked about it before, so he paid no attention to the fact that she continued to talk about it.

He wasn't exactly sure either when she started sitting right next to him while they watched television. It was her house, after all, and she could sit where she pleased, right? He wasn't even suspicious when Martha began leaving them alone in the living room all the time. Don't all old people go to bed early? Not that he'd ever call Martha old though. She was pretty sharp and spry for her age.

At Diane's insistence, he began attending the singles' group at church with her. He discovered he really enjoyed the fellowship and Bible studies. There were some good looking women in that group, and he'd even scoped out a few possible prospects—you know, in case he ever got the urge to start dating.

One night after he and Diane had gone to the theater and seen one of those mushy, romantic movies (seeing that movie wasn't his idea), they had stopped at a Denny's for pie and coffee. Probably because that movie was so sappy, Diane leaned across the table and tearfully told him, "I've almost given up on ever marrying and having babies."

Clearing his throat, he'd started to tell her what Connie had said, that maybe if she lost weight, she could find a husband. All he managed to say though was "You're so pretty." Before he could finish his sentence, Diane blushed, and grabbed his hand, saying, "Oh, Bill, thank you! That's so sweet!" He didn't have the heart to finish the sentence after that. Would you?

And just suppose he had only meant to say she was pretty, that in no way indicates an impending marriage proposal, does it? How Diane ever got the idea he was going to propose to her was beyond him. Just because she'd asked him several times if he thought he'd marry again and have more children, and he'd answered "Sure," that was not a declaration he was thinking of marrying her.

Of course, there was that time they were together in Wal-Mart, which is a whole other thing. How did he let himself get talked into going shopping with her…or any woman, for that matter?

Not knowing what to do while she shopped, he'd wandered over to the jewelry department—it was right next to women's lingerie, where he felt awkward, to say the least, to be hanging out with her. Shopping for that kind of stuff was purely a personal thing, and not something he felt comfortable with.

Anyway, he had been contemplating hocking his wedding band because Connie had married that man and wasn't coming back. He was curious about current prices on rings, and was just biding his time until Diane was finished. He never even saw her slip up behind him until she spoke. Just because she coyly asked what he was doing, and he replied "Pricing rings," why did she assume that meant he was buying one for her?

Now that he thought about it, it made perfect sense that that's what she thought because when he went over to eat dinner the next night, Martha was grinning from ear to ear, kept hugging him, and offering him more banana cream pie, his favorite. He thought perhaps she'd won the lottery or Publishers Clearing House or something.

The more he pondered all this, the more of a mystery women seemed to him. Saying that women were a mystery seemed more polite than what he really thought—which was that sometimes they behaved like they were a bit touched in the head. There could be no other explanation for all this confusion!

A case in point was that he never said he loved her, despite what she claimed. That misunderstanding came about while they just happened to be eating dinner one night while they watched a Suns' game. Absorbed in the game, he was startled when he swore she whispered "I love you" to him. He nervously glanced at her, but she just smiled and dug back into her dinner. He was relieved then, sure that what she must have said was "I love food." He smiled back at her, waved his fork around and said, "Me too."

The clincher, according to her, was when he kept telling her that he had a surprise Christmas gift for her.

"I can hardly wait, Diane. You're going to be so happy because it's something you've always wanted." He couldn't help it, he knew he was grinning like a little boy let loose in a candy store.

Why, this gift was as exciting for him as he knew it would be for her. Neither of them had ever been to an actual Phoenix Suns' game. Can you imagine that? Diane was forever saying how exciting it would be if they could go to a game, so when a friend gave him tickets to a Suns-Lakers game, he decided to take her as a Christmas gift.

Was it his fault she thought the surprise gift was an engagement ring? Why in the world would she even think that? Women are a mystery for sure!

So here he was, two days before Christmas, all alone at the Suns-Lakers game, befuddled, begging God's help on how to go about correcting this misunderstanding. Diane was so upset she'd probably never speak to him again. And what was with that Martha, glaring at him out the window as he walked away?

He just didn't know what he was going to do. He was positive this meant he wouldn't be welcome at their house for dinner on Christmas Day. He'd really been looking forward to that too.

One thing for certain, he'd better learn how to cook because those dinners every evening at Martha and Diane's weren't going to be happening anymore either.

No matter which way he examined all of this, for the life of him, he just couldn't figure out how he had gotten into this mess!

No More Stones, Please!

Jo Russell

It was just a few days before Christmas. I was sitting in the waiting room of a women's medical clinic. The toddler-sized Christmas tree winked with cheerful colored lights. I usually loved the season. Watching the palm trees outside wave in the sunny breeze might brighten anyone's spirit. Not mine. Not today.

Fear multiplied as one crisis after another hit me in less than two months. How could I manage? My life felt like it was at a dead stop. Soon, I would find out if I had breast cancer, a disease that ran in my family. I felt like I had been stoned and someone had just picked up a boulder to finish the job.

Count my blessings? What for? Six weeks before, my twin boys had been born. As the hospital representative had held one of my infant twins as if he were collateral, the baby cooed and she demanded, "How do you expect to pay the balance on this bill? It's about three years of your salary, and the second insurance carrier won't pay it."

Common in twins, both boys had been in intensive care fighting for their lives the first few weeks. Thanks to excellent care, they were now stable.

I wasn't. Divorce was pending. Bankruptcy loomed. Far away in my hometown, my newborns stayed with family to keep them safe. Now this medical test. *Oh, goody*, I thought sarcastically.

The waiting room was nearly empty. Close by was a mother-to-be, her belly round with an unborn child. She and her husband calmly held hands and looked into each others' eyes with love and concern. Soon they would share the birth of their child.

I was so jealous I couldn't look at them.

The two nurses at the desk smiled at the couple and said, "Go to the hospital and your doctor will meet you there." The door closed behind them. Then the nurses leaned toward each other, unable to see me or anyone else in the room. One asked, "That's a dead baby, isn't it?" The second nurse nodded.

As if I'd been pushed to the ground, I felt the breath knocked out of me.

Everything that had seemed so big to me now proved to be as small as a grain of rice.

Sometimes seeing others' pain makes ours seem less.

Season of Guinea Pigs

Jean Ann Williams

Times grew lean for our family of five, and my husband and I didn't see how we could provide the Christmas our children were accustomed to. We had inexpensive gift ideas for Jami, age ten, and Jason, nine, but we had no clue what to give four-year-old Joshua.

As the holiday season approached, my husband worked a temporary job with relatives three hours north of where we lived and the family invited us to spend Christmas with them. Our children became excited, as we counted off the days until they could see their cousins. One problem remained: what gift to give Joshua.

Jami told me her idea, which seemed a bit of a responsibility, though we decided Joshua would be thrilled. The weekend before Christmas, our family piled into the car and drove to the city. While the older children kept Joshua busy at the other end of the store, my husband and I picked out two furry pets.

That night after Joshua fell asleep, Jami asked, "Daddy, how are we going to carry the guinea pigs in the car so Joshua doesn't see them?"

"Or he doesn't hear them," I added. Everyone stared at the closed laundry room door. The two guinea pigs released their stored energy, racing in their box and squeaking to high heaven.

His face lit up. "We'll put them in the trunk."

"But, Daddy," Jason said, "will they get air in there?"

My husband patted him. "Don't worry, son, we'll stop a few times and open the trunk."

Jami's eyes grew large. "What if Joshua sees them?"

"I'll keep Joshua occupied," I reassured her, "and you guys check on the guinea pigs."

When the day came to drive north, we packed the car. As I kept Joshua busy, my husband carried the guinea pig box and placed it in the trunk. I saw the concern on my family's faces that Joshua might hear them during the trip. Jason and Jami agreed to act like they didn't hear a thing if the pets became too loud.

Once we arrived at our relatives' home, I breathed a sigh of relief. "Well, we made it without a squeak." My two older children's faces glowed.

Our relatives knew we had bought the guinea pigs and said we could keep them in the basement where Joshua would not be able to hear them. I checked on the little pets before retiring for the night and imagined the look on Joshua's face when he opened his present. In my heart, I felt sure our tight budget had produced the best gift ever for our youngest child.

On Christmas morning, after everyone opened their presents, my husband went downstairs and fetched the box. Everyone stared at the gift coming toward them, except for Joshua. He sat cross-legged by the tree, making motor noises as he played with his new toy cars. Smiles stretched across our faces as Joshua's daddy said, "We have one more gift, Joshua. Do you want to guess who it's for?"

He pointed at his brother. "Jason."

My husband laid the box at Joshua's feet. "No. It's for you, Son."

Joshua's eyes grew big as marble shooters and just as brilliant. "What is it, Daddy?"

"Open it, open it!" all of us sang.

Joshua ripped apart the candy cane designed paper and looked inside. He sucked in his breath, and his face softened. "Ahhh," he said.

His daddy said, "Sit down, and you can hold one."

Joshua smothered his face into the guinea pig fur. "He's so cute, Mama."

"They're girls," I corrected.

"Both of them?" my aunt asked.

"Oh, yes," I said, "two guinea pigs are enough."

She nodded. "Smart idea."

The guinea pigs became the highlight of the day, with the cousins taking turns playing with them.

Once we were home and settled with our new family members, Jami taught Joshua how to care for his "piggies" as he called them. He did a wonderful job of feeding them, cleaning their box, and changing out their water.

For the next few weeks, Jami made a habit of checking on the guinea pigs each morning before she left for school. She would hold each one and talk to them like they were her own. On a snowy January morning, Jami squealed, and yelled, "Mom, Mom, come see the guinea pigs."

I ran from my bed-making job and stood over the box. "There are five of them," I gasped.

Jami clapped her hands and ran into Joshua's bedroom. "Wake up, Joshua, your piggies had three babies."

Jason beat Joshua to the box. "I guess we got a boy and a girl, huh?"

Joshua peered in with a sleepy grin. He looked at me with question marks dancing in his eyes. "Mama? How did we get five?"

I knelt beside him and hugged him to me. "Honey, we got a boy and a girl, instead of two girls. Now they are a mommy and a daddy."

"Can I hold a baby?" he asked.

Jami interrupted. "Not yet, they're too small."

"That's right, Joshua," I said. "Let's leave them alone. We don't want to upset the mama."

His next words made us laugh. "Do the babies drink their mama's milk like I used to drink your milk?"

"Yes, Son."

He pursed his lips and smiled.

After the older children left for school that day, Joshua and I got a bigger box fixed up for the furry family of five. When we walked by and looked in on the guinea pigs, they'd squeak. I'd also find Joshua sitting next to the box and talking to them as though they were people. At one point, I smiled down at my son. We purchased two pets for Joshua from what little we had, and God gave the increase.

The Blue Woolen Blanket

Lenna Wyatt

It was 1946, a week before Christmas, and very cold. Jon and Brynie Alwyn snuggled close together in bed to keep warm under a blue woolen blanket given to them as a wedding gift before they came to America twelve years ago from Wales.

Every winter Brynie would cut off a strip from the sides of the blanket and make mittens, a muffler, and a head wrap for each of their three children as they got old enough to play outside in the winter.

Jon Alwyn's work delivering ice in their small northern Arizona town to those who had iceboxes came to an end each year in October. People discovered that by placing their perishables outside the windows in a tin box by the kitchen door, the cold and snow did as good a job preserving food as Jon's large chunks of ice. His truck would then sit idle until the warm weather set in again.

With only a few logs left of the large stack he cut from the forest in the early fall, Jon was beginning to worry if they were going to have enough wood for Christmas Day. The children were going to bed with their mufflers on, and it was becoming more of a challenge for Jon and Brynie to keep warm under the shrinking blue woolen blanket. But they trusted the Lord and were determined to believe that He would supply all their needs.

It was two days before Christmas as Jon placed a bundle of small sticks on the andirons and the last two logs on top. He carefully turned them to cause an air pocket around each so that by early morning there would still be some embers glowing among the ashes. They would be rationed between the cookstove and the fireplace.

For a month Brynie had been putting aside some flour, sugar, spices, a bit of oil, and a handful of raisins in a canning jar. For their little children, a Welsh cookie cake and five oranges Jon had traded for one log would be the extent of Santa's visit on Christmas Eve this year.

A few days before Christmas the children began to notice an old man with a long beard and coat and knitted hat walking past their house. His back was bent, it seemed, with the weight of two large burlap bags he carried over his shoulder. Now and then he would shift the bags, causing him to stagger a few steps on the icy street.

"There goes the stranger again!" the children cried as they peered out the window.

"I wonder where he's going?" said the oldest boy. "Every day his bags are bulging, and every evening when he returns, the bags are empty."

"I wonder what he has in those bags?" the oldest girl asked.

"He looks like Santa Claus except that his coat isn't red," said the youngest.

It was Christmas Eve. Jon went out the back door hoping to find a log he might have missed the day before. A new snow had fallen into small peaks. Taking the broom he swept away a few inches of snow where the firewood was kept. To his joy he discovered a small stack of firewood and beside it a bundle of kindling tied with a string. Excited, he ran into the house to tell his wife.

"I don't know where the wood came from, Brynie. It wasn't there yesterday."

There was enough wood for the fireplace and stove to last through Christmas. While Jon built a fire and got the stove going, Brynie poured the ingredients from the canning jar into a bowl and made five cakes. There was enough dough for two extra.

On Christmas morning each child found on their breakfast plates an orange and a Welsh cookie cake. As they bowed their heads Jon thanked the Lord for the firewood that only He could have supplied.

The day after Christmas the last logs were becoming embers and the family went to the back door hoping again to find a stray log. To their surprise the strange man in the long coat was placing firewood and kindling from his burlap bags by their door. His hands were red and chapped.

"Who are you, Sir?" Jon asked. "And why are you giving me this wood?"

The man bowed his head, then looked at Jon.

"Last summer I had no money to buy ice for my icebox and you gave me a twenty-five pound chunk. My wife was very ill and two times a week you continued to leave one for the rest of the summer. I vowed I would find a way to return the favor. As winter was beginning, my truck broke down for the last time, so I carry the firewood on my back and deliver it to my customers on foot. Two days ago I checked to see if you had any wood."

"Come inside," Jon said. "I have an idea. I have a truck, and I can't sell ice in the winter. You can't sell wood in the summer. What do you say we become partners delivering ice and wood in season?"

The stranger was overcome with joy. "My wife reminded me as I left the house today that the Lord would supply our needs. She was right."

"Wait a minute," said Brynie. She dashed into the house and returned with the two extra Welsh cookie cakes and gave them to him. "Merry Christmas."

"Oh," he exclaimed as he opened the napkin. "These look like Welsh cookie cakes. I haven't had one since we left Wales eight years ago. How kind you are."

"You're from Wales too? So are we. This is Brynie, and I'm Jon Alwyn."

"My name is Faren Dulay. Wait until I tell my wife, Gayna. This will be wonderful news. You see, she has been homesick for Wales for a long time. She knows I love America, though, and she never complains."

"Tomorrow," said Jon, "we'll take my truck and deliver the wood to your customers. And now, I'll drive you home."

At Faren Dulay's house he introduced Jon to his wife and told her of the events of their meeting. With grateful tears, she said, "Wait one moment," and returned with a package. "We received two of these at our wedding years ago and I want you and your wife to have this one."

At home Jon gave Brynie the package. It was a large blue woolen blanket. And now Brynie knew there would be mittens and mufflers and head wraps for all, including the Dulays, from the old woolen blanket.

Welsh Cookie Cakes

2 cups flour
¾ cup sugar
1½ tsp. baking soda
1 tsp. nutmeg
½ cup butter, mixed with
1/3 cup oil
1 egg
¼ cup milk
½ cup raisins or Craisins

Mix oil and butter into dry ingredients. Beat egg into milk. Add to flour mixture. Stir in fruit. Shape into patties and fry in ungreased pan until they're golden brown on both sides.

Christmas Miracles

*Everyday holds
the possibility of a miracle.
—Elizabeth David*

Angel on Ice

Barbara Russell Chesser

"Do you believe in angels?" my friend asked.

Funny, how a simple question can snowball into an avalanche of memories. One wintry incident jumped out at me, way ahead of the others. My friend asked me to tell her about it. And so I did.

The fall semester had just ended. Our daughter, Christi, was ten years old and as happy as Del and I were to be out of classes and to begin the holidays! She and I decided that the two of us would drive into town to do some Christmas shopping. At the time we lived on an acreage about three miles from the edge of Lincoln, Nebraska. Because winters could be treacherous in that part of the world, I checked the forecast—the temperature was bitter cold but no snow or ice was predicted.

Strolling leisurely through the mall, we enjoyed the congenial hustle and bustle of the other Christmas shoppers. Del planned to work all day at his office on the campus of the University of Nebraska. He wanted to finish grading student papers before Christmas. I had not left a note letting him know where we were, for I planned on being home before him. After enjoying some hot chocolate, Christi and I headed for the exit onto the parking area. What a surprise! Large, icy snowflakes were falling—not a good sign considering the sub-freezing temperature.

Just as I feared, the new-fallen, icy snow made the highway at the edge of Lincoln even slicker than the more traveled streets in town. I inched the car along as carefully as possible, knowing I would need to build up some speed to get over the first (and steepest) hill before turning off the highway onto the country road to our house. I approached the dreaded incline and accelerated. Just before reaching the top, all traction seemed to disappear. Since no other cars were behind us, I let our car slide slowly backward until it stopped. Putting the car in park, I got out and placed the large strips of carpet under my tires. (Many people carried strips of carpet or something in their cars for this very purpose.) This tactic got our car a little closer to the top of the hill, but again the car lost traction before topping out. So I tried the carpet again but with very little success.

Soon other cars were slipping and sliding on the icy highway approaching the top of the hill. Some men were pushing cars of a few elderly people to help them over the incline. Yet a few others, perhaps fearful of slowing down and not being able to make it over the hill, roared on past those of us stalled—with great risk of meeting someone coming over the hill from the other direction. I refused to give even a glancing thought to the possible fatal or crippling consequences for all of us on that icy hill. Our car was actually the first one in line to get over the hill, but most of the drivers were simply trying to get their own cars out of their dangerous situation.

Del would be worried about us. Cell phones were not widely available then so I told Christi to go to the nearby farmhouse and call him. But first we held hands and prayed—for our safety and the safety of the many other stranded drivers. I continued to pray as I watched Christi trudge bravely through the snow.

Just as soon as Christi returned and climbed back into the car, a pickup came over the hill from the opposite direction. In spite of numerous other cars spinning helter-skelter, the driver of the pickup pulled up alongside our car and shouted, "You ladies need some help?" With no hesitation, I replied, "We sure do." He turned his pickup around and hooked a heavy chain from his truck to our car and eased us over the hill. As he was disconnecting the chain, Del drove up. Seeing what had happened, he called out to the man, "What do I owe you?" The man turned his pickup around to drive back the same direction he had come, and called out, "Not a thing. Just have a Merry Christmas!" As my husband and the man made this brief exchange of words, I carefully jotted down the information on the Good Samaritan's license plate.

The day after Christmas I called the state office in charge of licensing vehicles. When I explained to the woman why I was asking for the man's name with this license plate, she said she would ask her supervisor. The supervisor came on the phone and asked who I was and where I worked. After telling her my name, I explained that my husband and I both taught at the University of Nebraska. The supervisor told me she would have to contact the driver and ask if she could give me his name and phone number, or possibly he would prefer to call me. I told her I understood, and she asked me to wait while she checked on the license.

After a long silence, the supervisor finally came back to the phone and apologized for taking so long. She asked if I was sure of the information I had given her. I emphasized how I had written the information and then checked it carefully. I was certain I had copied it correctly. She then told me that there was no license plate with that number.

Too stunned to say anything, I just let the scene on top of that cold, icy hill flash through my mind—how Christi and I prayed so hard and sincerely, how the man in that truck drove straight to our car as though he knew exactly where he was going, how he refused payment, how he waved good-bye and wished us a Merry Christmas, how he turned around and drove back the same way he had come, and how I carefully wrote down his license plate number.

Breaking the silence, the supervisor said, "I am sorry I cannot help you."

At that point, my friend interrupted me, "Didn't you feel bad that she couldn't help you?"

"She did help me!" I exclaimed. "Until that stranger appeared out of nowhere to rescue Christi and me from a very dangerous situation, I did not believe in angels. But when that supervisor could find no record of his license plate, that is when I began believing in angels."

Reprinted with permission from Keeping Christmas: Stories to Warm Your Heart Throughout the Year, Legacy Publishing, 2011 (Compiled by Barbara Russell Chesser).

Like Precious Silver

Patricia Childress

It seemed like the perfect Christmas gift for my friends and family—the purchase of a table for six to attend the Women's Christmas Brunch at church. As the hostess for my table, the china, flatware, and table decorations in keeping with the season would be my choice. When Marilyn, one of my guests, offered her set of eight sterling silver dessert forks to add to the ambiance of the table setting, I felt honored.

At the close of the program, Amy, a guest at my table, helped me clean up. We had to be cleared out by 4:00 p.m. in order for the maintenance crew to set up for another program. We hurriedly tossed the utensils, including the silver dessert forks, into a bag to sort and wash that evening.

Later at home, while placing the stainless pieces into the dishwasher, I recalled Marilyn's words, "Please don't put the silver forks in the dishwasher. They need to be washed by hand." The warning reminded me to be careful. Of the set of eight, two forks remained unused in the original bag, and I found five dirty ones to hand wash and return to the bag. *But where had the eighth fork gone?*

After examining the dishwasher, searching my car, and rummaging through the boxes of paraphernalia I crated back home, the missing fork could not be found. I dashed back over to the church and hunted through and around the building where we previously enjoyed our brunch that day.

Lord, I prayed silently, *please help me find that fork.*

A man, whose identification would later become apparent, noticed me looking around and asked me what I searched for. I told him about the missing fork. Although he appeared sympathetic and thoughtful, he didn't offer a solution.

When I returned home, I wrote an email to Sonya, the event leader, conveying my predicament and described the fork. She wrote back and said she would check around and keep an eye out for it.

That night slumber didn't come easy. My mind raced with thoughts about how to break the news to Marilyn.

The next morning, Sunday, I went to the information booth at the church where I asked if a silver dessert fork had been turned in. I kept praying, hoping against hope.

The information booth did not have it, so they directed me to the church librarian, who suggested the church kitchen where I frantically looked through the drawers of utensils.

Although feeling panicky, I continued to pray, *Lord, Marilyn values beautiful things. She is especially attached to those items that have sentimental significance for her. She entrusted those forks to me, and I have ruined the set by losing one of the priceless pieces. Please, Lord. Let me find that missing fork.*

I meandered one last time through the large hall where we enjoyed our brunch the day before and, with my cousin, looked through a waste barrel in the hallway nearby. Still, the missing fork didn't surface.

Then my memory traveled to a single moment during the Christmas program after the brunch when I noticed my dessert plate sitting on a corner of the stage with a mess of napkins on top. I forgot about it. While everyone cleaned up, it might have been thrown away with the napkins. *How would I ever tell Marilyn? How could I tell her my carelessness had caused her loss?*

All afternoon I braced myself for the dreaded task. But just prior to my leaving for her home, the phone rang.

"Is this Patsy?" the voice inquired.

"Yes," I replied.

"This is Sonya. They found the fork," she eagerly informed me.

"They found it!" I exclaimed. "How, where?"

"Well," she explained, "one of the landscapers, Mr. Woods, headed up a team. The men went out with a metal detector and searched through the trash and found it."

Overjoyed, I profusely expressed my gratitude through Sonya and jotted a thank-you note to Mr. Woods.

On Monday morning I went to the church office and was relieved to see for myself that the fork they recovered matched the set. With joy, I placed it into the Baggie with the others and rushed off to return the entire eight to my friend.

A few weeks later I met Mr. Woods at a Christmas dinner and recognized him as the gentleman I met in the empty church parking lot where I first began looking for the fork. Now I had the face-to-face opportunity to thank him.

"One thing you don't know," he replied. "The trash is usually picked up on Saturday. Strangely, on Sunday night, the trash was still there. The city had not picked it up on the usual day. That's why we were able to find the fork."

"Thank you," I told him again, and in my heart I said, "Thank You, Lord."

A Christmas Prayer

Carolyn Griffin

"I'm sorry kids, but we're going to miss Christmas this year. Mommy and I have made a few gifts. That's all there'll be." It was the day before Christmas, 1952. My five-year-old brother David and I (who was nine) listened with saucer eyes as our father gave us the bad news.

He shook his head. His eyes were sad. "Being a minister means I've a different kind of job than most daddies. I work for God and the church people." He glanced out the window. A sunbeam, shooting through an opening in the dark clouds, crossed his face, making it glow momentarily. "I get paid from the tithing. Most of them are farmers and since the dry summer ruined the fall crops, they don't have the money to pay tithes with."

Dad swallowed. I could tell this was hard for him. "Tonight," he said, "during prayers, would you both pray for food so we'll have a Christmas Day meal? I'd appreciate it."

We glanced up at our father and nodded. Of course we'd pray!

I sat in the overstuffed chair by the window, rubbing my fingers thoughtfully around a fat braid, and watched soft snowflakes fall gently to the ground. I thought about what my daddy had said and about God. *Daddy works for God…I mustn't wait 'til tonight! I won't! Now's the best time to talk to Him!*

I closed my eyes tightly and concentrated on the goodness of God, since I didn't exactly know what He looked like or how to picture Him, and prayed. "Hi, God. How're You doing?"

I grinned. *Of course, God's doing great! He's God, isn't He?*

"Okay Lord, here's the problem. Daddy doesn't have enough money for food." I thought a moment. "He doesn't even have enough for Christmas this year." (It was best to tell Him about that too, as long as we were talking.) "And God, it's really important to have food to eat—but it's most important to have Christmas! After all, Christmas is celebrating Your Son's birthday!"

I opened my eyes and watched white fluff cover the ground like the downy quilt that covered my bed, keeping me cozy warm on any bitter cold winter night. *God's keeping the earth warm, and all the little flowers to be, and the green grass we'll see in spring, and the fat worms so's when the robins come in May they can eat. God's very good indeed! He takes care of everything! Oh yes—He'll take care of us too!*

I whispered, "Thanks for handling things, Lord!" Then I went to my bedroom to play with my dolls.

That night during prayers I only added, "Thanks, God," before crawling into bed. I was positive He had some sort of arrangement in mind for us.

The next morning I tiptoed over to the bedroom window. Christmas Day—what a beautiful morning! The bright sun made the snow shimmer and sparkle. I drew my breath in quickly, hurriedly dressed and rushed downstairs to where it was warm.

David stood by the front porch window, staring outside, his brown eyes wide with excitement. "Hey, Sis," he hollered, "come and see!"

My parents and I hurried over to the window and peered out. All four of us gazed with amazement. The large deck was covered with boxes of food, bags of groceries, and wrapped presents. It was full from one end to the other with stuff, with Christmas stuff, that God had provided.

I looked and saw many footprints in the snow going from the street to the porch, and back to the street. Christmas had come, and food too. Oh yes, God had figured out how to handle a super big problem!

My family had a glorious Christmas that year. There were lots of presents to be opened, and Mom made a magnificent turkey dinner with an abundance of leftovers that fed us for several days.

Like Sherlock Holmes, Dad investigated. He discovered that the church families, having no money, gave what they had. Every household participated so that their pastor and family would have a nice Christmas. Dad explained to David and me, "Everyone who shared with us will be blessed. God'll see to that! They'll have a better Christmas themselves, because they did good to someone else."

The second week of January my father received enough money to pay bills and purchase an abundance of food. Things were better after that, and times were easier. Today, I often think back to when I first learned as a young girl what the Lord meant when He said, "Be anxious for nothing but in everything by prayer and supplication, with thanksgiving, let your requests be known to God" (Philippians 4:6).

Stolen Bikes and Grace

Lynn Hartke

Two weeks before Christmas, my husband and I rode our bikes to an art festival in downtown Tempe, Arizona. We locked them to a bike rack and walked around for two hours. When we got back, our bikes were gone, stolen by a thief who used bolt cutters to take our property. After standing around with a sick *I can't believe this happened to us* feeling, we found a police officer to take our report. After giving him descriptions, the officer had a few questions. Did we have the bikes registered? No.

Did we have the serial numbers recorded? No.

Did we have receipts? No.

Did we have photographs? Yes, at home.

We walked away knowing that the chances of ever seeing our bikes again were very slim—right up there with finding a snowman in the Phoenix area at Christmas. And even though we had used our bike lock for over a decade, we walked away feeling like idiots, that we should have known we needed a gigantic, super-duper lock.

So to say I was surprised when the Tempe police called three days later to say they had our bikes would be an understatement. They ID'ed the bikes from a piece of paper they found in one of my bike pouches. On it I had written my name and address in case I was ever in an accident.

Who gets their stolen bikes returned? Almost nobody. And without serial numbers and registration? An even smaller group of nobodies.

Suddenly, we found ourselves stumbling into a grace moment.

A grace moment. It's not planned. It's not on a to-do list. It's completely unexpected. We didn't find it among the Christmas items for sale at the booths at the art festival, because grace isn't like that.

It's not given because you are smart enough or rich enough or talented enough or because you remember to write down serial numbers. Grace can't be grace if it were dependent on any of those things.

Grace is free. It's undeserved. It's not from buying super-duper locks to keep the bad guys away. It's sometimes given even on days you feel like an idiot. Or a nobody. In fact, I think grace is especially given on days like that.

So what do you do in a grace moment? Maybe you will want to do what I did.

I bowed my head and said, "Thank you."

A House for Christmas

Donna Clark Goodrich

"Are we going to find a house before Christmas?" our six-year-old daughter, Janet, asked my husband and me as we returned from work one evening.

"And will we have a Christmas tree?" Patty, her four-year-old sister, chimed in. A Christmas tree was very important to her. There had to be a place for the presents she knew she would receive.

I couldn't answer—uncertain if there would be presents or a house. We had been in Arizona for three weeks and were still staying with my girlfriend and her family. I had called her several weeks before, telling her we were moving to Arizona because of my husband's health. "You can stay with us as long as you need to," she assured us.

"Oh, it'll only be a day or two," I replied rashly. I didn't know that we would be house hunting at the same time as thousands of winter visitors who were escaping the cold and snow of their home states.

We had sold all our furniture in Michigan, sent boxes ahead by Railway Express, and packed the rest in our station wagon. We didn't know how soon we could find work but housing, we figured, would be a cinch.

Deciding what we would take was especially hard for the children. Janet and Patty picked out their favorite toys and we laid the rest aside to sell at a garage sale. Robert, our seven-year-old son, wanted to bring his oversized plastic bowling set.

"We don't have room," I told him. "Besides it only has nine pins. We'll buy you another set when we get to Arizona." (I was to make that promise many times as we put more and more of their playthings on the "To Sell" pile.)

To my surprise, once we arrived in Arizona, finding a job was the easiest part. The personnel manager who hired for a chain of grocery stores just "happened" to be at a nearby supermarket when my husband put in his application. He hired Gary on the spot, our first day in town. I found a job the second day at a newspaper office.

However, our jobs were in different towns and our friend lived in a third town, miles away from both our jobs. Gary and I worked different shifts and it seemed all we were doing was taking each other to work and picking each other up, exchanging our one car all hours of the day and night.

In our spare time, we searched everywhere, but there were no houses to be found. Sometimes there would only be one house listed in the classifieds. We drove all over the "Valley of the Sun," screeching on our brakes when we saw an empty house and knocking on the neighbor's door to see if they knew who owned it.

Driving home from work every night, looking at the majestic mountains and Arizona sunsets, I gained strength. I felt if God wanted us to move to Arizona, He must have a house for us somewhere, but when? "Please, help us find one for Christmas," I begged Him.

Christmas came closer and closer and our family was getting more and more discouraged. One day I looked at a four-bedroom house. It was perfect except it was unfurnished and $240 a month—almost three times what we had been paying in Michigan. (Those prices sound ridiculous now, but we're talking 1969!)

After talking the landlady out of the security deposit and the last month's rent in advance, I went back to our friend's to talk to my husband. He finally agreed to look at it, but said, "You know there's no way we can afford that much rent and buy furniture too."

As we were walking out the door, the telephone rang. A friend's voice said, "Our daughter and family are moving to New York and wondered if you would like to look at their house in Mesa." Would we? That's where we wanted to live.

The house was in need of repair, but it was all furnished (including a piano!) and the rent was only $110 a month! It also had a basement, unusual in Arizona.

There was one drawback, however. "We won't be moving till January 15th," our friend's daughter explained, "so we don't want to say anything to the landlord yet."

January 15th! Three and a half more weeks with our friends who also had three children. No home of our own for Christmas. "Lord, you promised," I prayed desperately, and took new hope.

On December 23rd the phone rang again. "We've decided to move tomorrow instead of waiting till January," the voice said.

"I know it," I replied.

"How could you know? We only now made up our minds."

"Because the Lord promised us a house before Christmas," I told her confidently.

Now there was another catch. "You have to talk to the landlord. We just called and told him. He may already have someone else to rent the house."

We discovered she was partly right. As we marched into the real estate office and announced we wanted to rent the house our friends were vacating, the landlord laughed. "You and about twenty others." He held up a long list of names and my heart sunk.

"Sit down," he said. "I'll check these out."

He began calling: "Too high." "Too small." "Wrong neighborhood." "Needs too much work." "Already found a place." Finally he checked off the last name and said, "You must have someone looking out for you. The place is yours."

As I wrote out the check, he added, "I'll make out the receipt to begin December 28th. That's when their lease is up." Four days of free rent!

Driving thankfully back to our friend's house, we passed a Christmas tree lot. "Can we get a tree now?" Patty asked hopefully.

"We sure can," my husband said. "Let's stop here and look at one."

We saw a big "$2.50" sign above one bunch of trees and selected one, thinking we could pick it up later.

"That'll be $15.00," the salesman said.

"$15.00? But the sign says '$2.50'," we protested.

"That's $2.50 a foot. This is a six-foot tree."

Sadly, we put it back. "We can't afford one that expensive now," my husband told Patty. Then, looking at her eyes filling with tears, he reminded her, "But at least we'll have our own house for Christmas."

The next day, December 24th, we moved in the back door of our new house as the former occupants were moving their belongings out the front. The storage shed was full of boxes. "If there's anything you can use in any of those boxes, help yourself," our friend told us. "Otherwise, throw them in the trash."

"Look, Mom!" Robert yelled. "Bowling pins!" Sure enough, there was a set exactly like those he had left in Michigan, except this one had all ten pins!

Is God "able to do exceedingly abundantly above all that we ask or think"? Yes, indeed, for another item our friend's daughter left for us in the corner of the living room—in answer to a four-year-old girl's prayer—was a Christmas tree, all decorated!

About the Editor:

Donna Clark Goodrich is a freelance writer, editor, and proofreader. A native of Jackson, Michigan, she moved to Kansas City, Missouri at the age of 20 to work as secretary to the book editor at the Nazarene Publishing House. Typing a term paper for a seminary student led to her meeting Gary Goodrich, whom she married in 1960. Now residents of Mesa, Arizona, they have three children and two granddaughters. Donna began the annual Arizona Christian Writers Seminar in 1982 which she led for seven years. She has also been instrumental in helping to form Christian writers clubs in many cities. The author of 22 books and over 700 articles and short stories, she is a frequent instructor at Christian writers conferences across the United States. Her greatest love is working with beginning writers and helping them to spread the gospel through the printed page.

Donna's newest books are: *Healing in God's Time*, the story of gospel songwriter Dave Clark who has had 25 songs reach number 1 on the charts (including "Crucified with Christ" and "Mercy Said No") and *A Step in the Write Direction—the Complete How-to Book for Christian Writers*.

She also writes devotional and self-help books to encourage Christians in their daily walk with God, how-to books to train writers, biographies to tell other people's stories, short stories and poetry for readers' enjoyment, and personal experience articles to share how God has helped her through life situations.

Short Author Bio Notes

Lucy Neeley Adams, North Carolina, is author of *52 Hymn Story Devotions*. Married to a minister, they have 4 children, 14 grandchildren, 1 great grandchild. www.52hymns.com

Maria Magdalena Agullo is a Cuban-American author/illustrator residing in Winter Park, Fl. She writes children's picture books, adventure narrative poetry, and medieval fantasy.

Emily M. Akin, Union City, TN, is a staff writer and *Seniors Today* editor for a local lifestyle magazine

Margaret Albertson resides in Southern California with her husband and 1 of 4 adult children. Her mother was born in Scotland and taught Margaret the art of making shortbread.

Michael M. Alvarez has written and published numerous poems, short stories, novels, and articles on writing. He teaches writing at Pima Community College in Tucson, AZ.

Betty L. Arthurs has written numerous articles for magazines and several compilation books. She enjoys living in the Southwest and hanging out with her 7 grandchildren.

Betty Baker lives writes nonfiction in central Florida. She and her husband have 2 grown sons and 7 young grandchildren.

Millie Barger, author of 10 books and hundreds of articles, is a mother, grandmother, great grandmother in Phoenix, AZ.

Linda Boutin, graduate of San Diego State University's School of Journalism, worked as a copy editor/writer for *San Diego Home Garden & Lifestyles* magazine. http://tkdbasenji.blogspot.com/

Faye L. Braley and her husband, Jim, reside in Cottonwood, AZ. They have 2 children and 2 grandchildren.

From a military family, **John Brewer**, Gainesville, FL, attended 11 schools in 12 years. https://www.facebook.com/#!/profile.php?id=100000100173379&sk=info

Trained in Christian education and writer of poetry, **Rhonda Brown** of Mesa, AZ, has served on a church staff and, as a volunteer, taught high school English for 7 years.

Kathy Bruins is a Christian writer who has had articles published in magazines such as Outreach Magazine, Seek, and Rick Warren's Pastor's Toolbox. Kathy lives in Southwest Michigan. Find her blog at www.kathybruins.com

Rebecca Bruner, Mesa, AZ, has loved writing stories since she was a young girl. She enjoys spending time with her husband and 2 teen-agers and teaches women's Bible studies.

Debbie Burgett is a missionary with New Tribes Mission in Sanford, FL. She and her husband have 5 grown children. www.ntm.org/rand_burgett

Bill Butler lives in Phoenix, AZ. He served in the US Army for 8 years and supervised and trained vocational rehab counselors at the Samaritan Rehabilitation Institute.

Ellen Cardwell is a Bay Area transplant living in the Sierra Nevada foothills. She writes devotionals, and enjoys singing, gardening and spending time with her family.

April Smith Carpenter lives in Mississippi with her husband David and 2 children. She teaches aerobics and works with older adults at the YMCA. ww.godlycommunication.com.

Debbie Carpenter worked as assistant children's ministries director for 14 years in her church in Tucson, AZ. She and her husband have 2 daughters and 3 granddaughters.

Paige Carpenter, Gainesville, FL, is a graduate of Florida State University, and is a writer and illustrator. Visit her blog at http://roguedoe.wordpress.com

Rebecca Carpenter, Olive Branch, MS, recently retired after 37 years of teaching. She and her husband are now traveling the world on both pleasure and mission trips.

Dr. Barbara Russell Chesser, Waco, TX, is a New York Times bestseller author and an award-winning university professor. She has authored numerous books and anthologies.

Patricia Childress lives and writes in Sacramento, CA. She also enjoys decorating, patio gardening and, crafts, and is also a mentor and speaker.

Phyllis Ciarametaro, Fountain Hills, AZ, grew up in a small fishing community northeast of Boston, and has written several short stories depicting ethnic family life.

Liz Collard is a wife and mother from Orlando, FL. Author of the Building a Godly Marriage series, her heart's desire is to see families serving and glorifying God together.

Janet Ann Collins, Grass Valley, CA, is a feature writer, columnist, and author of books for children. She is also a teacher and a grandparent. www.janetanncollins.com

Virginia Colclasure, Jarrettsville, MD, is a retired librarian, writes book reviews and contributes to Portions of Grace http://portionsofgrace.blogspot.com.

Kelly Combs, Ashland, VA, is a wife, mother, and writer, published in various publications including *Guideposts, P31 Woman, and Love Is A Verb.* www.kellycombs.com.

Laurie Barker Copeland is a storyteller, actress and author of The Groovy Chicks series. She lives in Florida with her husband, John, and daughter, Kailey. Lauriecopeland@cfl.rr.com

Connie Coppings, Stanford, KY, and her husband recently retired after 25 years in ministry. When not writing, she loves to cook, garden, and play the piano.

Suzanne Courtney, Monroe, MI, is a retired teacher, mother of 3, and grandmother of 2. She loves to travel, collect antiques, and spend time with family. suzannegenecourtney.com.

Don Cunningham, Prescott Valley, AZ, is a retired social worker and licensed minister of pastoral care and outreach, currently conducting pastoral care ministry at his local church.

Mia Lynn DeBruyne, Fruitport, MI, is a "stay-at-home" mom who writes inspirational stories about family life for the online West Michigan Christian Newspaper.

Willow Dressel and **Jennifer Smetana**, Chino Valley, CA, are sisters, married with grown children. They love the outdoors, animals, children, and reading.

Terri Elders lives near Colville, WA, and is a frequent contributor to anthologies. http://atouchoftarragon.blogspot.com/

Diane Ellenwood, Adrian, MI, grew up in southeast Michigan and currently pastors a church in Michigan with her husband of 35 years. She has 3 children and 8 grandchildren.

Linda Rose Etter, Adrian, MI, taught school for 36 years in Michigan after graduating from Huntington College. In 2011 she published a devotional book, *Listen To HIS Heartbeat*.

Raymond Fenech, Malta, G.C., worked for leading newspapers including *The Times* and *Sunday Times* and edited 2 national magazines. His work has been published in 12 countries.

Sandra Fischer taught high school English and owned a Christian bookstore in Indiana for several years. She lives in St. Helena Island, SC, with her husband, Craig.

Phyllis Qualls Freeman is a freelance writer with more than 400 published articles. She and her husband, Bill, are making memories with their 5 grandchildren in Hixson, TN.

Margaret Dornan Gamber studied at Kent State University and the University of California, Riverside. She and her husband enjoy their 2 children and 5 grandchildren in California.

Annette Geroy, a lay minister with Mount Horeb House Ministries in Kerrville, TX, works extensively with women who have suffered sexual abuse.

Linda Gillis, Sun City, AZ, is an author of 3 books. She is a 2006 winner of the Guideposts Magazine Writer Workshop and author of three books. www.incidentsfrom.com

Donna Clark Goodrich, author of 22 books and over 700 published manuscripts, lives in Mesa, AZ, with her husband of over 50 years. www.thewritersfriend.net

Anne Grace belongs to the Hilton Head Island Writer's Network and Christian Women in Media Ass'n. She and her husband, Bob, have 4 children and 9 grandchildren. www.annesgrace.com

A retired school teacher, **Alice King Greenwood**, writes poetry, fiction, nonfiction, and music. She and her husband have 5 children and have lived in West Texas for over 50 years.

Cona F. ("Faye") Gregory-Adams, DeSoto, MO, writes poetry, children's stories, fiction, and nonfiction and has published in newspapers, magazines, poetry journals, and anthologies.

Carolyn Griffin, a wife, mother and grandmother in Tucson, AZ, enjoys arts and crafts, crocheting, drawing and painting, church and family activities, and especially story telling.

Nikole Hahn lives in Northern Arizona. She's a book reviewer, writer, outdoor enthusiast, and coffee addict who blogs at: www.thehahnhuntinglodge.com.

John J. Han is professor of English & Creative Writing at Missouri Baptist University in St. Louis, MO. He's the author of 3 haiku books and many haiku published in several countries.

Elaine Hardt is a retired teacher with 8 books and over 2,000 manuscripts published. She leads the Prescott Valley (AZ) Writers' Group. www.EncouragingU.blogspot.com

Barbara Haropolous (D.H. Barbara), Arvada, CO, loves to cook, read, and attend Bible study. Her novel, *Seasons Of A Life*, is available on Amazon.com.

Lisa Harris lives in Tucson, AZ with her 2 daughters, 7 cats, 3 dogs, 1 persnickety fish tank, and 8 tortoises. She works as a environmental consultant.

Lynne Hartke, Chandler, AZ, is a writer, preschool music teacher, mom, grandmother, and wife of a minister/city councilmember.. She blogs at www.lynnehartke.com.

Londa Hayden is a freelance writer and native Texan transplanted to Bartlett, TN with her husband and 3 boys. Her new book is titled *Date, Pray, Wait*. http://londahayden.com

Christine Henderson, Alta Loma, CA, writes picture books, inspirational pieces, and weekly skits for the children's ministry at her church. TheWriteChris.blogspot.com

Joanne Hendrix, Mesa, AZ, is a full-time wife, mother of 6, and grandmother of 5. She squeezes in teaching college English and is finishing up her second master's degree.

Irish born writer and musician, **Cora Holley** lives in Chandler, AZ with her family. She is a contributing author of *The French School, Bray, Remembered*, by Jennifer Flegg.

Annette Kathleen Hutchins, Durango, CO, is a graduate of Virginia Commonwealth University. She is a writer/illustrator of children's books and puppet show skits.

Multi-published **Gay Ingram** enjoys writing from the piney woods of East Texas. Recently she published Some Write Thoughts, a book for writers. www.gayingram.com.

Jewell Johnson lives in Fountain Hills, AZ with her husband LeRoy. They have 6 children and 9 grandchildren. Jewell has published 3 devotional books and over 300 articles.

Deb Kemper is a freelance writer and cake designer, currently completing her first novel. She lives near Kansas City, MO, with her husband, Ken, and 3 dogs. www.DebKemper.com

Loreen Marie Kollmorgen, Mesa, AZ, is married to Larry and has 2 children and 3 grandsons. She's a retired cosmetologist and has published a children's book *Animal Patrol*.

As a teacher, **Joyce Komar** watched students blossom when they discovered the joy of writing stories. Now retired to Arizona, she experiences that same joy with her own writing.

A former teacher, **Nancy Julien Kopp** lives in the Flint Hills of Kansas. Her writings appear in many anthologies, magazines, and newspapers. www.writergrannysworld.blogspot.com

Jennifer Kruse resides in Gilbert, AZ with her husband and 2 kids. A daughter, sister, wife, and friend, she pens the blog www.sisterchick.wordpress.com.

At age 51, **Jerri Clark Legler** realized her lifelong desire of earning her high school diploma. She enjoys writing short tales about people and incidents in her life.

Carin LeRoy, Orlando, FL, is a wife, mother of 4, and grandmother of 5. She works as a mission mobilizer with Pioneers, and enjoys family, piano, missions, and writing.

Kris Lindsey, Loomis, CA, enjoys any occasion that brings family and friends together, and especially scuba diving in Fiji. Kris holds a BA in Social Work. www.krislindsey.com

A studio painter, writer, and poet, **Barbara Boothe Loyd** of Tulsa, OK, is always inspired by beauty.

Frances E. Luymes is a USA citizen and also a resident of Trenton, Ontario, Canada after marrying a Dutch-Canadian. She and her husband met on the Internet at ages 79 and 80.

Brendalyn Crudup Martin, Phoenix, AZ, wife, mother, and grandmother, writes personal experience, fiction, and poetry and is the Poet Laureate of the Arizona Supreme Court.

Joyce McCullough, Manchester, TN, is a high school English teacher and a freelance writer. Her church pianist, she also teaches students in the church's LOGOS program.

Bruce McLeland, Prescott, AZ, is retired from real estate, also a former airman, heating and air conditioning designer, and missionary in the inner city of Newark and Chicago.

Carol Meeks, Tulsa, OK, is the 2009 Oklahoma Senior Poet Laureate from Amy Kitchener's Angels Without Wings contest. She and her husband Pat have 2 sons and 3 grandsons.

Anita Mellott, Suwanee, GA, has been published in India and North America. Her latest book is *School Is Where the Home Is: 180 Devotions for Parents*. www.anitamellott.com.

Danielle Mendenhall, Cottonwood, AZ, wife and homeschooling mom of 2, loves reading, writing, singing, and ballroom dancing. She's now studying Secondary English Education

Kathy Collard Miller, Indio, CA, is a women's conference speaker and author of 49 books. She has spoken in 30 states and 7 countries. www.KathyCollardMiller.blogspot.com.

Carol Moncado, Republic, MO, wife and mother of 4, teaches Poli Sci and writes romantic comedy. She is editor-in-chief of Pentalk Community Blog. www.carolmoncado.com.

Diane Morgan, of Mesa, AZ, is devoted to God and the Bible, her family, her friends, and her church. She is thankful for her day job as a paralegal, which funds her passions!

Peggy Halter Morris, Gilbert, AZ, is married with 3 children and 9 grandchildren. She writes material for teachers and counselors.

Sherrie Murphree, Odessa, TX, wife of Mel and mother of 2, is a Bible teacher, church musician, and writer of articles published in 30 magazines and 9 book compilations.

Juanita Wier Nobles, DeSoto, MO, is a retired teacher, published in newspapers, magazines, and anthologies. www.nobleschristianbook.com.

Ashleen O'Gaea is a mother, wife, and cat mommy who lives in Tucson, AZ. She is the author of several fiction and nonfiction books about Wicca.

Leola Ogle, Phoenix, AZ, is a wife, mother, grandmother, great-grandmother, and native Arizonan. She retired in January 2011, and now devotes her time to writing.

Deborah Onderdonk lives in the city in which she was born and raised—St. Augustine, FL, and works for the county property appraiser as a deed processor and mapper.

Ginger O'Neill, Seminole, FL, is a teacher, conference speaker, author, and graduate of the University of South Florida. http://www.gingeroneillministries.com

Noreen Ophoff lives in Grant, MI. Her farm upbringing connects her to strong family roots and a deep love for rolling land.

Betty Ost-Everley, Kansas City, MO, is a wife, mother, and administrative assistant. She serves as a church deacon, and is on the Advisory Board of the Heart of America Christian Writers' Network.

Andrea Arthur Owan is a freelance writer, speaker, and retired educator. She lives in Tucson, AZ, with her husband Chris and their youngest son.

Sharen Pearson, Cottonwood, AZ, is a pastor's wife, mother of 5, founder/teacher of Goof & Giggle Mom/Tot classes and the host/creator of BabyFirstTV's Baby D.I.Y. program. www.sharenpearson.com

Cherry Pedrick, Lacey, WA, is the coauthor of 7 books, including The OCD Workbook and The Habit Change Workbook. www.CherryPedrick.com/ocd-breakingfree.blogspot.com.

Connie Peters writes fiction, poetry, and nonfiction. She and her husband live in Southwest Colorado, have 2 grown children, and host 2 adults with developmental disabilities.

Tammy Pfaff of Prospect Park, PA, is a wife and mother of 4 children. A graphic artist, she studies journalism at DCCC. She loves writing, scrapbooking, and sunsets on the beach.

Peggy Blann Phifer lives in southern Nevada with husband Jim. She is an author, columnist, and a retired executive assistant. www.peggyblannphifer.com

Carol Mottinger Ramirez, retired educator, lives in Gainesville, FL with husband Fred. She is a MOPS mentor mom, and enjoys traveling and creating memories with family and friends.

Annette Rey, Arnold, MO, is president of the Writer's Society of Jefferson County (MO). She is eager to share helpful ideas and hear your suggestions at http://www.annetterey.com

Jane Riley (pen name of Mary Lou Cheatham), award-winning author of Louisiana and Texas, has enjoyed careers as a teacher, and registered nurse. She is the mother of 1 daughter.

Lorilyn Roberts lives in Gainesville, FL. She has published 3 books and is the founder of the John 3:16 Marketing Network. http://lorilynroberts.com.

Natalie K. Rodriguez, Palm Beach, Florida, is a Puerto Rican Hispanic mother to 4. She has a BA in Comparative Religious Studies and English Literature and a Master's in Health Law.

Janet Roller, Forest City, NC, Miss South Carolina 1997, is a singer, speaker, writer, and worship leader. Wife and mother of 2, Janet shares with others through music and writing.

Pat Rowland, Cordova, TN, is a retired corporate director for Patient Affairs. Married, with 1 daughter, she's a writer and Bible teacher. She blogs at: http://patlrowland.wordpress.com/

Jo Russell, who lives in a small NE Arizona town, is a writer, columnist, Sunday school teacher, and speaker and has been published in many magazines. Button-to-God.com.

Joanne Sandlin, Prescott Valley, AZ, is a member of the Northern Arizona Word Weavers and author of a cookbook titled *The Front Burner With Family and Friends*.

Patti Schieringa, Holland, MI, helps people smile, to be glad, to make them laugh. When her late husband grew a white beard, she became Mrs. Claus. pattikayck@yahoo.com

Debbie Schmid, mother of 1 and grandmother of 1, has written 2 books and many short stories and articles. She enjoys writing, speaking, teaching, and scrapbooking in Tucson, AZ.

Reba Cross Seals, writer, teacher, and artist, lives with husband, David, in Alpine, TX. She is writing a book on living through grief, and also monitors alternative certification teachers.

Verna Simms, Festus, MO, a retired librarian, mother and grandmother, has been published in magazines, anthologies, and the local paper. She is now working on 2 novels.

Karen Strand lives in the beautiful northwest with her husband, Paul. She has been published in several magazines, including, *Focus on the Family* and *Guideposts*. www.karenstrand.com

Nanette Thorsen-Snipes, Buford, GA, has published more than 500 articles, stories, and devotions. Her stories are in more than 50 compilation books. www.nanettesnipes.com

Donna Collins Tinsley, wife, mother and grandmother, lives in Port Orange, FL, and has been published in several magazines and book compilations. http://thornrose7.blogspot.com

Freda Hatfield Tong and her husband Peter were missionaries to Taiwan for many years. They now live in Fontana, CA, where both are involved in writing projects.

Janis Van Keuren, Oro Valley, AZ, is a wife, mother to 2 adopted sons, a special education teaching assistant, and a published writer of stories of hope to encourage other women.

Coleene VanTilburg co-leads a writer's group in Chino, California, and works at the local high school as a special education aide.

Josephine (Jo) Walker, is a wife of 50 years, mother of 3, and grandmother of 11. She's been a stay-at-home mom, a business owner, a caregiver, and a writer in Cody, WY.

Anna Roberts Wells was born and raised in Arkansas. She is a retired teacher and social worker living with her husband near St. Louis. They have 4 children and 4 grandchildren.

Connie Wesela, Gilbert, AZ, is a retired educator. The mother of 2 adult children, Connie writes nonfiction, personal essay and short stories. Wesala-mythirdlife.blogspot.com.

Cass Wessel is a retired minister, currently living in rural Pennsylvania where Amish buggies rattle along the macadam roadways. She enjoys writing, supply preaching, and her garden.

Christy Williams is a freelance writer, blogger, and stay-at-home mom of 2 boys in Mesa, AZ. She enjoys scrapbooking family photos, volunteering with church teens, and cooking.

Jean Ann Williams writes, and also raises goats and one dog and a cat in a quaint valley in Southern Oregon with her husband. http://joshua-mom.blogspot.com/.

Liane Williams has warm memories of cold West Michigan Christmases. She still treats her children to real trees and cardamom bread. She enjoys sharing her heart through writing.

Deb Wuethrich, Adrian, MI, works as a staff writer for the Tecumseh (Michigan) Herald. She has been published in many magazines and is a 2003 Amy Award recipient.

Lenna Wyatt lives in Scottsdale, AZ. The mother of 5, grandmother of 7, and great grandmother of 2, she enjoys writing "Erma Bombeck" type stories, poems and songs.

The Writers, Editor, and Publisher wish you a Merry Christmas!

CPSIA information can be obtained at www.ICGtesting.com
Printed in the USA
BVOW072243021211

277245BV00002B/15/P